The Effectiveness of EU
Business Associations

The Effectiveness of EU Business Associations

Edited by
Justin Greenwood

ERNST & YOUNG
ASSOCIATION MANAGEMENT   palgrave

First published 2002 by
PALGRAVE
Houndmills, Basingstoke, Hampshire RG21 6XS and
175 Fifth Avenue, New York, N.Y. 10010
Companies and representatives throughout the world

PALGRAVE is the new global academic imprint of
St. Martin's Press LLC Scholarly and Reference Division and
Palgrave Publishers Ltd (formerly Macmillan Press Ltd).

ISBN 0–333–96412–8

This book is printed on paper suitable for recycling and
made from fully managed and sustained forest sources.

A catalogue record for this book is available
from the British Library.

Library of Congress Cataloging-in-Publication Data

The effectiveness of EU business associations / edited by Justin Greenwood.
    p. cm.
"Ernst & Young Association Management"
Papers presented at a conference.
Includes bibliographical references and index.
ISBN 0–333–96412–8
1. Trade associations—European Union countries—Congresses. 2. Pressure
groups—European Union countries—Congresses. I. Greenwood, Justin.
II. Ernst & Young Association Management.
HD2429.E87 E34 2001
380.1'06'04—dc21   2001036523

10 9 8 7 6 5 4 3 2 1
11 10 09 08 07 06 05 04 03 02

Printed and bound in Great Britain by
Antony Rowe Ltd, Chippenham, Wiltshire

Contents

List of Tables and Figures   viii

Acknowledgements   ix

Abbreviations   x

Notes on the Contributors   xiii

1 Introduction: Conference Issues and Themes   1
   Justin Greenwood and Alfons Westgeest

Part I   Understanding the Environment   **13**

2 Factors Influencing the Effectiveness of Business
   Associations: a Review   15
   Robert J. Bennett

3 European State Formation and its Impact on Associational
   Governance: Will Business Interest Association (BIA)
   Systems become Centralised at the EU Level?   30
   Frans van Waarden

4 Governance and the Role of Associations in Economic
   Management: a Response from an EU Public
   Affairs Practitioner   46
   Daniel Guéguen

5 The Importance of Institutions to Associations:
   Evidence from the Cross-National Organisation
   of Business Interests Project   53
   Wyn Grant

6 Large Firms and the Transformation of EU Business
   Associations: a Historical Perspective   64
   Maria Green Cowles

7 Challenges and Opportunities for Business Associations:
   Autonomy and Trust   79
   Rudolf Beger

8   The Changing Environment for Trade Associations
    and Strategies for Adaptation   85
    Mark Boléat

Part II   Change Agents and Managing Change   99

9   The Impact of the CEFIC Reforms upon the Associational
    Sector   101
    Jean-Marie Devos

10 The Case of EURELECTRIC: the Impact of Deregulation
    upon EU Business Associations   109
    Paul Bulteel

11 The Impact of Changing Sectoral Definition upon
    Associability: the Convergence of Business Interests
    in the Information and Communications
    Technology Sector in Europe   115
    Oliver Blank

12 The Impact of Sector Change upon EU Business Associations 122
    Jan J. F. Timmerman

13 New Models of Large Firm Collective Action   126
    Christophe Lécureuil and Simon Ward

14 EU Business Associations: Meeting the needs of
    Europe's Service Sectors?   131
    Irina Michalowitz

15 Association Management Companies as Change Agents   143
    Alfons Westgeest and Bruno Alves

Part III   Cross Sectoral and Employers Organisations   155

16 Employer vs. Product Market Associations: Different
    Dynamics in Associational Governance?   157
    Franz Traxler

17 National Members and their EU Associations   171
    Zygmunt Tyszkiewicz

18 How SMEs can Influence the Effectiveness of
    European Business   182
    Hans-Werner Müller

19 The European Round Table of Industrialists: Still a
    Unique Player?   194
    Bastiaan van Apeldoorn

Part IV   Conclusions   **207**

20 Globalisation and the Future of Associational Governance   209
    William D. Coleman

21 Conclusions   223
    Justin Greenwood and Alfons Westgeest

Bibliography   234

Index   243

List of Tables and Figures

Tables

2.1   Percentage of membership for each type of association
from different size businesses   16

2.2   The percentage of associations of each main type offering
services of each category   18

2.3   Main route for lobbying and representation in Europe   26

2.4   Percentage of a sector's members lobbying directly to
Brussels by type of association and its membership size   27

3.1   Phases of formulation and implementation of EU
regulations and directives, with their respective levels
of government   37

6.1   Development phases   65

9.1   CEFIC's main external contacts with public bodies/official
organisations   103

10.1   Organisational trends in the European electricity industry
associations 1997–2000   112

16.1   The problems of associational governance   158

16.2   The relationship between associational governance
and interest categories   160

20.1   Variations in supranational governance arrangements   218

20.2   International policy environments, policy community
types, and the policy process: rank order of importance   220

Figures

2.1   Increase in predicted probability of using business
associations for each additional staff member per 1000
businesses in their sectors or areas   22

2.2   Increase in predicted probability of the type of impact of
business associations for each additional staff member
per 1000 businesses in their sector or areas   23

10.1   Percentage electricity market opening by
member-state, 2000–2003   111

10.2   Member/Secretariat mix in the European Electricity
industry associations, 1997–2000   113

Acknowledgements

The Editor would like to thank all the staff of Ernst & Young Association Management (EYAM) who worked on the conference and this post-conference product, and in particular to Alfons Westgeest, Wills Hughes-Wilson and Bruno Alves. Thanks, also, goes to Nicole Schulze, the conference administrator from The Robert Gordon University who worked with the EYAM team on site in Brussels, and to Linda Strangward for her help in the preparing the manuscripts ready for the publisher. Finally, the Editor would like to thank the European Commission for providing the funding for the conference (under Framework Programme V, High Level Scientific Conferences), and the event sponsors. These were: Wirtschaftskammer Österreich; the European Voice; Adamson-BSMG Worldwide; Shandwick International; the European Information and Communication Technologies Association; the European Public Affairs Directory; the European Information Service, and European Centre for Public Affairs Brussels; and EurActiv.com. Finally, thanks go to all the contributors of this volume.

The author and publishers are grateful to Frank Cass publishers for granting permission to reproduce Table 2.3 from *West European Politics* by R. Bennett, 1999 and to Blackwell Publishers for granting permission to reproduce Table 2.4 from *Political Studies* by R. Bennett, 1999.

Every effort has been made to trace copyright holders but if any have been inadvertently overlooked, the publishers will be pleased to make the necessary arrangements at the first opportunity.

Abbreviations

ACC	American Chemistry Council
ACEA	Association des Constructeurs Européens d'Automobiles
ACOM	Consultative Assembly of Member Companies
AFEG	Consultative Assembly of Affiliated Groups
AFEM	Consultative Assembly of Member Federations
AMC	Association Management Companies
AMCHAM-EU	The EU Committee of the American Chamber of Commerce
AMUE	Association for the Monetary Union of Europe
ASAE	American Society of Association Executives
BDA	Bundesvereinigung der Deutschen Arbeitgeberverbände
BDI	Bundesverband des Deutschen Industrie
BTW	Bundersverband der Deutschen Tourismuswirtschaft
CBI	Confederation of British Industry
CEEP	European Centre of Enterprises with Public Participation and of Enterprises of General Economic Interest
CEFIC	European Chemical Industry Council
CEO	Chief Executive Officer
CET	European Ceramic Tile Manufacturers Federation
COGECA	General Committee of Agricultural Cooperation of the EU
COPA	Committee of Agricultural Organisations in the EU
COREPER	Committee of Permanent Representatives
DG	Directorate General
EBA	European Banking Association
ECOSOC	Economic and Social Committee
ECTEL	European Telecommunications and Professional Electronics Industry
EEC	European Economic Community
EEG	European Enterprise Group
EFPIA	European Federation of Pharmaceutical Industry Associations
EICTA	European Information and Communications Technology Industry Association
EITO	European Information Technology Observatory
EMRA	European Modern Restaurant Association

ERT	European Round Table of Industrialists
ESF	European Services Forum
ESN	European Services Network
ESPRIT	European Strategic Programme in Information Technology
ESRC	Economic and Social Research Council
ETAG	European Tourism Action Group
ETNO	European Public Telecommunications Network Operators' Association
ETOA	European Tour Operators Association
ETUC	European Trade Union Confederation
ETUI	European Trade Union Institute
EU	European Union
EURELECTRIC	Union of the Electricity Industry
EUROPIA	European Petroleum Industry Association
EYAM	Ernst & Young Association Management
FBE	European Banking Federation
FDI	Foreign Direct Investment
GATS	General Agreement on Trades and Services
GBD	Global Business Dialogue
GBDe	Global Business Dialogue on e-commerce
GdP	Group des Présidents
HOTREC	Association of Hotels, Restaurants and Cafes in Europe
IACA	International Air Carriers Association
ICCA	International Council of Chemical Associations
ICRT	International Communications Round Table
ICT	Information and Communications Technology
IGN	Intergovernmental Negotiations
ISO	International Organisation for Standardisation
IT	Information Technology
MLG	Multilevel Governance
MORI	Market and Opinion Research International
NGOs	Non Governmental Organisations
NORMAPME	European Office of Crafts, Trades and Small- and Medium-sized Enterprises for Standardisation
NTA	New Transatlantic Agenda
OBI	Organisation of Business Interests
R&D	Research and Development
RSPB	Royal Society for the Protection of Birds
SMEs	Small- and Medium-Sized Enterprises
TABD	Transatlantic Business Dialogue
TECs	Training and Enterprise Councils

TNCs	Transnational Corporations
UEAMPE	European Association of Craft, Small- and Medium-Sized Enterprises
UNICE	Union of Industrial & Employers' Confederations of Europe
US	United States
USA	United States of America
USP	Unique Selling Point
USSR	Union of Soviet Socialist Republics
VAT	Value Added Tax
WKÖ	Wirtschaftskammer Österreich
WTO	World Tourism Organisation
WTO	World Trade Organisation
WTTC	World Travel and Tourism Council

Notes on the Contributors

Bruno Alves is a consultant with Ernst & Young Association Management.

Robert J. Bennett is Professor of Geography at the University of Cambridge.

Rudolf Beger is the former (founding) Executive Secretary of the European Automobile Manufacturers Association, and has been an EU lobbyist for Exxon Chemical Europe, General Motors Europe and Citigroup.

Oliver Blank is the Director of EICTA – the Brussels-based European Information and Communications Technology Industry Association. With a background of political science, he has worked for VDMA and EUROBIT in the past, living in Germany, France, the UK, the US and China.

Mark Boléat is a consultant specialising in trade associations and the handling of public policy issues. His previous positions include Director General of the Association of British Insurers and the Council of Mortgage Lenders.

Paul Bulteel was appointed Secretary General of UNIPEDE and EURELECTRIC, in May 1997. The two organisations were merged in December 1999 to form the Union of the Electricity Industry – EURELECTRIC. EURELECTRIC represents the European Electricity Industry at expert, strategic and policy-making level. He is the author of several publications on environmental policies, the development of co-generation, and challenges and opportunities for the Electricity Industry.

William D. Coleman is Professor of Political Science and Director of the Institute on Globalisation and the Human Condition at McMaster University. He continues to do research on the impact of globalisation on the organisation of business interests.

Maria Green Cowles is an Assistant Professor at American University and co-editor of two books, *Transforming Europe* (Cornell, 2001) and *The State of the European Union* (Oxford, 2001). She has written extensively on the political activities and impact of multinational corporations in EU policy-making, the Transatlantic Business Dialogue (TABD), and, more recently, on the Global Business Dialogue on e-commerce (GBDe).

Jean-Marie Devos is Executive Director and General Counsel of the European Chemical Industry Council.

Wyn Grant is Professor of Politics at the University of Warwick and first published on the subject of EU business associations in the early 1970s.

Justin Greenwood is Jean Monnet Professor of European Public Policy at the Robert Gordon University, Aberdeen. He is the author of a number of titles on EU public affairs, including *Representing Interests in the European Union* (Macmillan, 1997) and *Inside the EU Business Associations* (Macmillan, 2002).

Daniel Guéguen is the Managing Director of the Brussels based CLAN Public Affairs. He founded the first European school of lobbying, has written several books of reference on European topics, including *A practical guide to the EU labyrinth*. He has served as chief executive officer of COPA-COGECA, the head organisation of the farmers associations and agricultural cooperatives of the European Union, and one of the largest lobbying groups in Europe.

Christophe Lécureuil is Director of Corporate and Regulatory Affairs for GPC International.

Irina Michalowitz is currently undertaking her Ph.D thesis on European Lobbying Strategies with the European Doctoral College. She is a freelance lecturer at the Brussels-based United Business Institute, and has worked for the public affairs department of Preussag AG, until the end of 2000.

Hans-Werner Müller has been the Secretary General of UEAPME since November 1992. He is also the President of NORMAPME and the Treasurer of the Avignon Academy. Before he was a member of the German Parliament (CDU) from 1976 to 1994 and between 1976 and 1979 also a member of the European Parliament.

Jan J. F. Timmerman is General Secretary of the European Petroleum Industry Association.

Franz Traxler is Professor of Industrial Sociology at the University of Vienna. He has recently coauthored with S. Blaschke and B. Kittel *National Labour Relations in Internationalized Markets* (Oxford University Press, 2001) which includes a comparative analysis of the activities, structures and performance of business associations in 20 OECD countries.

Zygmunt Tyszkiewicz is currently President of the Swiss-based Lanckoronski Foundation which finances educational and cultural projects connected with Poland, and from 1985 to 1998 was Secretary General of UNICE, the main European business association based in Brussels. Before that he spent 28 years with Shell, working in Latin America, Africa and Europe.

Bastiaan van Apeldoorn is Lecturer in International Relations and European Integration at the Free University of Amsterdam. He has published several articles on the role of transnational business in the new Europe, and his book, *Transnational Capitalism and European Integration*, is forthcoming (Routledge).

Frans van Waarden is Professor of Policy and Organisation at Utrecht University, and currently fellow at the European University Institute in Florence. He has published widely on business interest associations.

Simon Ward is Chairman of the European Modern Restaurant Association.

Alfons Westgeest is a partner of Ernst & Young Association Management in Brussels, leading an international team of over 20 professionals who represent and manage a dozen EU and international business associations and interest groups. He serves on the Board of both the American and the European Society of Association Executives.

1

Introduction: Conference Issues and Themes

Justin Greenwood and Alfons Westgeest

The context

We are pleased to present a selection of keynote contributions to a conference on 'The Effectiveness of EU Business Associations' held in Brussels from 18 to 22 September 2000.

The conference was designated an official 'EuroConference' under the 'High Level Scientific Conference' section of Research Framework Programme V of the European Union (EU) following a partnership application by us under competitive conditions in 1999, and this was the principal source of funding for the event held in the names of The Robert Gordon University and Ernst & Young Association Management. Under the funding programme, the European Commission seeks events which ensures knowledge transfer to a new[1] generation of researchers. To this objective, we added the task of knowledge transfer between analysts of EU business associations, primarily based in universities, and those who work in, for and with EU business associations, whether as staff, contract managers, members, or the EU institutions. This 'academic-practitioner dialogue' has never been undertaken on such a scale before, and in this sense the event was quite unique. We wanted academics to have access to the 'coal face' experiences and information that practitioners could provide, and to subject their interpretations and analyses to the acid test of practice. Similarly, we wanted practitioners to have access to some of the overviews and interpretations that academia could provide. We recognised at the outset that establishing a dialogue between 'practitioners' and 'academics' would be a challenging task, and encouraged each of our speakers and authors to present and write in a way that would be accessible to each of these audiences. In this book, we have sought to meet this challenge,

1

and have drawn together authors who include those drawn from the highest level of EU business associations, and academic analysts, many of whom have been key contributors to the subject matter over a substantial period of time. For instance, among our authors are the past and/or present chief officers of UNICE,[2] AMCHAM-EU,[3] UEAPME,[4] and CEFIC,[5] which is the largest of all EU business associations.

In the spirit of the event, we were delighted to welcome the names of Adamson-BSMG Worldwide, the Austrian Federal Economic Chamber, the European Information and Communication Technology Association, European Voice, Shandwick International and the United Business Institute to our team of financial sponsors, and those of EurActiv.Com, the European Information Service/European Centre for Public Affairs Brussels, and the European Public Affairs Directory, as our media partners for the event. The event attracted around 50 speakers of the highest calibre and 150 registrations during the week, with the outline presentations and abstracts available on the conference web site, http://www.ey.be/EYBE/Site.nsf/Pages/EnconfFrame. The second event in the conference series is scheduled for May 2002.

The issues

A well documented factor to which all associations can be subjected to is the potential that its positions might be no more than the 'lowest common denominator' of those of its members. Our focus was to investigate the conditions under which EU business associations vary in their abilities to move beyond these. In the first section of the conference, and in the contributions that follow, we examined factors in the external environment of associations held to affect the ability of an association to come to cohesive positions in a timely manner, whether these are factors affecting all associations, or those that explain the variation in associational performance. A second section examines change agents and case studies in managing change, and in particular the extent to which management, leadership and design of associations can make a difference to their performance, particularly within the context of the constraint factors in their external environments. A final section examines these factors in relation to the special position of cross-sectoral and employer organisations.

Our subject matter is of importance for those who work in, and with EU business associations, and those who study them. Business people are acutely aware that the world in which they operate is full of industries which are 'economic giants and yet political dwarfs', and are anxious to find ways of maximising the performance of their representative organisations. EU policy-makers also need and want organisations with which they can engage which are strong enough to deliver good quality information, advice and collective opinion, in that effective policy-partners can help deliver good EU governance and contribute to the wealth creation process. Yet beyond this, the study of effective EU associations is of wider significance. First, a recent initiative of the Commission has launched a debate about a modernised form of democracy, searching for ideas that will inform a 'White Paper on Governance'. Part of these questions concern the ability of associations to organise and regulate markets, and in doing so perform wider public goals, while another set of questions search for new forms of representative participation in EU policy-making, and the extent to which collective organisations with which policy-makers engage are both representative and accountable. Second, some accounts of European integration place business interest associations at the heart of a mechanism which explains how member-states are encouraged to transfer competencies to the European level, and how the EU institutions acquire extensions to their working domains. Third, there are unresolved questions about the extent to which EU associations assist economic performance through their ability to undertake certain tasks of economic governance, or whether they interfere with the wealth creation process and the free operation of markets through extracting from public authorities special privileges. Finally, for academics, there are unresolved questions about what drives firms and/or their representative organisations to act together, and whether it is automatic or problematic for them to do so.

There is no business domain in which relations between the EU and business are conducted wholly through an associational intermediary. At least 900[6] EU business associations (of which 750 are based in Brussels) operate alongside 350 large firms (of which around 250 are based in Brussels)[7] with EU public affairs capacities. Associations struggle where there are large firms, or other members, active in a public affairs environment that welcomes them. The official position of the European Commission towards outside interests is that:

> The Commission has always been an institution open to outside input. The Commission believes this process to be fundamental to the development of its policies. This dialogue has proved valuable to both the Commission and to interested outside parties. Commission

officials acknowledge the need for such outside input and welcome it.

SEC (92) 2272 final

The 'outside input' referred to above includes that from collective
entities (such as associations) and from individual entities (such as
firms). This 'free for all' welcome represents a relatively disorganised
form of dialogue with outside interests when compared to some
member-states. In some countries, there are explicit policies favouring
collective dialogue with business through their representative associations, rather than with individual firms, and ways in which states can
provide incentives to firms to work through associations for dialogue
with governments. In Austria, for instance, membership of the Federal
Economic Chamber is compulsory for firms, while governments can
provide selective incentives for companies to join and work through
associations by providing these associations with official status or
functions to undertake, such as self-regulation or economic development tasks.

The European Union only has a limited ability to provide the institutional patronage that associations need to derive their strength from.
First of all, the EU is not a 'state' at all, but a fragmented architecture of
multilevel governance in which there are a plurality of access points for
outside interests, ranging from national governments to the variety of
EU institutions. The result tends to be a 'lobby free for all' rather than an
organised system of dialogue with business. In its early days, while the
European Commission may have tried to develop EU associations by an
'official' policy to favour them as dialogue partners in preference to
companies and national associations, it has never been in a position to
enforce it. Through its own practices and reliance upon companies for
resources such as market and product expertise, and for the legitimacy
that dialogue with household name companies bring, it has long
allowed its dated policy to fall into disuse. While the European
Commission still tries to encourage the development of representative
EU associations by delegating functions to them, such as information
generation or self-regulation, few industries are in a position to undertake the most significant of these functions, such as self-regulation
on a European level, and these may not be consistent with national
requirements. There are some important exceptions to this, such as in
the advertising, and environmental protection domains, where associations have been invested with regulatory authority, and in turn these
have served to strengthen the associations concerned. Whether new

initiatives under consideration within the framework of the current 'White Paper on Governance' for self-regulation to be embedded within a system of 'coregulation' will strengthen, or weaken, the ability of EU level associations to undertake public policy functions remain to be seen. Some initiatives in the field of environmental improvement have also involved EU associations in a central role. In any event, the aggressive pursuit of competition policy rules by the European Commission in recent years has severely limited the extent to which associations can add value for their members by organising and regulating markets. In developing countries, business associations typically have high membership density because they are 'licensed' by governments to undertake economic development activities, such as sector upgrading, managing overcapacity, or export relationships. Under European competition policy, most of these activities would be forbidden, and indeed some EU associations have been implicated in hefty anti-trust penalties, or have had to adjust their constitutions in response to objections raised by DG Competition of the European Commission. Consequently, there are restricted ways in which EU associations can provide assistance to their membership constituencies. EU associations thus only have a limited ability to organise and regulate markets.

The above factors are common to all EU associations. Yet which factors explain variation in the ability of associations to be cohesive and add value for their members?

- *Patronage of political institutions*: While there are common factors system wide limiting the role of EU level associations, there are also variations in different sections of EU institutions exhibiting different capacities, policies and behaviour towards associations. For instance, some provide access to advisory committees, through which membership of the EU association provides the sole gateway for business. This introduces a second factor of variation.
- *The degree of EU regulation*: Many associations formed in response to the stimuli of EU regulation (such as the EU electricity association EURELECTRIC, initially formed to oppose electricity deregulation), or to seek it. In sectors where this stimuli is not present, there seems little reason to participate in the EU association for potential members.
- *The scope of the interest organised*: It is easier for business to act in highly specific, sometimes issue-based, associations, where there are a small number of members in the interest category with highly defined interests. In these circumstances, business associations can be homogenous. Hence, EU associations such as the Alliance for

Cartons and the Environment, or the branded products association AIM, are highly regarded external and internal to the organisation. The EU association with the most difficult portfolio is perhaps EuroCommerce, which organises retailers, distributors, wholesalers, and even some producers, and whose membership within these categories contains firms of highly diverse size.

Related to this factor is the degree of identity in the product chain. 'Upstream' producers often have quite separate interests from 'downstream' producers over issues such as transaction price or the flow of goods, and those associations which limit their scope to a specific position in the product chain often find an enhanced ability for cohesiveness. This introduces a fourth factor, relational to other interests:

- *Common enemy*: This may be another interest in the product chain, or it may be a labour union in respect of employer interests, or a public interest group which is perceived as an opposing interest by members. Campaigning environmental groups, for instance, provide cohesiveness to many associations in the chemical sector.

A related factor concerns the extent to which a sector is surrounded by issues of sufficient controversy that require a 'collective cloak' to reduce the exposure of an individual member.

- *Geographical scope of markets*: Markets which naturally cross national boundaries are easier to organise than those that are essentially nationally contained in scope.
- *The product cycle and nature of the product*: Sectors at a mature point in the product cycle are often highly concentrated and sometimes need to manage overcapacity. In these circumstances, there are natural tendencies towards collective action. These are exacerbated in commodity product sectors, where it is difficult to differentiate products other than through price, providing incentives for unlawful collective behaviour. Over the years EU associations in the steel, cement, pulp, and broadcasting sectors, for instance, have been implicated in competition policy decisions, having served as warning examples to all other trade associations.

In newly emergent sectors, division can be caused by companies clustering around competing technologies and a quest to gain market acceptance of one product standards, such as divisions that emerged between VHS and Betamax standards. Where new product standard agreements have been driven by associations organising interests at an early stage in the product cycle, the sectors concerned tend to have a relatively high degree of maturity and are well established globally (such as IT).[8]

- *Other sectoral characteristics*: Other characteristics of sectors that have been held to promote associational cohesion include the degree of sectoral concentration (not too much or little), and similarity of firm size and ownership structure (Bennett, 1999). Significant merger and acquisition activity has been held to be disruptive to associations by changing the resource base and distribution of influence inside an association.

The presence or absence of the above conditions predict the likely cohesiveness of an association. Thus, sectors where favourable conditions for associational effectiveness apply, they typically embrace the more concentrated upstream arenas, while the more fragmented downstream arenas face less favourable conditions. Hence, sectors such as pharmaceuticals, chemicals, steel, cement and gypsum; and chemicals do well, while unfavourable conditions apply in tourism, retail, and downstream construction.

'Management' and 'Leadership' are unlikely to make a considerable difference in unfavourable conditions. Yet the 'governability' of an association – that is, its ability to unify its members interests and to seek member compliance for these (Traxler, 1991) – is not wholly a product of a sector's external environment features. Some associations are able to exercise leadership with their members by *shaping their perceptions of what their interests are*. This is an extremely sensitive tightrope on which association General Secretaries walk, trying to provide leadership to their members, while at the same time being seen to represent their articulated wishes without walking too far ahead of them. Yet for those able to walk the tightrope, it is a key mechanism for associations to gain autonomy from their members, which in turn enhances their effectiveness, and their utility in public policy through their ability to be flexible and pro-active. Associations that are too closely controlled by their members are often riddled by internal disputes, are used by their members for control and damage limitation purposes, and are only able to react to the agendas of others.

These considerations draw attention to the ways in which design features of associations can influence cohesiveness.[9] For associations to develop autonomy, they need some degree of independence in their resources, from any individual member or category of member. Hence, some associations have developed rules requiring members to give long notice periods to exit, or constitutional rules which ensure that the association does not depend upon secondments from its members in order to staff the key positions of associations. Independence from a potentially dominant member can be ensured through the weighting of votes carefully between members. Nonetheless, large firms may be discouraged if they do not carry sufficient weight in the position of the association relative to smaller members, and an informal settlement needs to be reached whereby larger members carry a disproportionate burden for resourcing the association in return for a relatively higher degree of influence. The trick is to balance this alongside safeguards which secure the independence of the association from being over dominated by a small number of members.

The high degree of control exerted by members in some associations is often a function of lack of trust between them, and between the secretariat and members over the handling of commercially sensitive information. In these circumstances, membership of the association is not driven by the positive benefits an association can offer, but more by a desire to prevent the association, and its positions and activities, from damaging the interests of a company. On the part of this member, the purpose of membership is therefore driven by a desire to keep the association from damage, leaving the member free to undertake their own political representation work in the EU institutions. In these circumstances the association becomes reactive rather than active, and highly prone to 'lowest common denominator' type positions. This raises an entire series of questions as to whether some analytic order can be imposed upon associational membership.

In recent years businesses attention to the role of their associations has provoked a fresh look at the governance and leadership issues. The limited availability and cost aspect of corporate CEOs and technical experts have led to significant changes. The imperative of a more professionalised management started in particular in the US, leading to increased competitiveness among trade associations and the emergence of highly qualified Secretary Generals. These professionals are often relatively mobile within the business association domain,[10] and whose activities may lead to a more frequent and in-depth review of membership which is association driven.

What is the basis of EU association membership?

The above section has indicated a number of circumstances that explain variation in associational cohesiveness. In the right combination of circumstances, EU association membership can be highly attractive. Yet even in unfavourable circumstances, membership is still often the norm – driven *not by the positive benefits of membership*, but by *the costs of non-membership*.

The preceding statement implies the presence of reason, or rationality, to membership. Yet hard and fast 'reasons' may not be in the forefront of membership behaviour. Most EU business associations include national associations, for whom acting together – that is, membership – is normal political behaviour, and indeed reflects their very own *raison d'être*. In these cases, no special 'reasons' are required for members to join associations – they just do it automatically. While there are exceptions where national associations do not belong to EU associations, there are more cases where the opposite applies, where national associations remain in membership despite failing to participate for years. Because pure associations of associations (federations) still account for the majority of EU associations, a conclusion can therefore be drawn that in most cases, membership of EU associations is a relatively unproblematic concept that does not require extensive investment on the part of the association in selective incentives to attract and retain members.

Despite the current predominance of federations, there has undeniably been a clear trend in recent years to admit companies directly into membership of EU associations, either alongside national association members, or in associations dedicated solely to direct company representation. In these associational design formats, the near automatic basis of associability may seem less sure. Of interest is that most EU associations report that their direct company members are hard headed, cost-benefit calculators of their membership, often undertaking annual appraisal. Yet this claim is not borne out by the author's research among 42 large company members of 25 EU associations. Here, it was found that most undertake no evaluation, and for many respondents the question 'why are you a member of x association' provided them with the first opportunity to identify and articulate a set of 'reasons.' For most firms, once they join an association (often 'the thing to do'), there is nothing resembling a 'decision' to continue – continued membership is more like 'habit', or 'auto-pilot'. While there may be an initial membership 'decision', continued membership rarely resembles anything like a 'decision' at all. In some cases of membership renewal involving direct debit like procedures, there is nothing resembling a decision window. It is also possible that the membership decision is an 'historic' one, perhaps taken by someone who no longer works at the member company. Some multiproduct companies with decentralised divisional structures also have no centralised capacity to coordinate their EU association memberships, and in some cases there is no one in the company who is aware how many EU association affiliations they hold, bringing the risk with it of unknowingly taking up contradictory positions in different associations. One story was recounted to the author about a representative of a large, high profile American firm who was extremely active in her trade association, being informed during a committee session of the association that her company had resigned its membership on the grounds that no one in the firm ever heard from the association. Despite claims among associations that American firms were more likely to be hard headed cost-benefit calculators, firms of US parentage were found to be no more likely than European firms to evaluate their membership. One interpretation for the difference in perception between trade associations, and companies, is that firms may engage in convenient exit rhetoric inside association committees as a means of getting what they want, but which in reality may not be a sole guide to their behaviour.

Association membership is undoubtedly driven by a vast array of features.[11] Many of these can be categorised as membership 'incentives' which are only accessible by joining the association and which are not 'free rideable' by outsiders, whether for reasons that are positive to the member (such as access to influential decision forums), neutral (e.g. encouraged by EU institutions), or negative (e.g. ability to prevent the association from taking up a damaging position). Yet membership is not always driven by incentives. This introduction has indicated that continued membership of EU associations may be driven just as much by 'auto-pilot' type behaviour than by 'incentives', and has offered a categorisation of factors which influence both the likelihood of associability and association cohesiveness. Chief among these are the degree of specialism of interest domain and position in the product chain, the characteristics of a sector that make it prone to 'cartel' like tendencies, the extent of a 'common enemy', and the extent of autonomous and professional leadership of the staff and the Board of the association.

The chapters ahead test these propositions, and extend them by assessing the extent to which factors in the external environment of associations, and factors of management, leadership, and design, can explain variation in the ability of EU level business associations to be strong and cohesive organisations. We invite the reader to join us on our journey of discovery.

Notes

1   Defined in Commission rules as those of under 36 years of age.
2   Union of Industrial and Employers' Confederations of Europe.

3 The EU Committee of the American Chamber of Commerce.
4 European Association of Craft, Small- and Medium-sized Enterprises.
5 European Chemical Industry Council.
6 This figure has been arrived at following calculations made in the summer of 1999 derived from a composite of 6 Directory sources, using the most recent editions of the *European Public Affairs Directory* (Landmarks, 1999), the *Directory of 9300 Trade and Professional Associations in the EU* (Euroconfidential, 1999), the Union of International Associations' *Yearbook of International Organisations* (UIA, 1999), the European Commission web directory of interest groups (European Commission, 1999), and Butt-Philip and Gray (1996).
7 Figures for large firms in and out of Brussels are based upon entries in the *European Public Affairs Directory* (Landmarks, 1999). They should be treated with some caution because firms can choose not to be listed in the directory if they so wish, and the presence of an 'EU public affairs office' for a company is more difficult to define than an association. Some EU public affairs functions may, for instance, be carried out on an *ad hoc* basis by 'jet in jet out' staff from a remote general public affairs or other type of office using the premises of a subsidiary based in Belgium.
8 One example is the standards association for PC-Cards (PCMCIA) which from the start in 1989 was formed as a truly global initiative by a handful innovative companies – and in a few years successfully launched a common interface card for laptop computers, interactive TV and so on. A recent example is Bluetooth, an interface for electronics, attracting thousands of companies in the one or two years since its inception. They may also 'by-pass' established organisations such as IEC, ISO, and CENELEC.
9 In these circumstances, and in the case of emerging or small- and medium-sized associations, the option of contracted out Association Management can provide a solution. In the EU, Ernst & Young Association Management is currently the largest provider of this service.
10 The American Society of Association Executives (ASAE), based in Washington DC, organises regular seminars and publishes practical guidelines for the both elected leadership and full time association managers.
11 For a review of these see Jordan (1997).

Part I
Understanding the Environment

2
Factors Influencing the Effectiveness of Business Associations: a Review
Robert J. Bennett

This chapter addresses the factors that influence the effectiveness of business associations, focusing on their role as producers of economic services. Using British material from surveys of associations and Small- and Medium-sized Enterprises (SMEs), it demonstrates the existence of *internal economies of scale* and the existence of a 'critical mass' threshold to achieve significant market penetration for representation and services use, or to have major service impact on their business members. *Internal economies of scope* are also demonstrated to exist as a result of service 'bundling'. *External economies of scale* also exist in some specific contexts. The economics of service production is demonstrated to influence the extent of membership, use of services and service impact of business associations. Other factors influencing associations are the environment and diversity of the sector covered by the association. These factors together are also shown to have a strong relationship with how sector associations operate in Europe. In the case of lobbying, sector diversity and association character both influence the choice between company 'direct' lobbying, use of the 'national route' through national business associations, or use of a 'European association' route. Implications are drawn for association managers, government and the European Commission.

A key argument used below is that in order to understand associations, they must be analysed not solely through the lens of associations themselves, but also through the motivation and dynamics of their membership. In addition, it is argued that it is necessary to go beyond looking at trade associations and the old economy, to understand smaller businesses, the new economy and the diversity of businesses and their members, and hence the diversity of the types of associations that evolve in the contexts of different sectors, locations, and business

15

size classes. Most importantly this requires the addition of understanding of the specifics of SMEs and the economic motives and sociology of business managers. In Britain the membership of business associations is drawn 48 per cent from owner-managers or professionals, 50 per cent from SMEs of under 100 employees, and only 1.7 per cent from businesses of 100 employees and over (Bennett, 1999b: Table 1). Therefore, it is essential in understanding associations, that professional associations and director associations are included, as well as trade associations. An overview for the diversity of associations in the British case, is shown in Table 2.1.

First, the chapter outlines the underlying structure of association services to be expected from the ideas of management economics. Second, it demonstrates their relevance empirically. Third, evidence of

Table 2.1 Percentage of membership for each type of association from different size businesses (measured by number of employees)

Association type	Percentage of membership from each size class of business (number of employees)					
	>200	100–199	10–99	2–9	Individuals, self-employed and sole traders	Total density of membership (% of sector's businesses)
Corporate trade associations	2.8	1.4	57.7	32.8	5.2	61.7
Associations of owner-manager	0.7	0.2	27.3	39.6	32.1	40.1
Associations of self-employed	0.1	0.0	2.9	6.5	90.5	50.5
Professional associations	0.9	0.3	18.5	26.8	53.4	n/a
Mixed bodies	1.4	0.4	19.9	31.3	47.0	41.3
Federations	3.9	2.3	52.6	41.0	0.2	68.0
Total (sector associations)	1.2	0.4	21.1	28.9	48.4	53.4
Local chambers of commerce	5.3	5.1	29.3	51.1	9.2	11
Overall total	1.2	0.5	21.2	29.4	47.7	43.0

Note: British Chambers of Commerce (BCC) Census statistics use different size criteria and have been interpolated. The professional association membership cannot be readily collated from the surveys used, but is probably higher than for any other sector, on average. Hence the overall total density is probably underestimated in the table.
Source: Original surveys of associations and BCC Census; Bennett, 1999b.

relations of associations with European issues is examined. This allows associations to be placed within the wider context of other exchange relations of business-to-business alliances and networks, business-to-government/EU relations, and exchanges of business-to-other agents. Hence, for example, the direct links of businesses to government or EU bodies ('the direct route') are investigated as well as the national, European or international association routes of exchange. In each case the example of Britain is used for detailed discussion, but this is set in a wider context.

The economics of supplying association services: 'bundling' and critical mass

The emphasis in this chapter, on understanding associations through the dynamics of their membership, leads naturally to trying to understand the economics of these organisations. The discussion here seeks to understand associations in the normal terms of management economics that would be applied to any other professional service supplier. The economics of supply of association services, whether collective or individual, like any other service derive from the interaction of the fixed, variable and communication costs of delivering services. For the supply of most professional services the main costs are the variable costs of core staff (Mills and Margulies, 1980; Kotler and Bloom, 1984; Perry, 1992; Wilson and Smith, 1996). This may include highly specific staff skills. In addition there may be some variation in levels of fixed costs for different services arising from the IT and communication systems required, library and documentary sources, and any specialist equipment. Variable costs, however, including staff as well as transport, communication and delivery costs, are usually the main cost element of most professional service businesses.

Although the main costs are *variable costs*, there is usually a critical threshold of volume that is required to make the support service viable and allow market entry. This depends on the interaction of fixed costs with variable costs across the market of potential demand, which in turn depends on the level of market penetration (see e.g. Phillips *et al.*, 1998). This has been referred to in a number of contexts as the need for a 'critical mass' of both supplier services or resources, and sufficient potential demand and depth of market penetration in order to justify the investment required for service development (see e.g. Chandler, 1990; Bennett, 1993; Harrison, 1997). This critical mass will be determined by the aggregate number of clients, transaction costs per unit of service, the influence of economies of scale and scope, and agglomeration economies. The critical mass may vary for different mixes of services supplied.

In practice, because of the interaction of fixed and variable costs with the level of demand and market penetration between different types of services, which determine critical mass, most associations have developed trade-offs between services, particularly between collective representation services (which are beset by free-rider problems where non-members can consume the benefits of a service for no costs), and other services. Olson (1971) refers to this as a bi-product problem. More generally it can be understood as generating the need for a supplier to *bundle* the services they supply (Paun, 1993). For associations this means that they have to bundle representation and other services.

The bundling of association services that occurs in Britain is shown in Table 2.2 for trade and professional associations, and local chambers of commerce. The mixed pattern of service provision confirms the need to understand the interplay between (i) the 'logic of individual services'; (ii) the 'logic of influence' and representation; (iii) the logic of excludable collective services; (iv) the forces from the market for control

Table 2.2 The percentage of associations of each main type offering services of each category (multiple responses included)

	Corporate trade associations	Professional associations	Chambers of commerce
Excludable individual services (e.g. advice and consultancy)	95	63	100
Excludable collective services (e.g. group insurance, group marketing and purchasing)	95	95	100
Non-excludable collective services (e.g. surveys and information dissemination, training lead bodies)	94	72	100
Non-excludable collective lobbying and representation:			
UK	84	60	100
EU	64	30	8
Self-regulation (e.g. qualifications, branding, benchmarking, accreditation)	26	45	43

Source: Surveys of associations; Bennett, 1999b.

(business size, concentration and organisation) which affect exit, voice, loyalty and involvement; and (v) forces from associability (sociological, geographical) which also affect exit, voice, loyalty and involvement (see Hirschman, 1970, 1982; Streeck and Schmitter, 1985a).

The *fixed costs* of business association derive from the need to operate a basic entity that can respond to enquiries, administer its member/client database, develop influence, and operate its most basic services. This requires a certain minimum staff, premises, communication and associated office costs. The basic minimum of fixed costs to allow the development of each association is probably very small. Certainly there are many business associations that exist with only a single member of staff, and indeed many operate purely with volunteers. Market entry does not seem to be a major problem for sector or local chamber associations. Many have no full time staff. In the case of such small bodies it proves possible to operate support organisations with a tiny core staff incurring fixed costs, with all other costs variable in line with the volume of members dealt with, or clients advised, or activities generated. For example, member businesses may carry some of the costs of increasing volume. Alternatively, external consultants and advisors may operate on a self-employed contract, charging and thus generating costs for members only when they are used. This approach is used by many small business associations.

The generally low fixed costs of providing business support, and hence low market entry barriers, result in a multiplicity of rival associations developed in Britain and most other countries. As a result the concept of 'critical mass' for business support organisations tends to depend less on the need to overcome fixed costs and enter the market, than on the need to develop a significant 'weight', 'clout' or level of market penetration (breadth of encompassing). This requires a level of visibility, dissemination of information about the association, and marketing of its unique selling point (USP). To the extent that this type of critical mass element feeds into costs, marketing and brand development become important aspects of fixed costs. Moreover, the level of use (market penetration) and the value or impact of the service received by the client become key indicators of the extent to which critical mass has been achieved.

Beyond the level of the normally rather low basic fixed costs for a business association to exist, variable costs will be the most important aspect influencing association development. These may increase linearly with volumes. However, it is likely that there will be some internal or external economies of scale and scope.

Internal economies exist when unit increase in the capacity of the organisation lead to more than proportional increase in output or decrease in unit costs of service provision (Harrison, 1997). This can derive from the diminishing cost of the mix of factors needed to supply a single specific service (internal economies of scale), or to cost reductions across a bundle of related services (internal economies of scope). For business association services both scale and scope economies chiefly result from the benefits of increased market penetration, with economies of scope being particularly important in allowing a customer link, once established, to be diversified into further custom, thus potentially economising on marketing and related costs. Thus internal economies of both scale and scope may contribute to the development of further benefits deriving from the development of a 'critical mass'. Alternatively, it may be the case that once a threshold to achieve a critical mass is crossed, the benefits of further internal economies of scale and scope are small or indeed may be negative if the customer perceives the organisation to be too large, too remote, or too generalised to be useful to provide its specific needs. The form of these economies is largely an empirical question dependent on market testing.

External economies arise for associations from a number of possible features. For local bodies such as chambers of commerce there may be external economies of localisation and agglomeration. These arise from locations where other important organisations exist to provide the benefit of 'knowledge spillovers' (Pred, 1977). The concept of locational 'clusters' of related and supporting industries (Porter, 1998) can also be equally applied to associations, as to other businesses. For sector associations, external economies may be sought in collaborations and federations, or other networks of inter-business and inter-association activities.

Empirical evidence

While economic principles may help us to understand the possibilities for internal and external economies of service supply, it is an empirical question how far associations can actually realise these possibilities in what is a crowded and highly competitive market for professional services. This market is crowded not only with other private sector service businesses (banks, accountants, lawyers, consultants, etc.), but also by public sector bodies seeking to help businesses. Even in the field of representation to governments, there is a high level of competition, from the private sector, where consultants and lawyers have made this an important part of their portfolio nationally and in Brussels; from the public sector where many executive agencies and government departments play their own games of trying to influence decisions; and from social partners, NGOs and non-business organisations that compete to put alternative views.

The empirical evidence of association effectiveness is presented below using survey evidence from business users and from association managers. The survey and business users derives from a University of Cambridge ESRC Centre for Business Research survey of 2500 SMEs, surveyed in 1997 and 1999 for the whole of Britain (see Cosh and Hughes, 1998). This survey of businesses allows analysis of the factors influencing both use and impact. These factors are estimated using logit and ordered logit regression models and are reported in detail in Bennett and Robson (2002), Bratton *et al.* (2002) and ongoing research. Only the key findings are reported here. Similarly, surveys of trade and professional associations undertaken in Britain in 1996 are used to address the question of external economies of scale and 'bundling' of European representation activities (see Bennett, 1999b,c). The range of factors influencing use and impact of associations is analysed. The analysis focuses in turn on internal economies, external economies, and other factors.

Internal economies and 'critical mass'

A key finding of empirical assessments using the business survey is a series of estimates, derived from the actual use by businesses of associations, of the probabilities of using a business association, while controlling for other factors. The change in these probabilities with the size of an association is shown in Figure 2.1. The measure of size used in all cases is the number of staff (full time equivalent) since, as argued earlier, human resources expertise is the key aspect of most professional service, and usually the dominant cost. Three types of association are examined: sector associations, local chambers of commerce, and the hybrid public–private body of Training and Enterprise Councils (TECs).

Figure 2.1 demonstrates a number of features of the effect of internal economies. First, market entry barriers are very low for each body, as expected. Use of an association begins at very low staff sizes. However, market penetration (use) increases rapidly as staff sizes increase from very small to only slightly larger levels.

Second, for local chambers and TECs, a very definite critical mass threshold appears to exit at between about one and two staff per thousand businesses. For sector associations the critical mass level is higher,

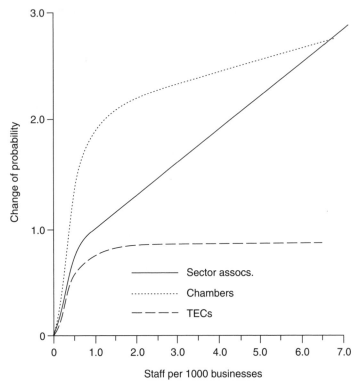

Figure 2.1 Increase in predicted probability of using business associations for each additional staff member per 1000 businesses in their sectors or areas (The probability levels are estimated from logit regression model).

at about five staff per thousand businesses, but sector bodies increase their use to higher levels than local bodies before reaching this threshold, indicating their easier market entry and capacity to develop internal economies over a greater range of small association staff sizes.

Third, there is also strong evidence of the continually increasing probability of use with increasing staff size after the critical mass threshold has been reached for chambers of commerce and sector associations (see Figure 2.1). This suggests that they experience significant nonlinear internal economies of scale which can be interpreted as chiefly arising from synergies between services (i.e. 'bundling') for the largely self-selecting group of customers that elect to become association members. For TECs, however, once the critical mass threshold is reached, returns to scale are linear with staff size. Each TEC service thus appears as discrete, with little or no benefits of bundling. Significantly, this suggests that TECs have not been able to develop an effective coordinated business support strategy for their areas.

The impact of business association services differs from that of use. TECs show no influence on impact of increasing staff sizes. Sector associations and chambers, however, do show a significant influence of staff size on impact, but with a tendency for there to be diseconomies at larger staff sizes (Figure 2.2). This implies that while market penetration can be increased with larger staff sizes by sector associations and chambers (Figure 2.1), over a certain size they can become too remote and with the result that their services to clients are judged to be less intense and satisfactory in terms of impact.

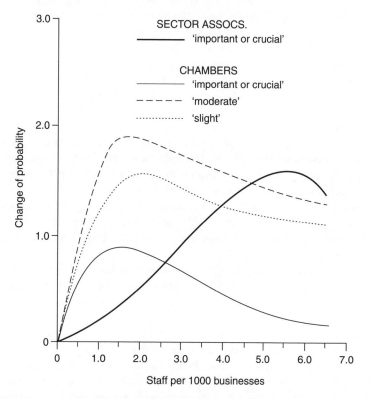

Figure 2.2 Increase in predicted probability of the type of impact of business associations for each additional staff member per 1000 businesses in their sector or areas (Probabilities calculated from ordered logit regression model).

External economies

It has been proved possible to assess external economy effects for sector associations only from surveys of associations themselves. For these, multivariate regression estimates suggest that federation services and cooperation are a positive influence on association market penetration, rate of joining and reduced rate of lapsing (Bennett, 1999c). However, these results are in no case highly statistically significant. The external economies of inter-association cooperation thus appear minor, at best.

More detailed empirical assessment can be made for SME use of local chambers and TEC services. Using the same large sample survey, there is clear evidence of external agglomeration effects from location in large cities and traditional industrial areas. In the logit regression, chambers are significantly more likely to be used in these concentrated locations suggesting that it is easier to meet a critical mass threshold where there are business clusters and industrial agglomerations. However, the more general variable of distance from a business centre is not significant, suggesting that it is only in the case of location in or close to the most concentrated urban and industrial centres that *external* economies of scale and scope operate for business associations to increase use and market penetration (Bennett *et al.*, 2001). This result is an interesting contrast to private sector professional services which are highly distance constrained, as evidenced from the same survey data (Bennett *et al.*, 2000) and in other surveys in Britain and other countries (see e.g. O'Farrell *et al.*, 1992, 1993; van Dinteren, 1987; Illeris and Rasmussen, 1992; Illeris, 1994; Tordoir, 1994; Coe and Townsend, 1998). The differences appear to result from the fact that local associations such as chambers and TECs operate over a specific territory.

Also of significance among the locational influences on association use, however, is the eligibility for EU structural funds and financial aids. Both chambers of commerce and TECs in areas eligible for EU structural funds experience greater levels of use, after controlling for other factors. This suggests that local business associations benefit from the cost supports that these aids offer. The improved financial base allows the critical mass threshold of business associations to be met at a lower level of effective demand and/or lower levels of market penetration. Thus a larger staff and/or range of services will be available than would be the case under market stimulus alone.

The 'environment' of the association

The environment of associations relates to the character of the trading environment and broader economic and political factors. In a multivariate analysis of a large scale survey of sector associations to assess these factors the following statistical characteristics are evident (Bennett, 1999c):

- The level of sector concentration/consolidation and organisation is a major positive influence on association market penetration.
- The predominance of large companies encourages greater market penetration and other companies are attracted by this large company membership.
- The range of an association's services has little effect on market penetration, but does increase the rate of joining.

Other factors of significance are (Bennett, 1999c):

- The management structure of an association has only a minor influence suggesting that an executive-driven structure (rather than a member on council-driven structure) marginally increases market penetration and joining rates. This gives mild confirmation to Boléat's (1996) arguments.
- The size of an association is a negative influence on market penetration, larger associations tend to have lower densities of membership.
- The age of an association is generally a positive but small influence on market penetration, evidencing some effects of competitive advantage deriving from historically established positions.

Association diversity and European 'representation'

Major EU representational activity by British businesses and their associations generally follows more than one route, as shown in Table 2.3. The national route, working through the British government and institutions, is the most common; European associations are also used extensively, and ranked first by federations. European associations are also felt to be the most open to influence. A Brussels strategy through use of an office or other direct activities with the EC and other institutions is also widely used, as well as direct lobbying by member companies. This spread of routes accords with other findings (Greenwood *et al.*, 1992; Mazey and Richardson, 1993; Pedler and van Schendelen, 1994; Bennett, 1997).

The interrelation between a business's lobbying strategy, the form of its association and the size of the business is demonstrated in an analysis by Bennett (1999d) for the case of Britain. This confirms that a higher

Table 2.3 Main route for lobbying and representation in Europe

	Corporate trade associations	Owner-manager associations	Self-employed associations	Professional associations	Federations	Total
'Brussels Strategy'						
(1) Member company direct lobbying	13.1	2.7	40.0	4.1	10.0	10.9
(2) Association direct lobbying	18.6	13.5	0	11.1	10.0	16.5
Through European association	24.1	35.1	20.0	27.8	50.0	27.4
'National Strategy' (through UK government etc.)	40.0	43.2	40.0	50.0	30.0	42.1
Mixed/other	4.1	5.4	0	0	0	3.0

Note: Percentage of each association type rating each option as their main route; columns sum to 100 per cent.
Source: Bennett, 1999a.

proportion of larger businesses directly lobby than smaller businesses, but only for corporate businesses, within the category of 'trade association'. The density of membership (encompassing) generally does not significantly influence the extent of direct lobbying. In contrast to the suggestion by Olson (1971) and Streeck and Schmitter (1985a), the extent of encompassing does not influence the extent of direct lobbying, except in the corporate sector for large companies. Nor does the sector's degree of organisation or weight ('clout' as measured by scale of a sector's turnover) have statistically significant influence on the degree of direct lobbying. This is a contrast to the finding of Greenwood (1997). The main contrasts between the extent of lobbying for each association type and two association sizes are shown in Table 2.4.

The main results of the statistical estimation of these effects using multivariate regression (Bennett, 1999d) demonstrates that the main features explaining the extent of direct business lobbying are the size of an association and the type of business. For most businesses, and for most associations, direct lobbying is not an option. But for large corporate businesses in small associations direct lobbying is a major activity. Moreover it is an activity that increases in scale the higher is the proportion of members of the association that are also large corporates. This applies both as a proportion of the sector's businesses and as a proportion of the association's members.

The tendency for large corporate businesses in small associations to lobby directly indicates a form of the phenomenon recognised by Hirschman (1982) and Useem (1984), that large firms seek involvement *and* control. However, it is surprising that this search for direct benefits and control is stronger the more that the presence of large corporates is

Table 2.4 Percentage of a sector's members lobbying directly to Brussels by type of association and its membership size

	Size of association membership		
	≤70	>70	Total
Trade associations	47.2	3.6	26.9
Owner-manager associations	–	0.25	0.25
Professional associations	–	–	–
Mixed associations	–	1.4	1.4
Federations	–	1.6	1.6
Total	47.2	2.4	18.7

Source: Bennett, 1999d: Table 1.

merged with other large corporates in the same association. The findings demonstrate a clear constraint on the potential of associations to
act for businesses collectively in those cases where the businesses are
large and weighty in a sector that is highly concentrated. In contrast,
however, for SMEs, micro businesses and professional association members, direct lobbying is largely impossible and national or European
associations are the key lobbying route.

Conclusion

This chapter has restricted *empirical* discussion to British business associations. However, its findings have wider application. The chapter has
shown the importance of understanding the economics of associations
and the diversity of businesses and of their associations. The Chapter
has confirmed the importance for associations of key economic management criteria:

- Low barriers to market entry.
- Rapidly increasing internal economies of scale.
- A critical mass threshold for market penetration and impact on business members.
- Non-linear increasing economies of scale, after the critical mass
  threshold has been reached, only for pure private sector business
  associations.
- An absence of economies of scale for public–private bodies above
  their critical mass thresholds which demonstrates that they do not
  operate a strategic approach that allows service bundling. Although
  specific to TECs, these results may also be indicative of the economic
  behaviour of public law associations or those with substantial public
  contracts or supports.
- The existence for chambers of commerce of significant external
  economies from local agglomeration of businesses in large and
  traditional cities.
- The importance of the 'environment' of associations, particularly:
  – Sector concentration/organisation;
  – Larger sized company membership which stimulates other busi-
    nesses to join.

With respect to European activities, the chapter shows that most
associations combine 'Brussels routes' with European association routes,
national strategies and direct action by their member companies. There
are, however, important differences between associations of different
types and by types of membership sizes and company sizes.

Acknowledgements

This research has been undertaken with the support of a Leverhulme Trust Personal Research Professorship, the use of the BCC Census. Some aspects have the support of the ESRC Cambridge University, Centre for Business Research Survey and help of Paul Robson and William Bratton through an ESRC Studentship No. S00429637024.

3
European State Formation and its Impact on Associational Governance: Will Business Interest Association (BIA) Systems become Centralised at the EU Level?[1]

Frans van Waarden

Interest Associations as rent seekers or instruments of economic governance?

Organised private interests have often been seen as threats to the common good, particularly in the US. James Madison, one of the founders of the American state, talked already of the 'mischiefs of faction'. Ever since, American economic and political science literature has abounded with descriptions, analyses and criticism of the private abuse of public power. The choir of critics has been politically diverse, from Marxists (Baran and Sweezy, 1968) to liberals sociologists (Wright Mills, 1956; Domhoff, 1967, 1970), political scientists (Schattschneider, 1962; Bachrach and Baratz, 1970; Shonfield, 1982; Chubb, 1983), 'capture' theorists (Bernstein, 1955; Mitnick, 1980) to conservative representatives of public choice theory (Buchanan *et al.*, 1980; Olson, 1982) and the economic theory of regulation (Stigler, 1971; Posner, 1974). The common thrust of these approaches has been to view economic interest associations are rent seekers, and any influence of them on public policy tends to pervert such policy. They abuse public authority for their own particularistic interests at the expense of the common good. Rather than a democratic state there is a capitalist state, a trade union state, an automobile association state, or a corporatist state, depending on ones political prejudices. At the very best, the influence of opposing particularistic interests may offset each other, allowing public authorities to follow their own course, serving the public interest. This was the theory of pluralism.

Two research projects on business interest associations (BIAs) in which I was involved, have taught us that interest associations, even BIAs, can also have positive functions, can also contribute to the common good. The first project was the so-called OBI project (Organisation of Business Interests project), which was conducted under the leadership of Streeck and Schmitter (see for the design Streeck and Schmitter, 1981) in the first half of the 1980s, and which produced a number of country and sector case studies of BIAs. This project studied the functioning and structure of 352 associations at one specific point in time, around 1980, in four sectors and in nine different countries. The second project was the HDI-project (History of Dutch Interest Associations), a historical study of BIA in The Netherlands in between 1890 and 1980 (van Waarden, 1989, 1992; Unger and van Waarden, 1999). What were these positive functions of BIAs?

First of all, such systems of interest associations can perform positive *political* functions, both on the part of civil society and of the state. Interest definition and aggregation are functional imperatives in politics, and the institutions of parties and parliament have certain disadvantages in doing so. They have to aggregate a great variety of interests on a great number of issues rather 'quickly', thus inhibiting the separate institutional representation of specific interests on specific parties. Voters have to give a general mandate to individual candidates for political office and cannot be certain on how their stand will be on specific issues. Some positions of those in office they may like, others they may find contrary to their own interest. A way out has been the formation of single issue parties, pro-ecology (green parties), pro-cars (the Swiss car party), or anti-foreigners (extreme right wing parties). However, those parties that got into parliament and were able to stay there, had to develop policies on other issues decided on in parliament as well, thus developing towards all-round parties. Nevertheless, citizens apparently still felt a need for spokesmen of their interests as consumer, worker, automobile driver, or clean air breather. Hence they also organised outside of the parliamentary arena in interest associations. These associations have not so much become rivals and threats to preference aggregation through parliament, but have formed an alternative channel and carefully monitor and check the performance of parliament, cabinet and the bureaucracy. As such they have become part of the system of checks and balances in the polity. In time, many of them have come to share in the political functions, not only of preference aggregation, but also of policy implementation.

Second, interest associations can also have positive *economic* functions. They can correct for 'market failures'. Many market failures can obstruct the economic process, or lead to perverted outcomes. Information and power asymmetries between partners in economic transactions can tempt one of the partners to behave opportunistically, to cheat or fraud. And already the fear that the other may do so may inhibit the less informed or powerful partner from engaging in the transaction. And of course where there are no transactions there is no economic welfare and growth. Fierce or even ruinous competition may enhance the temptation of partners to cheat. It may also prevent economic actors from investing in sectoral collective goods such as vocational training, generic R&D, or generic health and safety at work facilities, out of the fear that competitors may turn out to be free riders and poachers. Some form of regulation is needed to correct for such market failures.

Of course the state can do so, and it has done so extensively through its social and economic regulation. However, besides 'market failures' there are also 'state failures'. State authorities often lack the necessary sectoral information and expertise to regulate markets in detail. And they may lack the power and organisational resources to effectively administer and enforce such regulations. As the state intervened more intensely and in more policy areas, it developed a greater need for information from civil society, not only technical information, but also information about the preferences of those concerned.

'Buying' the cooperation of the subjects concerned by involving them in policy-making had various advantages, the state could make good use of their knowledge and information; and the involvement of associations tended to increase the legitimation base of public measures. This was even more the case where state agencies delegated regulation and/or implementation to interest associations, provided that safeguards had been built in to protect the public interest. Thus associations aided the state in one of its main functions, that of bringing about social, and in particular economic, order. Both the OBI and the HDI project found many cases of associations compensating both for 'market failures' and for 'state failures' through associational self-regulation.

Structural preconditions for associational governance

The OBI project also found that associations were best able to perform such functions when they satisfied certain structural conditions. The associations had to be more than mere mouthpieces of individual member interests. They had to be able to rephrase and redefine member interests, taking some distance to highly particularistic interests, to aggregate them to more general business' interests, and to take account of what was acceptable to opponents and interlocutors such as the state or trade unions. In negotiations with interlocutors they had to be able to give and take, to make concessions, and to defend these for the membership. Rather than following the membership they had to be able to assume a position of leadership in interest definition. This required a certain autonomy *vis-à-vis* the membership. Associations had to develop a position of necessary intermediary between the (prospective) membership and interlocutors such as the state or trade unions. They had to do so by creatively managing what Streeck and Schmitter called the 'logic of membership' (the exchange relations with members) and the 'logic of influence' (the exchange relations with interlocutors). Resources acquired from one party had to be employed in the relation with the other party. Financial resources, information, loyalty, discipline in boycotts or lock outs, and concessions, acquired from members could be used to pressure interlocutors for concessions. Conversely, subsidies, information, and concessions attained from state agencies could be used to get members to accept certain compromises or to make certain sacrifices.

Such strategic management of the logic of membership and the logic of influence was facilitated by certain organisational conditions. Favorable ones were, for example, a certain distance between the leadership and the members (indirect elections, certain oligarchical constructions, fixed terms of office during which leaders could not be deposed); centralisation of decision-making and of control over important resources (lock out and boycott funds, information); the availability of – or even exclusive, almost monopolistic, control over-goods, services or other resources highly valued or needed by members (e.g. export licenses, guarantee funds); and large size and broad definition of the membership domain. Large interest associations which harbored a wide diversity of interests, also called comprehensive or inclusive associations, found it more difficult to externalise the costs of radical and particularistic demands, as those who might have to bear such costs were also members. Large comprehensive unions were more restrained in their wage demands, as the costs of strong wage increases – inflation – would be born in large part by their own members. The positive function of such comprehensive interest associations has in the mean time also been realised by many economists (Olson, 1983; Calmfors and Driffill, 1988; Teulings and Hartog, 1998).

History has shown that business associations were often not able to acquire such organisational capacities for self-discipline on their own.

Such capacities developed with the logic of influence strongly affecting the logic of membership. Members were often only inclined to accept more central coordination and control by their association when their interests were threatened by trade unions or the state. Thus large scale strikes in the past have induced employers to accept centralisation of decision-making in their associations.

The crucial role of the state in the development of (systems of) interest associations

The OBI-project, and even more in detail the historical project which I carried out, has shown in particular the importance of the state for the development of organisational capacities for associational governance, and which allowed such associations to perform the positive political and economic functions listed above. The state thus played an import-ant role in many societies in structuring the system of BIAs. Negatively, in the sense that the threat of state intervention has often induced business to preempt this by organising and engaging in self-regulation of their markets, and in providing the organisational conditions, includ-ing the capacity to enforce such regulations among the members. And positively, by providing access, recognition, and concessions, the state provided BIAs with resources which they could use in their logic of membership, to offer collective or selective goods to members, and to discipline them if necessary. In turn the state has often taken initiatives historically to organise or to reorganise (the system of) business associ-ations. Much of national social and economic legislation and market ordering regulation has been developed over time in either close cooperation or conflict with business associations. Therefore, the system of statutory social and economic law has both been a product of state–BIA relations and has influenced it again in turn. Quite clearcut examples are competition law and rules that regulate access to markets, by setting qualification standards for business. These have directly affected the goods that BIAs are legally allowed to deliver. This holds in particular for corporatist systems of interest intermediation, and for trade associ-ations (as distinguished from employers' associations).

If the state at the national level has been so important for the development of systems of interest associations, what could possibly be the effect of the gradual formation of a European state on the struc-ture of interest associations? That is a question which comes directly out of the findings of the OBI-project and which will be the concern of the remainder of this essay.

The emergent European state

European integration can be considered a new phase in the European history of state formation. It produces new state structures and new or at least different forms of state intervention into markets, which significantly modify the structures and strategies of the older 'nation-states'. The clearest manifestation thereof is the gradual development of a system of European law, with new institutions and organisations like the European Court of Justice, and with increasingly large bodies of both codified statute law and case law. This supersedes and changes national legal systems. Given the importance of state structures, policies and law for BIAs, this change should affect such associations. Let us look a little closer at dimensions of European state formation which could affect the structure of interest associations.

1. The development of a European state has first of all brought about *changes in state structures*. State power/sovereignty becomes increasingly *differentiated, diversified, and fragmented*, both vertically and horizontally. The vertical differentiation, that is, the increase in the number of aggregation levels at which state actors are found, is obvious. But also horizontal differentiation or segmentation between policy arenas and policy communities increases, if only because the EU intervenes more actively in some policy areas than in others. This leads to an asymmetry in the vertical differentiation of different policy areas. Added fragmentation and complexity is provided by the court system and comitology.

The introduction of judicial review with the European *legal system*, which has been new to a number of member-states (like GB, NL), has increased the complexity of 'checks and balances' within the EU. European courts are increasingly assuming political roles, a common phenomenon in the US. As citizens, firms, and associations increasingly try to get their way through the court, courts are forced to take more or less political decisions. Indicative is that this is happening even in a traditionally non-litigious culture as The Netherlands. A recent landmark case has been decision of a Dutch court to annul the agricultural minister's decision to reduce the national pig staple by 20 per cent, at the demand of the agricultural statutory trade association. This development in Europe seems to be part of a 'global expansion of judicial power' (Tate and Vallinder, 1997). With the courts becoming more important, the system of courts becomes more differentiated, multilevel and specialised. Not only the ECJ applies European law; so do increasingly national courts.

State complexity is also increased by the burgeoning of *comitology*, the development of networks of committees, bridging European, national and regional policy-makers, and involving often experts, some of whom are related to interest associations. In particular the creation of EU-regulatory agencies has enhanced this trend. The European agency for regulating access of medicine to the market EMEA has formed a network of committees around it to advise and help in decision-making, which involves up to 1500 experts from the worlds of medicine, the pharmaceutical industry, and the national regulatory agencies.

These processes of vertical and horizontal differentiation of state power have led to a complex and fragmented network of public, semi-public and private agencies and actors, that are more or less involved in the exertion of public power.

2.   So far the EU has primarily been a *regulatory state*, as distinguished from a distributive state (Majone, 1994). But it should be noted that this is somewhat of an artificial distinction. Many rules and regulations have distributive consequences. Some citizens and firms profit, others bear the costs. In any case, there is enough reason for BIAs to try to influence such regulation.

The regulatory character of the EU state implies that the aforementioned differentiation in state structures revolves especially around the various *phases in rule formulation and implementation*.

European regulation and directives affect national, regional and municipal state actors in various ways. EU law is becoming increasingly important, but often has to be transposed into national law. By now, almost 50 per cent of all acts passing Dutch parliament are transpositions of EU law. National and subnational state agencies have tasks in implementation, administration and enforcement. These have often overlapping and competing jurisdictions, or cooperation may be required. In the implementation of the Seveso II directive (on safety of dangerous chemical substances) in The Netherlands at least three ministries are involved, and several municipal agencies (police, fire brigade). In Spain the regional governments have the main responsibility for implementation (Versluis, 2000). Only rarely (e.g. in the case of competition law) does the EU Commission implement and enforce itself. However, it does check and control national agencies, often through specialised bodies (e.g. in meat inspection).

The following phases of formulation and implementation of EU regulations and directives, with their respective levels of government, can be distinguished.

Table 3.1 Phases of formulation and implementation of EU regulations and directives, with their respective levels of government

Regulatory phase	Responsible state agencies
Developing of draft regulations and directives	Civil servants of the European Commission, and advisory committees filled with civil servants of member-states
Enactment of regulations and directives	EU Commission, Council, Parliament
Transposition of directives in national law (= legal implementation)	National ministries and parliament
Operationalisation of such laws in norms, procedures, and administrative ordinances, work manuals for inspection	European regulatory agencies like EMEA; National and regional ministries; inspectorates; courts
Administration	European regulatory agencies, national, regional and municipal agencies and inspectorates
Enforcement	National, regional and municipal/ general and specialised inspectorates, police, etc. Supervision and control by EU agencies
Sanctioning	National, regional and municipal authorities, public prosecution, courts
Handling appeals	Administrative appeal, national courts, ECJ

Many of these regulatory phases are still responsibilities of agencies of the member-states. The distance between the basic EU directive and the actual enforcement practice in the member-states is still a long one. This implies that there are still many possibilities for influencing the realities of European regulation within the member-states.

3. European directives and regulations affect national state agencies also, in that they imply *new forms of supervision and accountability of nation-states* to a higher authority, the institutions of the EU. National governments are responsible for the right implementation and enforcement of EU directives. Many European rules have direct effect, that is, European citizens can directly deduce rights from them and can claim compensation in court if their rights are negatively affected by

negligence of the state. In addition, the Commission can fine and sue national governments for negligence. This has made national governments more reluctant in delegating the implementation and administration of public tasks to self-regulation by private associations. A case in point is the directive on packaging waste disposal (Haverland, 1998). Whereas this issue was regulated before in The Netherlands through self-regulation by industry – within the context of a covenant, a private contract between the state and industry – after the acceptance of the EU directive the Dutch government saw itself forced to replace the covenant under private law by a public statute.

4.   European integration has also brought about *changes in the nature of state intervention into markets*. New rules on market ordering have been introduced, regulated sectors such as the former public utilities are being deregulated, and competition law is being stiffened. European integration has often been considered a 'large deregulation project', as negative integration, that is, the requirement to break down non-tariff trade barriers (and barriers against the free movement of production factors) has outlawed many national regulations including self-regulation by industry. The legal doctrine of 'mutual recognition' has threatened to undercut many such national public or private regulations. However, their place is being taken by an increasingly sophisticated system of EU norms and standards: competition, food quality, environment, sector-specific regulations in, for example, transport or industry and so on.

Such EU substantive rules have had direct effects on markets, but also indirectly, through their influence on national regulations. A case in point is competition law. European competition law has direct effect on what is allowed in terms of inter-firm collusion – in so far as it affects inter-state trade. However, EU law – in this case mostly case law – has also led to a gradual convergence of national competition laws (Drahos, 2001; Drahos and van Waarden, 2001). Several national systems have changed from an abuse system to a prohibition system. Forms of collusion that were forbidden under EU law for inter-state trade are also increasingly becoming illegal on the domestic market.

5.   European integration is also enhancing a trend of increasing *juridification* of social and economic relations. This happens in various ways:
- The new possibilities for judicial review and administrative appeal, introduced by the EU-legal system (something typical for federal states in general, as distinct from unitary ones: political courts are created to adjudicate in conflicts between levels of government).

- New layers of courts, which may increase fragmentation of the legal system, and offer more possibilities for enterprising lawyers.
- The internationalisation of the market for legal services, and with that the internationalisation – and growth in size – of legal firms, as part of the globalisation/Europeanisation of business professions (lawyers, accountants, consultants). Such larger international firms employ lawyers who know the case law from different legal systems. This has led to a tendency in which lawyers are using case law from one country to derive arguments c.q. even precedence from, for cases they are arguing in other countries. This also enhances a certain convergence in the substance of national law.
- The larger international law firms are also introducing a more aggressive American style of case acquisition and case argumentation; in part because they employ American lawyers or legal advisors.
- Market liberalisation and deregulation of social and economic public law, in the wake of European economic integration, has as a consequence that contracts tend to become more important, especially in the absence of a codified European civil law. This requires lawyers to draw them up, monitor, and enforce them.
- Privatisation, also driven forward by European integration, has also enhanced this increase of importance of contracts, now between the state and private providers of, for example, public transport, energy, or telecom services. These contracts can be extremely detailed and lengthy. In addition, privatisation has enhanced juridification in the sense that where formerly public monopolies were informally regulated, now they have to be formally supervised by sector-specific regulatory agencies, which add to the contractual rules increasing numbers of rather specific semi-statutory rules (Vogel, 1996).

European state formation and BIA systems

These changes in the state structures and activities and in the legal systems are likely to affect BIAs. Relevant questions to be asked in this context are:

- What are the interests of these various state-levels and state agencies in cooperating with BIAs; what could they expect/get from BIAs? How important are (potential) resources of BIAs (information, acquiescence, cooperation) for them? Do they have an interest in sponsoring interest associability; in the formation of more comprehensive, or, to the contrary, rather more specialised, associations?

- Which state levels have which resources (for associations) to spend? (finance, access, recognition, monopoly recognition, concessions).
- How important are these resources for (potential) BIAs?

The following are some hypotheses regarding how these changes in the European state(s) and their legal system(s) could affect national BIAs.

Regarding centralisation of authority to European-wide BIAs

I expect that a possible tendency for EU-level centralisation of BIA systems, that is, for EU-level associations to become more important, will remain limited for the time being. For various reasons:

- As long as much of the realisation of EU directives and regulations is the responsibility of national and subnational governments and agencies, there is still quite a bit of room for national (or subnational) BIAs to influence the realisation of such regulations. And indeed there are still many differences in the national implementation of EU directives in the different member-states.
- More in general, the increased differentiation and fragmentation of the state could imply less of an impetus for centralisation of the BIA system.
- Many economic sectors are still mainly domestic sectors, which are as yet less affected by EU law. This holds, for example, for construction, retailing, and many of the business and social services, which, by the way, are increasing in importance for employment and GDP.
- There are however exceptions, where one would expect EU-level associations to become more important, namely in those sectors which:
  - Are strongly affected by European regulatory agencies (e.g. the pharmaceutical industry through the activities of EMEA).
  - Are particularly strongly affected by EU directives and regulations. For example, the chemical industry, through European environmental law; or the transport sector through environmental and transport law.
- However, it should be noted that increasingly formerly domestic sectors are becoming internationalised, in part as a result of pressure of the EU, and that it hence could very well be that there will be more and more of such 'exceptions'. Such internationalising sectors are banking and insurance, air transport, or book publishing and retailing.
- The EU offers possibilities to some national associations to exert influence. Some well resourced ones, with lots of staff, know how, and experience in a certain field, from countries whose government has regulated their sector extensively in the past, have a competitive

advantage where it comes to expertise, which is highly valued by both sister-associations in other member-states, and by the European Commission. This can give them substantial influence. It seems that such is, for example, the case with the German Zentralverband des deutschen Handwerks, which is quite active in trying to influence European SME policies. In this respect, the German legalistic tradition, which has resulted in quite detailed legislation in many fields, could be of an advantage to German BIAs, when it comes to exerting influence in Brussels.

Regarding resources

- Specific subsidies or other forms of financial support which national governments used to give to specific BIAs (sometimes in return for specific services such as the provision of statistical information, or of advice to SME firms) could be or come in conflict with European competition law.
- The same holds for the provision of a monopoly to a specific BIA to distribute specific selective goods to business firms (licenses, training certificates, 'warm' restructuring of industries, social security benefits); or for the recognition of exclusive representational monopolies of some associations.
- Such monopolies may also be undercut by the differentiation and fragmentation of state power. Where is the sovereign which could distribute monopoly rights?
- New activist international law firms could offer new services of professional 'lobbying' to business. Many BIAs began from individual lawyer offices, at least in The Netherlands. Some of these lawyers became veritable 'political entrepreneurs', and have furthered business associability in their own interest. As the associations eventually became bigger, they hired specialised staff to replace the more broadly oriented lawyers' office. Could it perhaps be that 'BIAs go back to their (lawyers) roots', with the increasing specialisation among lawyers, made possible by juridification and the increase in the size of lawyers' offices? Lawyers after all offer the important resource of a neutral arbiter among business firms who want to cooperate but remain competitors.

Regarding activities/output of national BIAs

- Several activities have already been and/or could become illegal under the developing European law.

- Competition law has already banned exclusive trade agreements in the 1960s, formerly an important sanction for BIAs to discipline members and support forms of self-regulation. By now also all horizontal price, market entry and market division agreements have become illegal, either directly under EU law, or as a result of the convergence of national competition law. These were important activities and sources of resources, for example, Dutch construction associations.
- The liability of national governments for the rightful implementation of EU directives and the resulting reluctance of such governments to rely on private contracts (covenants) with, and self-regulation by, industry, has also undercut such forms of self-regulation.
- Deregulation and privatisation of certain economic sectors makes other forms of self-regulation by national BIAs more difficult (e.g. road and river transport, social security).
- However, as I have argued earlier (van Waarden, 1995), the danger of European integration for BIAs has so far been less great that expected, for example, by Schmitter (1981).

Regarding state–industry relations

- The differentiation and fragmentation of the state, including courts, on the one hand offers greater variation of possible interests of state actors as regards cooperation with BIAs. On the other hand it offers firms and BIAs more and different 'berthing' spaces for access to and concessions from the state(s). In addition to local, regional and national governments, ministries and agencies now associations can also turn to the Commission (with different DGs), the European Parliament, their national minister in the Council, the European courts, and specialised European regulatory agencies. There are more alternative roads to follow in trying to get one's way. If firms do not get it from a national regulatory agency, they can try again with the Commission (with different DGs), or appeal to courts applying European law. That is, there are new and more possibilities for business and for the state to play off the other party against each other.

  This could very well lead to more adversarial relations, quite distinct from the consensual tradition of state–business relations in many member-states. The ongoing trend of juridification, enhanced by European integration, will certainly strengthen any such tendency towards more adversarial relations.

Forces pro and con centralisation of BIA systems at the European level

Finally, how will European state formation affect the centralisation of BIA systems at the EU level? How likely is further centralisation? Here we can perhaps learn from the earlier historical phases where local and regional associations merged and/or centralised at the national level. What do the OBI and the HDI projects teach us about this? The HDI project showed that at least in The Netherlands business usually organised first at the local or regional level. The cotton industry, the metalworking branch, the dockyards, the food industry, or the construction sector all organised first on a municipal level. These local associations persisted for quite some time. Only gradually did concentration and centralisation at the national level come about. What were the typical forces hindering or fostering such centralisation? What were the incentives and constraints of political entrepreneurs who tried to bring about such a centralisation? And could they also be of relevance for a possible centralisation from national to European associations? Under what conditions could European BIAs become more important?

Many factors have worked to keep associations small and local. Hindrances for forming national associations were among others:

- Problems of collective action were easily solved in smaller groups. Long before Mancur Olson associations were very aware of this. The Amsterdam construction association listed Olson's arguments almost literally in an anniversary study of 1915. The arguments for small size being:
  - each member's contribution to the common cause was still recognisable and necessary.
  - there was more mutual social control in smaller local groups.
  - face-to-face relations allowed for the development of mutual trust.
  - there was a shared identity of belonging to the local elite.
- The local level provided several external supports for cooperation, for example:
  - business was also organised in clubs which provided important solidaristic goods (local society, year clubs).
  - there was a shared common culture, for example, religion. At least many Dutch associations had originally a catholic or calvinist identity (and these were regionally differentiated in this country).
  - support was received from local government.
  - trade unions were at first a particular threat at the local/regional level. Most strikes were local.

The arguments of less collective action problems due to smaller numbers, less heterogeneity and a shared common identity and culture now also hold for national associations. Due to mergers and concentrations the number of firms in many sectors has decreased dramatically, thus giving national associations now a size (in terms of numbers) comparable to the former local and regional ones. Cultural identity is perhaps even stronger at the national level than it was formerly at the local one, as it is strengthened by differences in language and by customs and institutions of the different countries.

The history of associations has taught us that these hindrances to centralisation at the national level could only be overcome under certain conditions and through the influence of certain factors. Principally, factors among these were:

1 A common enemy, for example, trade unions which started to play off employers in different cities against each other. This happened among others in the construction and the dock industries. A precondition was the earlier centralisation of the trade union movement, that is, centralisation of unions also forced employers to centralise.

2 Strong state intervention in their sector, with central government agencies directly implementing and enforcing their own regulations, that is, with no room for local government.

3 A central state which needed assistance by BIAs. For example, during the First World War and during the crisis of the 1930s, the Dutch state helped business to form national trade associations to help it in implementing state policy. Cases were the distribution of export licenses (the First World War) and subsidies (1930s), and the authorisation of self-regulation to control market entry and reduce ruinous competition, for example, through the statutory extension of cartels (1930s).

4 Some BIAs went national where self-regulation/authoritative goods were only effective when all national firms were involved in certain cartels, such as export market distribution, or exposition cartels (RAI).

5 Other associations gradually developed selective or commercial goods (e.g. advice on labour relations, job classification and wage systems), which were attractive to larger group of firms, also in other parts of the country, and which allowed for the use of economies of scale and scope.

6 The activity of political entrepreneurs, like lawyers, who had a personal interest in forming larger associations. Many mergers of

regional associations into national ones were the work of such entre-preneurs.
7 External support for BIA centralisation, for example, by the catholic church; and of course by the national government.
8 Finally, and perhaps most importantly, the reduction in the number of firms, through the decline of a sector (e.g. cotton, shipyards), or through mergers (chemical industry).

Only a few of these factors are likely to work towards centralisation of sectoral associational systems at the EU level, notably factors 2, 5, 6, and 8. Therefore, centralisation at the EU level now seems less likely than centralisation to the national level in the past. However, given the nature of these factors it is likely that there will be differences between sectors. Most affected will be sectors that are already strongly interna-tionalised, which are strongly affected by EU regulations and regulatory authorities, and which are made up of relatively small numbers of larger firms. Examples are the pharmaceutical and chemical industries, which indeed seem to be already relatively well organised at the EU level.

Note

1 This is a slightly revised title from my original conference presentation which was included in a section entitled 'Governance and the Role of Associations in Economic Management: a Response from an EU Public Affairs Practitioner'. This title is still used by the author of the next chapter, Chapter 4, who participated in the same section of the conference.

4

Governance and the Role of Associations in Economic Management: a Response from an EU Public Affairs Practitioner

Daniel Guéguen

For nearly 25 years, I have been professionally involved in European issues, initially as Director General of the European sugar lobby; then as General Secretary of COPA-COGECA, the largest European lobby, for farmers and agricultural cooperatives; finally as General Manager of a consultancy company for European affairs.

But where are the French?

Reading the programme for this conference is an edifying experience, most of the speakers are Anglo-Saxon, with a few Dutch and Germans. But where are the French?

In the context of the Anglo-Saxonisation of European thought, reading the 'European Public Affairs Directory' is enlightening. To start with, the guide only exists in English. Moving on to the 38 pages of the 'European trade and professional associations' heading, about 1000 European professional associations are listed. The main ones such as UNICE, CEFIC, CIAA, COPA and so on are well-known. What do these acronyms mean? Union des Confédérations de l'Industrie et des Employeurs de l'Europe, Confédération Européenne des Fédérations de l'Industrie Chimique, Confédération des Industries Agro-alimentaires, Comité des Organisations Professionnelles Agricoles and so on. Even today, 2/3 of the European associations have French names.

What about their leaders? For more than 20 years, the French mono-polised the secretary general positions of the most important European associations. Today, the situation has been reversed, with the exception of the European Association of Beetgrowers and the European Committee of Sugar Manufacturers which are still in French hands, the posts of secretary general of the EU trade associations have been entrusted to Belgian, Dutch, British, and German nationals.

In the European vision and practice, the year 2000 was the exact opposite of 1999. A 180° turnaround. Nowadays, Brussels speaks English, often an English volapük, and Brussels in particular thinks in English at all power levels, Commission, Parliament, media and business circles. The former vision of a federal Europe of a small group of countries united by a common, political vision is now prehistory.

The European future is today crystal clear, at least in its objectives, enlargement prevails over deepening. The goal today is to create a well-structured, free trade area encompassing 30-odd countries from the Atlantic to the Urals. Exit the 'Community'. *Pauvre* Delors, poor France.

Extreme fragmentation of the interest groups

The European lobbying landscape is extremely fragmented over 1000 EU trade associations, as we have already said, but that's not all, to be precise, we should add:
- Around 750 NGOs (which represent consumers, ecologists, religions, families, Third World aid, etc.);
- European representative bodies from around 500 major companies;
- 130 regional offices (each European region has its own representative organisation in Brussels);
- 130 specialist law firms working on European law (the large majority of which are of British or American origin, as owing to the predominance of the WTO, Anglo-Saxon law has now become primordial);
- An unspecified number of consultants of all natures, many of whom specialise in regulation and community finance programme monitoring.

Altogether, it can be estimated that there are around 3000 lobbying structures in Brussels, which is considerable.

Why has there been such a proliferation of lobbies in Brussels?

First of all, and quite rightly, because Brussels has become an enormous centre of power:
- As Jacques Delors said in his day, 80 per cent of national legislations today are of European inspiration;
- All of the major issues such as, the Common Agricultural Policy, the WTO, food safety, public health, aeronautics, transport and so on are now managed by Brussels;

- Over 1000 Committees and Expert Groups assist the Commission in the preparation, adoption and enforcement of Union regulations and directives;
- With 1000 journalists, Brussels has become – by far – the world's leading press centre.

But this explanation is only partial and far too simplistic. Other reasons, which are just as important, should be put forward:

- First of all, the absence of a legal framework for lobbies and interest groups, 40 years after the signature of the Treaty of Rome, there is still no appropriate legal framework for European associations... Owing to this fact, at least 1/3 of the NGOs and EU trade associations are *de facto* associations with no legal existence.
- The total absence of rules for exercising the profession of lobbyist should also be pointed out, there is no obligation for competence, no obligatory code of ethics and no penalty in the event of professional misconduct. It is – in my opinion – important and urgent to regulate the profession of lobbyist in the form of a professional order comparable to that of lawyers or architects.
- The amount of European subsidies provides a clear incentive for the profusion of European associative structures to make the most they can out of the Community manna. In this respect, we can neither understand – nor admit – that the European Commission should continue to allocate public subsidies to European interest groups which are organised in the form of *de facto* associations, that is, with no legal existence.... An urgent solution has to be found to this astonishing situation.

A major U-turn in the consultation process

Once there was a time when the Commission genuinely consulted socio-professional circles and where the Economic and Social Committee (ESC) had a major influence. Be it on agricultural matters or social issues, the ESC was a heavyweight in Community policies. Furthermore, it demonstrated on a daily basis its capacity to bring together workers' syndicates, employers and consumers around common points of view. This situation is no more, and even if the ESC's opinions remain 'technically interesting', they no longer have any political influence.

And what can be said of the Committee of the Regions? Poor old Committee of the Regions without power or fame. Each Inter-Governmental Conference on institutional reform promises increased subsidiarity, a new source of regional powers and a new dynamic for the

Committee of the Regions. Alas, they are only promises... Both the Treaty of Amsterdam and the Nice Summit abandoned the Committee of the Regions right where it is, nowhere....

The situation is no better for the consultative committees, especially for agriculture. Being highly expensive, they are nowadays devoid of any influence. These consultative committees are nevertheless based on a good idea, to bring together within one consultative organisation all of the parties involved in the agriculture sector such as farmers, food and drink industries, workers' syndicates, ecologists, consumers and so on. In the past, these consultative committees, which were places for discussion, consultation, proposals and constructive opposition, are now – with a few rare exceptions – dead structures.

The representativeness of EU trade associations has evolved greatly over the past ten years, and certainly not in the right direction.

In 1990, when the Commission wanted to find out the opinion of a professional sector, it went to the competent European association. At the time, the EU trade associations were few and far between, generally speaking, there was only one per activity sector. One for the car industry, one for sugar, one for milk, one for banking, one for insurance, and so on.

Thus, everything was simple, at the top of the pyramid, there was the EU trade association made up of the national associations, which were in turn made up of companies. This EU trade association had the monopoly on representation of the sector with regard to the European Institutions. In this golden age, no business leader or national association would have dared – or even dreamt of – conducting their own lobbying in Brussels and short-circuiting the EU trade association. At that time, it was all simple, coherent and let us admit it, effective.

Nowadays it has all changed. Brussels is teeming with lobbies. And all of them are behaving like flies around a honey pot. Multiplication of EU trade associations, multiplication of NGOs, direct involvement by companies and national associations in the Commission, and so on. From now on, everyone is playing their own game and attempting to influence their specific interests, taking ever less account of the collective interest of the profession.

The consequences of this situation are threefold:

- It considerably weakens the consultative process. The Commission is of course continuing to consult socioprofessional circles as it is obliged to do. But these consultations no longer contribute to the legislative process. As we have already stated, the role of the Economic and Social Committee has become marginal. The same applies to the Consultative Committees.

- To develop its proposals, the Commission is continuing to consult professional circles. But on a case by case basis, in an *ad hoc* manner. It could be said that it is less official and more personal. The Commission services currently tend to choose contact people according to their personal expertise.
- This evolution is crucial. It demonstrates that the effectiveness of lobbying now no longer lies in representativeness, but in credibility. This point will be developed further.

The difficult relations between companies and the EU trade associations

For a company, belonging to an EU trade association is essential for two reasons:
- On the one hand, the EU trade association remains the official representative body for a profession with regard to the EU Institutions (all with their consequent advantages in terms of obtaining information and invitations to official meetings).
- Furthermore, the EU trade association is a crucial meeting place for national members (all for a generally modest annual subscription).

We can therefore state that a company and even a large company cannot easily sidestep an EU Trade association. This statement is confirmed by the recent experience of a major French food company which had decided to retire from its European professional association and is now finding itself cut off from various information sources in Brussels.

It is not therefore a matter of large companies leaving the EU trade associations, all the more so since they exert an increasing amount of power....

In the 1990s, decision-making power in the EU trade association was held by the national member associations. Currently, it is the large companies who are running the show.

This takeover of the EU trade associations by the big companies has come about gradually:
- Increasingly, the Chairman of the EU Trade association is from a big company;
- Very often, the EU trade associations have accepted to create a major companies' Club within them (often having a seat on the EU trade association committee);
- The choice of General Secretary is clearly influenced by the big companies;

- The big companies contribute to the EU trade association's budget (special subscription, project sponsoring, provision of a member of staff, etc.).

This situation suits everyone and offers numerous possibilities in terms of lobbying. Thus according to the issues, the big company will wear the EU trade association's hat when it has an interest in doing so. Conversely, it will undertake its own lobbying actions when this is to its advantage.

Increasingly frequently, the large company will undertake a 'lobbying mix', combining the action of the EU trade association focused on the joint interest and its own action focusing on its corporate interest. This is what is known as a dual lobbying strategy.

Towards new lobbying techniques

In a somewhat caricature manner, lobbying strategies can be defined in three categories:

1 Negative strategies consisting of a face-on opposition to Commission proposals or by proposing untenable counter-proposals, the farming lobbies provide the best illustration of these opposition strategies.
2 Reactive strategies in which prudence triumphs over action, no initiatives, no conflicts, and so on. Most of the EU trade associations restrict themselves to this minimum service, a little monitoring, a few meetings, and a small amount of public relations.
3 Pro-active strategies consisting of working with the Commission in a spirit of partnership, credibly and constructively. And with foresight. In the past, sugar symbolised this strategy. Nowadays they are partially implemented by certain NGOs.

Statistically speaking, reactive strategies are in the majority, followed by negative strategies. Conversely, pro-active strategies are rare and almost the exception.

This situation is anachronistic. And it explains why corporate lobbying is developed alongside the traditional EU trade association lobbying.

Without any doubt, the future belongs to pro-active strategies, in which the lobbyist offers the legislator an authorised, technical opinion and credible proposals. As Paul Lannoye, the Chairman of the Greens Group in the European Parliament said: 'A good lobbyist provides valuable assistance for the legislator; a bad lobbyist is a nuisance.'

Influence with the European Institutions and particularly the Commission no longer depends on size or representativeness, but the project and credibility. This positive evolution is opening up enormous potential for influence for companies and . . . for consultants.

A final word, credibility also involves companies' and industries' capacities to build European alliances with consumers and ecologists. Facilitating the Commission's work to a maximum, proposing it pre-negotiated solutions, this is the way for the future. A real cultural revolution for 99 per cent of EU trade associations.

5
The Importance of Institutions to Associations: Evidence from the Cross-National Organisation of Business Interests Project

Wyn Grant

The Organization of Business Interests (OBI) project, coordinated by Wolfgang Streeck and Philippe Schmitter, was the largest comparative project ever undertaken on business interest associations. It encompassed a range of countries in Europe and North America – Austria, Canada, Denmark, Germany, Italy, The Netherlands, Spain, Sweden, Switzerland and the United Kingdom. There was an associated group of researchers in the United States. Attempts to find participants from France were unsuccessful. Although the present data were collected over 20 years ago, many of the basic features of business associations identified at the beginning of the 1980s remain in place. Moreover, the theoretical perspectives developed in the project continue to be relevant to the study of business associability.

In the absence of much systematic empirical data, the project was first concerned with finding out how business interests organised at a national level. The project did not cover European Community levels of organisation. In some countries, there was a very clear demarcation between employers' organisations (dealing with industrial relations issues and engaging in collective bargaining) and trade associations (dealing with commercial issues) which fed through to distinctive peak associations, for example, Germany. In some countries, territorial forms of organisation assumed a greater significance, for example, in Italy and in Spain.

However, the project was not simply concerned, with the tasks of categorisation and classification. A central theme was to investigate how business interest associations achieved higher levels of organisational development which was seen as a necessary condition of greater effect-iveness, both in serving their members and acting as partners with government. Schmitter and Streeck (1981: 124) defined the concept in the following way:

> Organizational structures are more 'developed', the more encom-passing they are in scope and purpose (the more 'external effects' and interdependencies they 'internalize'); the more specialized and co-ordinated they are internally; the more safely their supply of strat-egic resources is institutionalized; and the greater their autonomous capacity to act and to pursue long-term strategies regardless of short-term environmental constraints and fluctuations. Thus, the concept can be seen as resting on two focal points – the degree to which the complex organisational arrangements to be found in a sector are *ordered* and *coordinated* and the degree to which associations are *autonomous* from their several environments and thereby suited to the assumption of an independent policy role.
>
> (Coleman and Grant, 1984: 212)

The first criterion draws attention to the space the association seeks to represent and how it is organised. Thus, for example, a more developed association would have a functionally differentiated inter-organisa-tional division of labour and would be integrated and hierarchically ordered. The second criterion focuses on the resources available to an association and how they are converted into outputs. A more developed association would not be solely reliant on member subscription or fees as its source of income. In determining strategy, members would be one of a number of environments taken into consideration. Such an associ-ation would take a long-term perspective. (These criteria are developed more fully in Coleman and Grant, 1984: 213.) In summary, a less developed association is likely to be reactive; a more organisationally developed association is likely to be pro-active.

The logic of influence

The OBI project made a basic conceptual distinction between the logic of membership and the logic of influence. The logic of membership is concerned with the characteristics of the type of sector being organised. For example, is it capital or labour intensive? How competitive is it? Do large firms predominate or are there large numbers of small and medium sized enterprises? Any organisational design for a business interest association is going to have to take some account of logic of membership factors. However, an effective association is likely to pay more attention to logic of influence factors. These are concerned with the characteristics of the target of the association's activity. Depending on the association, these could include trade unions, suppliers or customers, but the most usual target is government (broadly defined). This chapter is concerned with logic of influence factors rather than with the logic of membership, although the two are closely interrelated.

Schmitter and Streeck conceived of the logic of influence as an exchange relationship. Associations seek to develop in a way which optimises 'the probability of exploiting the existing (or emergent) configuration of state authority, interests and needs for their own purposes.' The state rewards or punishes organisations for acquiring organisational properties which increase the probability of it achieving its own goals. Schmitter and Streeck went on to use an implicit 'strong state–weak state' model, arguing that the logic of membership would be more influential in cases where the state was dispersed, dependent and relatively easily penetrated (Schmitter and Streeck, 1981: 86). In the EU case, one might argue that there is a considerable amount of institutional differentiation and internal competitiveness and that the Commission has quite high informational needs. However, the very complexity of the structures and processes creates a high political entry price and hence a need for associations that are attuned to the logic of influence.

At the national level, there is a simple checklist of questions that may be applied to the targets of association activity. First, is the form of government executive led? This is the characteristic form of government in European states and leads to a concentration of representative activity on ministers and other heads of executive agencies, but more particularly on the bureaucracy. In a system like that of the United States where the legislature has a much greater role in decision making, there will be a different allocation of resources.

Second, it makes a difference whether a country is a unitary or a federal state and, if it is a federal state, how decentralised the exercise of authority is. Decisions taken by subnational legislatures may play an important part in agenda setting, as with the case of the so-called 'California effect' in the United States where California pioneers new regulations or standards which are subsequently adopted elsewhere. In the United Kingdom, the creation of a Scottish Parliament and Executive and a Welsh Assembly has faced business associations with new and difficult questions about how they can best deploy the scarce resources available to them for representative activity.

Third, it makes a difference whether a country can be classified in ideal typical terms as a company, associative or party state. (These terms are explained more fully in Grant, 1993.) In a company state, direct representation by firms is regarded as legitimate, perhaps even to be encouraged, for example, Britain and the United States. In an associative state, continuing emphasis is placed on the key role of associations as intermediaries between business and government, for example, Germany. In a party state, there is a highly factionalised dominant party, for example, Japan. It may be suggested that the European Union (EU) combines elements of the company and associative state models. Business therefore needs to develop representative capacities at both the firm and association level.

Multilevel governance

It is more difficult to apply such a simple checklist to the complex operating environment of the EU. Decision-making in the EU can be fluid and unpredictable and the balance of influence between institutions can change from one issue to another. In Europe as a whole, a system of multilevel governance has developed. 'MLG analysis amounts to the claim that the EU has become a polity where authority is dispersed between levels of governance and amongst actors, and where there are significant sectoral variations in governance patterns.' (Rosamond, 2000: 110).

Multilevel governance theorists may be said to make a number of key propositions. A central proposition is that 'decision-making competencies are shared by actors at different levels rather than monopolized by state executives' (Marks *et al.*, 1996: 346). This means that the relatively simple world in which representative activity can be directly primarily at a national executive has disappeared. Nor can that be replaced by simply directing activity at the European Commission. The system is more complex horizontally and vertically. Authority at the EU level is dispersed between the Commission, which is generally perceived to have been losing ground; the Council of Ministers and the Committee of Permanent Representatives; the European Parliament; and other institutions, most importantly the Court of Justice. It is then divided vertically between the European level (but also an international level above that), the member state level and various subnational entities. The 'subnational actors operate in both national and supranational arenas, creating transnational associations in the process.' (Marks *et al.*, 1996: 396). The member state level remains a significant level of political activity. However, 'States do not monopolize domestic and European actors, but are one among a variety of actors contesting decisions that are made at a variety of levels.' (Marks *et al.*, 1996: 396).

Business associations have to contend with a situation in which authority is both dispersed and overlapping. The logic of influence implies a set of clear, hierarchically ordered targets which can then be used to shape the pattern of associational activity.

However, such an ordered system is no longer available to structure strategic choices. Associations are no longer dealing with 'the state', but a series of entities possessing statelike properties. The building in which the conference on which this book was based was held is called 'Scotland House'. It is not, of course, an embassy as Scotland is not a sovereign state, but it is nevertheless entitled to its own representative focus at the geographical heart of the European Quarter in Brussels.

A further layer of complexity is that there is considerable sectoral variation. In agriculture, for example, the pattern of bargaining in the Council of Ministers remains predominantly intergovernmental with complex trade offs between different national interests, including the frequent resort to ameliorative side payments. Some attention to the national level therefore continues to make sense. As the number of member states has grown, and the complexity of interests increased, it has proved increasingly difficult to maintain the coherence and effectiveness of the European level organisation, COPA (Comité des Organisations Professionelles Agricoles).

In contrast, if one looks at various aspects of trade policy, such as the conduct of negotiations in the World Trade Organisation (WTO) or the application of anti-dumping rules, there is much more supranationalism in the sense that the EU operates as one entity, taking key decisions and implementing them on behalf of all member states. Industries which have key interests in the area of trade, such as chemicals and motor vehicles, need to operate effectively at the European level and to be able to arrive at clear common positions. These sectoral variations create a continuing and important role for the industry level association which has an understanding of the particular politics of its own sector.

The complexity of a system of multilevel governance represents both an opportunity and a threat to business interest associations. It particularly represents a threat to the less organisationally developed business association which may find it difficult to understand and respond to a complex and rapidly changing operating environment. It does demand more sophisticated management of associations. The days when senior association staff could be drawn from company managers nearing the ends of their careers, or from retired bureaucrats or diplomats, are over. One needs staff with a range of competencies and skills who, ideally, have had some experience of government from the inside.

In such a complex operating environment, in which matters may be handled at as many as five levels of government (city, region, nation-state, EU, and global governance agency) it is more difficult to demonstrate to members a clear link between activities and outcomes. Members understandably want a demonstrable return for their subscriptions, but they also need to be educated in the complexity of the operating environment and the subtle and sophisticated way in which it needs to be handled. There is a danger that associations may fall into the trap of the logic of membership, responding to the short-term demands of their members and failing to develop a long-term strategy which may reap greater, if less immediate, rewards for members.

One temptation into which associations can fall at a national level is to consider that they must appear as 'business like' as possible, generating as much revenue as possible from fee based services such as specialist seminars or training courses. In pursuing this route, they enter a crowded market in which there are already many providers with considerable expertise. Even if they are relatively successful, the association might become just like a consultancy firm. It may lose the unique characteristics of an association which is to act as an *intermediary* between its members and government, understanding the needs and priorities of both and bridging them in a way which creates positive sum outcomes for both sets of participants.

There is, of course, an opposite danger that the association becomes too much like the bureaucracy it is trying to influence, sharing its assumptions and becoming too preoccupied with the routines of its working procedures. Even the government relations representatives of firms were sometimes perceived to have 'gone native' in Brussels, becoming too preoccupied with the shifting balance of influence within the Commission rather than the priorities of their employers. This is why association staff with good strategic vision are so important. They will be responsive to their members, and also be able to spot opportunities to advance their interests. They will have a sense of the long-term strategic needs of the industry they represent and how those needs mesh with the goals of the European institutions.

Associations operating at the European level need to have a understanding of the ways in which the roles of the European institutions are developing and changing. Practical questions have to be faced, such as what proportion of the available organisational resources should be devoted to representation at the European Parliament. Should this be handled 'in house' or delegated to a specialist firm?

However, the contemporary logic of influence does not just mean being alert to changes in political structures and processes and the effect that these have on the distribution of influence. It is also important to be sensitive to the broader and changing political context within which representative activity is conducted.

The politics of production and of collective consumption

A distinction may be drawn between a politics of production and a politics of collective consumption with a long run shift towards the latter, 'new age' form of politics. (Grant, 2000). At the heart of the politics of production is a struggle between management and labour over the control and distribution of the fruits of the production process. This need not be an adversarial conflict as management and labour may realise that there are 'win–win' gains from mutual recognition and a structured bargaining process based on agreed rules of the game. Very often a politics of bargaining emerges in which there is a series of negotiating exchanges which produce mutual learning about each other's expectations and limits. Adjustments at the margin often produce acceptable solutions. Above all, there is a commitment to the centrality of the production process itself.

The politics of collective consumption is concerned with the externalities of the production process. At its core is a concern with public goods, or at least goods which have some of the characteristics of public goods. It is a politics which is less amenable to elite bargaining which can make policy adjustments at the margin. Indeed, many of the core values of the production process are called into question.

The techniques used in this type of politics often involve various forms of direct action. Traditional channels of exercising influence are either avoided altogether or treated with extreme caution. Because those involved are often driven by a sense of moral outrage, the action almost because more important than its effects. They see it as an end in itself rather than a means to an end.

The politics of production offers many opportunities to the well organised business association. Typically it involves detailed negotiations in private with broadly sympathetic bureaucrats. Thus, the Commission may wish to pass a directive on, say, a particular pollution control problem. However, it does not have all the information it needs about the technical issues or the availability of pollution control equipment. Also, it does not wish to make European industry less competitive than its counterparts elsewhere in the world. It therefore enters into a dialogue with the relevant business associations who are able to supply technical information which shows that the directive will have to be set up in a particular way to make it technically feasible and economically acceptable. This is the world of what one contributor to the conference on which this book is based called 'Rond Pont Schumann' man. His (and he was usually male) great days were during the development of the single market. He was well plugged into technical committees and had a good relationship with Commission officials. However, he had no media skills and could not cope with, for example, a challenge to a particular product or production process being allowed at all.

The politics of production has not been displaced altogether. It continues to flourish in many areas of EU activity. Indeed, the argument was made in the conference that environmentalists had so far been able to frustrate the deployment of only one new technology, genetically modified seeds. That of itself is a significant development, as there are no prior examples of a major new technology being halted by political action. More important, the number of challenges of this kind are likely to increase and it is important that associations adapt so that they are able to respond to them.

Fundamental political challenges arising from 'new age' politics are particularly likely to be apparent in the food processing sector. There are a variety of reasons why this should be the case. Given the continuing problems of BSE, it is relatively easy to suggest that health risks are associated with a new food technology, even if the evidence is purely speculative. 'We are what we eat' is a slogan which resonates readily with the public. Sometimes slogans may even be invented by firms within the food chain, as was the case with the vivid image of 'frankenstein foods' which was used to describe foodstuffs containing genetically modified ingredients by a British retail firm seeking to move into a new market niche. The media are always ready to run a new food scare story, often with scant regard for any relevant scientific evidence.

The food processing industry has a highly fragmented associative structure at the European level (and also often at national level), significantly affected by logic of membership factors (Grant, 1987). It may be possible for multinational firms in the sector involved in large numbers of associations and committees to exert pressure for a more rationalised and focussed structure. However, customer–supplier tensions in the food chain can be a significant factor, for example, those between sugar beet growers and sugar farmers and the industrial users of sugar. One way forward may be the kind of lean and mean associative structure evolved by the European Modern Restaurant Association representing what are sometimes referred to as 'fast food' retailers. This body operates to a large extent electronically and focuses on a few key issues which are of central concern to this highly competitive sector.

The politics of collective consumption requires a reorientation of associative activity to adjust to a new political setting. If one was writing the research design for a organisation of business interests project today, one might include a logic of protest alongside a logic of influence. In order to consider appropriate strategies for business associations in this changed environment, it is first necessary to explore the underlying conditions which have produced the growth of 'new age' politics.

It is evident that there are long run changes in society which underpin these developments, although their relative importance remains the subject of disagreement. The old social class formations on which the politics of production were based have largely dissolved, creating a vacuum at the heart of the political process. One consequence is a decline in the membership of political parties relative to that of pressure groups. Two-and-a-half times more people are members of the Royal Society for the Protection of Birds (RSPB) in Britain than are members of the Labour Party. Political parties have to aggregate a wide range of demands whereas pressure groups are concerned with much narrower interests or causes.

'Hierarchy of needs' theory would suggest that once basic needs are satisfied in a prosperous society, the political agenda shifts towards a range of 'postmaterial' goals. Higher levels of education can lead to a questioning of established values and procedures. Changing gender roles in society may also be more important. For example, 'An interesting facet of the animal protection movement is the role played by women.' (Garner, 1993: 66). Garner estimates that in Britain and the United States around 70 per cent of the animal protection movement consists of women. He speculates that 'the culturally defined role of women, with its emphasis on nurturing and caring, and the greater consciousness women have of their political status, has led many to lend their weight to a cause with which they can identify.' (Garner, 1993: 67).

More specific factors help to turn these underlying social changes into new forms of politics. The electronic media in particular like the strong visual images produced by direct action, particularly if animals are involved. Their use of them is often rather undiscriminating and not balanced by any critical comment. Technological developments have made it easier for groups to mobilise. In the petrol protests in Britain, mobile phones and the Internet were used extensively.

Perhaps the most worrying development from the perspective of business associations is the extent to which non-governmental organisations are trusted to a greater extent than either firms or government or, for that matter, scientists. A survey carried out by MORI in Britain asked 'Thinking about pollution, which two or three, if any, of these sources would you trust most to advise you on the risks posed by pollution?' The most popular answer in the 'trust most' category was 'pressure groups' (61 per cent), followed by independent scientists (60 per cent). Private companies received a score of 4 per cent. The 'trust least' category was headed by government ministers (48 per cent), followed by politicians (36 per cent) and private companies (33 per cent). Only 8 per cent of respondents gave a 'trust least' reply for pressure groups (Figures from Jordan and Davidson, 2000: 67).

This high level of trust for organisations like Greenpeace is not confined to Britain. Research by Edelman Public Relations in Europe found that almost one-third of respondents trusted non-governmental organisations to do the right thing. In contrast, only one-fifth trusted government and 15 per cent business. (*Financial Times*, 6 December 2000).

Jordan and Davidson comment (2000: 68) that 'the perception appears to be that [pressure groups] are defenders of the public interest, presenting neutral, value free accounts of issues and problems . . . this is a naïve interpretation of reality.' There seems to be little recognition by the public that pressure groups have their own agenda to pursue. In part this is determined by their ideology and goals, but it is also influenced by their survival goals as organisations. Ultimately, they are reliant on public subscriptions (or legacies). A particular crisis can produce a new series of newspaper advertisements asking for donations.

These public attitudes are unlikely to shift in the short run. It may be that a better short run strategy is to focus on opinion formers. Shell has designed its first coordinated global corporate communications programme 'to reach a wide range of opinion-forming stakeholders, from fund managers, journalists and business peers to academics, politicians and NGOs.' Opinion research suggests that favourability ratings towards Shell amongst global opinion formers went up from 48 per cent in 1997 to 69 per cent in 1999 (Shell, 2000, unpaginated).

As far as business associations are concerned, there needs to be a dual strategy of refuting the claims made by the more extreme groups and entering into a dialogue with those with a more constructive outlook.

More generally, there needs to be a debate about the role of non-governmental organisations in politics. This is beginning to happen. There is an increasing realisation that non-governmental organisations are often not very internally democratic organisations; the level of their support is often unclear; and they have not been through a process of election like politicians. As one think tank report refers to a growing chorus of complaint that sees NGOs as unrepresentative, unaccountable and often plain uninformed – distorting the democratic process, eroding the authority of elected officials, and excluding the voices of those directly affected by global change in favour of an urban, middle-class minority of armchair radicals, based largely in the industrialised world (Edwards, 2000: 2).

New age direct action can degenerate into a form of lifestyle politics which trivialises important political issues. Politics becomes another form of consumption in which one takes part in an action simply as an experience. Campaigning organisations become protest businesses which market a particular identity and lifestyle choice to consumers (Jordan and Maloney, 1997). At its worst, one can have a kind of infantilist politics in which people think their demands are morally superior and should be satisfied immediately, regardless of the preferences of others.

Nevertheless, it needs to be recognised that there are genuine concerns behind the demands made by environmental and other groups. All too often, the European project seems to be a technocratic, elitist one, driven by the preferences of a political class out of touch with public opinion. The effective business associations of the future will be those that can recognise this changed operating environment, engage constructively with public concerns and develop strategies which do not rely simply on influencing political elites. A logic of protest now sits alongside the logic of influence and the logic of membership.

6

Large Firms and the Transformation of EU Business Associations: a Historical Perspective

Maria Green Cowles[1]

When examining the effectiveness of EU business associations, one must ask 'which associations?' There are, of course, the traditional associations found in Brussels since late 1950s – the 'associations of associations' model. UNICE, whose membership includes the national industry associations, is a classic example of such an association. Yet, today one finds many different kinds of business groups: direct-firm associations (e.g. the EU Committee of AmCham), 'mixed' associations comprised of associations and individual firms (e.g. CEFIC), Chief Executive Officer (CEO) organisations (e.g. the European Round Table of Industrialists (ERT)), and ad-hoc organisations (usually comprised of companies) whose purpose and existence may change based on the policy issue at hand (e.g. the ENERG-8). In recent years, one can also find EU business associations that are actually transatlantic or global in membership (e.g. the Transatlantic Business Dialogue (TABD) and the Global Business Dialogue on e-commerce (GBDe)).

How and why did these different EU business associations come about? How can one understand the evolution of business associations? As this chapter points out, the answer largely lies in the mobilisation of large firms in Brussels policy-making – firms that were largely dissatisfied with the effectiveness of the traditional EU business associations and/or lobbying practices in Brussels given the economic, political, and technological developments of the time.

The purpose of this chapter is to provide a brief historical overview of the transformation of EU business associations by large firms.[2] I will examine five broad historical eras (Table 6.1) during which large firms (and/or their CEOs) organised themselves in Brussels. The chapter concludes with some reflections on the general effectiveness of existing EU business associations, and potential future transformations of these groups that may arise.

Table 6.1 Development Phases[3]

Phases	Format	Example(s)
1950s–1960s	Association of associations	UNICE
1960s–1970s	Informal groupings of public relations representatives and CEOs	The Ravenstein Group; the Groupe des Présidents
1970s–1980s	Format A: Direct Firm/Direct CEO Memberships	EU Committee of AmCham; European Roundtable of Industrialists (ERT)
	Format B: Mixed Associations	CEFIC
1990s	*Ad hoc* Direct Firm Memberships	ENERG-8; ICRT
1990s–2000	Global Direct Firm Associations	Transatlantic Business Dialogue (TABD); Global Business Dialogue on e-commerce (GBDe)

1950s – once upon a time[4]

Looking at the Brussels political landscape today, one might forget that the Common Market was largely forged without the influence of business – and definitely without the support of big business. EU founder Jean Monnet, after all, thought large companies were too nationalistic to support his European project and distrusted them in part to the real or alleged activities of some of the large companies during the Second World War.[5] Business, for its part, largely distrusted the unfolding integration efforts of the founding fathers. Indeed, UNICE (the Union of Industrial and Employers' Confederations) was created in 1958 as an organisation designed to monitor and hopefully prevent the expansion of the integrationist policies in Brussels.[6] French industry in particular envisioned UNICE as a defense mechanism against the High Authority (today's Commission).[7] Consequently, it is not surprising that relations with the Commission were rather strained during this period.

UNICE was forged by bringing together the national industry associations from the six founding members of the Community. As such, UNICE was a very 'intergovernmental' organisation – each national association represented its own national constituency. Because there was little emphasis on supranational compromise, the members often found it difficult to agree on EU-wide industry positions. As a result, UNICE usually commented on Commission legislative action after it was proposed – or even, in some cases, passed into law.

While large companies were generally absent during this period, a few firms made their first entrée into Brussels during this period. For example, FIAT attempted to build bridges to the Commission largely due to Giovanni Agnelli's personal belief in the European project. By the 1960s, Unilever and Royal Dutch Shell began to send representatives to speak with Brussels Eurocrats every couple years. There was no lobbying in the traditional sense. As an ICI official noted, company representatives often attended cocktail meetings with Commission officials after hours to learn about general Community developments. In short, the qualifications for a business representative in the 1960s was to be 'a nice guy who could properly handle a glass of sherry.'[8]

The 1960s–1970s: informal groups

The Community's unanimous voting system, reinforced by the 1967 Compromise of Luxembourg, meant that there was little incentive for associations or firms to develop stronger supranational institutions in Brussels. Associations could simply follow the 'national route' by encouraging their national government to veto legislative proposals not to their liking.[9]

Given this environment, one would expect little change in business representation. Yet, significant developments did occur with the creation of the first CEO group and a number of important public affairs/lobbying groups. While any number of factors contributed to these changes, two stand out in particular. The first was the arrival in Brussels of American firms. These companies often employed British representatives who shared their Anglo-Saxon approach to lobbying. The second factor was the realisation in the business community that Brussels policies could, in fact, impact corporate activity – the national veto withstanding.

The latter factor led to the creation in 1967 of the Groupe des Présidents – an informal grouping of CEOs who met to dine and discuss EEC issues with Commission and national officials. The group was created at the behest of a former Philips official, M. Von Geldern, who worked in Euratom. Von Geldern was appalled that corporate leaders in Europe paid little attention to the Community. The secretive Groupe des Présidents survived for over two decades when in 1988 it was disbanded when some members decided to join the European Roundtable of Industrialists (ERT) (69).

Beginning in 1975, a number of organisations for Brussels public affairs officials were created to discuss Community legislative activities and to encourage a 'professionalisation' – some would say 'Americanisation' – of the Brussels-based lobbyists. The surge in American activity in Brussels can be attributed to growing US foreign direct investment in Europe in the aftermath of the EEC's creation, and the decision by many US companies to set up their headquarters in the Belgian capital. In 1975, the IBM government affairs representative founded the Ravenstein Group (named after the famous restaurant/chateau where they met) to 'sharpen up ideas' about how to approach the Commission. Three years later, the representative of the US company Merck Sharp & Dohme, created the Internal Public Affairs Forum – better known as the 'Longin Group' after its founder – to encourage stronger lobbying skills. That same year, the representative of Rank-Xerox created the Industry/Government *Ad hoc* Council to enable company representatives to meet with officials from national governments and the Commission during biyearly meetings.[10]

The 1970s–1980s: direct firm, CEO, and mixed associations

Some scholars have suggested that the most significant changes to EU business associations occurred in the aftermath of the Single Market program in the 1990s. While the 1990s did witness an explosion in the quantity of interest group – including business association activity – I would argue that the more significant developments occurred more than a decade earlier. While Europe was supposedly 'sick' during the economic malaise of the 1970s, large companies began to mobilise in important ways in Brussels, creating new types of business associations, and transforming others. In the process, at least one of these new business associations – the European Roundtable of Industrialists – played no small part in the launching of the Single Market program itself.

As discussed below, there were a number of developments that arose during this time period that prompted large firms to pay closer attention to EU activities. At the same time, it became clear to these companies that traditional industry associations such as UNICE were ill-equipped or unable to address these new developments. As a consequence, the informal business groupings of the 1960s gave way to important new business organisations in the 1970s and 1980s.

In 1973, the Commission developed its 'multinationals programme' that sought to place some controls over the burgeoning activities of multinational firms – namely, American firms – in Europe. Since most national industry associations did not allow American firms in their membership rosters, the interests of US companies could not be represented through UNICE. That same decade, the European Court of Justice began to issue its first competition policy cases against large companies – notably, American firms. The 1979 Vredeling proposal – a precursor to the Work Councils directive of the 1990s – proved to be the 'final straw' for US companies. Some American firms viewed the proposal as a form of industrial espionage that would enable Europeans to learn US company secrets due to work councils reporting requirements. A planeload of Washington, DC-based lawyers and lobbyists – most of whom had never been in Brussels before – descended upon the Commission to lobby against the proposal. Needless to say, the American entourage and 'aggressive' US lobbying tactics were not well-received in the EU capital. In the aftermath of this public relations fiasco, Brussels-based representatives of US firms vowed to create their own EU business association. What began as a small committee inside the US–Belgian Chamber of Commerce in 1978, became a separate institution – the EU Committee of AmCham – in 1985.[11] As one of the first direct-firm associations in Brussels, the EU Committee developed the reputation in the 1990s as one of the most powerful business voices in Brussels.[12]

The Anglo-Saxon influence in Brussels was strengthened in 1973 with the arrival of the UK – and thus, the Confederation of British Industry (CBI). The British organisation differed in important ways from its continental counterparts. The CBI, for example, was anxious to benefit from the European Community and to develop a Brussels industrial policy. In addition, the CBI was organised quite differently from other national industry associations. Whereas the German industry association, the Bundesverband des Deutschen Industrie (BDI), is a national association of sectoral associations, the CBI allowed for sectoral associations as well as direct firm memberships. And since there were more multinational corporations in the UK than in any other country on the continent, there were a large number of multinational firms active in the British business association, most notably in its 'Europe Committee'.[13]

The CBI and its large companies soon became frustrated with UNICE and its reactive orientation to Brussels policy-making. By 1980, there was still no UNICE committee set up to address the Vredeling proposal or the Commission's programme on multinationals. Thus, a core group of large British firms, in alliance with other companies in Brussels, undertook a programme to transform UNICE. Over time, the group became known as the European Enterprise Group. Its goal was not to get rid of UNICE, but to make it a proactive organisation by placing individual firms on UNICE policy committees and working groups, and creating new rules on position papers that allowed for consensus agreements (with disagreements noted in the appendix). In addition, recognising that the national associations' financial contribution to UNICE's operations was rather meager, the companies sought to strengthen UNICE financially in hopes of rendering it a more effective organisation. By creating a special fee-based membership group within UNICE, the UNICE Advisory and Support Group, firms are able to contribute to the organisation's budget while strengthening their voice, albeit in a rather minor way, in UNICE policy matters.

Today, despite these changes, EEG's success in transforming UNICE should not be overemphasised. The national associations still jealously guard their representation in the organisation and keep a ceiling on direct firm financial contributions. The EEG itself is now a forum in which members of the EU Committee, UNICE, and the ERT occasionally meet to discuss their mutual concerns.[14] At the same time, however, the firms have left their imprint on other Brussels business associations. For example, several of the same firms involved in the creation of the EU Committee (Esso) and the European Enterprise Group (ICI) were key movers behind the 1991 transformation of the European Chemical Industry Council (CEFIC) that divided the association into two bodies – one of associations, the other of firms.

Arguably the most important development in the transformation of EU business associations occurred in 1983 with the creation of the European Roundtable of Industrialists (ERT). Whereas the EU Committee of AmCham and the EEG emerged as efforts to thwart Commission activity (i.e. the Vredeling proposal) and to promote more effective lobbying efforts in Brussels, the ERT was created at a time when certain Commission officials began to work closely with large firms to develop responses to various industrial crises. The path-breaking activities of Industry Commissioner Etienne Davignon – dubbed Steve Wonder by his colleagues – led to more congenial, if not mutually supportive, relations between large firms and the Commission. In 1978, for example, Davignon assisted in creating the Information Technology Roundtable comprised of CEOs of major European IT firms. Discussions between the Commissioner and industry leaders led to the European Strategic Programme in Information Technology (ESPRIT).[15] In 1982, Davignon met with Pehr Gyllenhammar, CEO of Volvo, the Swedish automaker, to discuss efforts to create a CEO group that would speak out on EU industrial matters in light of the economic malaise at the time. A year later, Gyllenhammar brought together a group of leading European CEOs and Board Chairmen to form the ERT. In time, the ERT, with leadership from Wisse Dekker of Philips, led the effort to relaunch the European economy with a major industrial initiative – namely, a Single European Market.[16]

In doing so, the ERT emerged as a novel kind of EU business association comprised of CEOs and Chairmen of the Board, not public affairs representatives. Moreover, unlike the Groupe des Présidents which disbanded in 1988, these company heads were politically active individuals who were willing to speak out on EU initiatives at both the national and European levels. ERT members appeared with top-level Commission officials to launch European initiatives, sent coordinated responses to heads of state and government, and carefully used the media to advance their projects. While the ERT's influence was most evident during the Single Market era, as noted by Bastiaan van Apeldoorn in this volume, the group continues to leave its imprint on EU policymaking. Most recently, for example, the ERT helped spearhead the Lisbon package on competitiveness.[17] The ERT has become a CEO-based model for future EU business associations in the decades that followed.

The 1990s – formalizing the *ad hoc* organisations[18]

The 1990s witnessed the emergence of important *ad hoc* organisations. To be certain, *ad hoc* groups were not new. The Ravenstein Group and the EEG began as *ad hoc* groupings, and remained fairly informal organisations. Moreover, *ad hoc* associations had long been in existence at the national level in countries such as the United Kingdom. What was different in the 1990s, however, is the emergence of a new form of *ad hoc* associations at the European level that dealt with vertical issues, that is, specific policy issues. Moreover, these groups were 'corporatised' with professional managers, substantial funding, and, more often than not, the involvement of CEOs who contacted high-level Commission officials at key phases in the legislative process.

The maturation of the Single Market program coupled with the use of qualified majority voting were key factors leading to the creation of these groups. By the mid-1990s, the EU had already passed a significant amount of single market legislation. EU policy-makers were thus turning their attention to: (1) those issues that initially were too sensitive to tackle; and (2) those areas where general directives now require more specific legislation. As a consequence, large firms began to coalesce around these 'new' issues. At the same time, companies and other societal groups recognised that they could not rely on government vetoes to protect their interests. Instead, they needed to build coalitions of like-minded groups or firms to send their message to any number of national governments.

One such *ad hoc* group was – and continues to be – ENERG-8, a coalition of eight energy intensive manufacturing companies created in 1995–6. The purpose of the coalition was to enter the debates on the internal energy market that had largely been dominated by the key producers of energy – nationalised firms or dominant private companies that were predisposed to protecting their national monopoly. Indeed, the voice of the energy consumer was largely missing from the debate. Therefore, eight powerful companies – Akzo Nobel, BASF, Daimler-Chrysler (then Mercedes-Benz), Dow Europe, ICI, KNP BT, Pilkington and Thyssen – decided to pull their resources and create the industrial consumers' voice. The existence of ENERG-8 prompted energy producers, who have traditionally relied on their ties with national government to influence EU legislation, to become more organised at the European level. While there is disagreement over ENERG-8's influence in this debate, the *ad hoc* group was recognised by officials in the Santer cabinet as an important new voice in Brussels. Interestingly, ENERG-8 has reinvented itself in recent years as a new 'multinationals' voice' in the Climate Change debate.

Another example of an *ad hoc* group is the International Communications Round Table (ICRT). Calling itself 'an informal, cross-sectoral grouping', the ICRT is a diverse group of leading companies from the publishing, media, computer, and communications industries, including Bertelsmann, Dun & Bradstreet, IBM, ICL, Microsoft Europe, Reuters and Sony Entertainment, among others. Creating the group in 1994, ICRT companies sought to influence the debate over intellectual property protection, electronic commerce and encryption in Europe. While informal, the ICRT hosts two plenaries a year in which the ICRT CEOs could discuss priorities and meet with prominent European policy-makers. Over the years, the ICRT has become increasingly global in orientation. Indeed, several ICRT CEOs and companies became active in more global dialogues later in the 1990s.

The 1990–2000 – going global

Until recently, the development of EU business associations has been rather 'evolutionary' in perspective. Developments in the mid-1990s, however, have proven to be more 'revolutionary' as EU business associations move from being national or European participants, to more global players in the international trade and regulatory game. Indeed, European firms are not only 'going global' in their market operations, but in their political realm as well. One could argue that the rise of the Transatlantic Business Dialogue (TABD)[19] and its related organisation, the Global Business Dialogue on e-commerce (GBDe) have prompted renewed strains between large firms and national industry associations and reinvigorated business–government relations with the Commission and the US government.

A number of factors set the stage for the emergence of these groups. One factor was the increasingly global economy where international investment far surpasses international trade. Nowhere were the linkages in this global economy more apparent than in the US–EU relationship. In 1995, for example, EU firms held approximately 58 per cent of all foreign direct investment in the United States, and US firms owned about 44 per cent of FDI in the EU.[20] The growth in the global economy was matched only by that in the 'new' or 'networked' economy linked to the Internet, wireless, and computer-driven technologies. A second factor were the changes in the size and scope of European companies themselves. With the creation of DaimlerChrysler, for example, there now existed a European company that would rival that of large American corporations. At the same time, companies such as Nokia and Ericsson were leaders in market share and at the forefront of this new economy. Yet a third factor was the growing realisation of government officials that they were ill-equipped to manage the global economic developments, to understand the changing market forces, and to regulate accordingly.

The origins of the TABD, in fact, can be traced to a government official, Ron Brown, the late US Commerce Secretary in the Clinton administration. At an EU Committee of AmCham-sponsored meeting in Brussels on 15 December 1994, Brown laid out his idea to encourage a dialogue among US and EU firms on global trade and regulatory issues.[21] Brown believed that companies were far ahead of governments in their thinking of international markets and trade liberalisation. American officials also were concerned that EU companies were less active in external trade matters. Several believed, for example, that greater market liberalisation would have occurred had these firms been involved during the Uruguay round negotiations.

After close consultation with Commission officials, a joint US–EU steering committee comprised of government and industry officials met for the first time in Brussels in July 1995. A decision was made to launch a Transatlantic Business Dialogue conference in Seville, Spain, in November 1995 to develop recommendations on removing obstacles to trade and investment. The idea was to incorporate these recommendations into a joint US–EU initiative at the Madrid US–EU summit a month later – an initiative that became the New Transatlantic Agenda (NTA).

The Seville conference proved to be very successful, not only in terms of the recommendations made, but also in terms of the relationships forged between the US–EU business communities. TABD officials note that over 60 per cent of the TABD Seville recommendations were later incorporated in the NTA. The success of Seville laid the groundwork for annual conferences that have been held in Chicago (1996), Rome (1997), Charlotte (1998), Berlin (1999), and Cincinnati (2000). During this period, the TABD has influenced a number of developments including the signing of the Mutual Recognition Agreements in 1997, the creation of an industry agreement on Third Generation Wireless standards, and the consensus reached on the Information Technology Agreement.[22]

As mentioned above, the TABD is also notable for its impact on business associations in Brussels. In the first place, the TABD directly challenges the role of national industry associations – and therefore, UNICE as well – in external trade matters.[23] Historically, external trade matters were the purview of national industry associations and UNICE. Many of these associations, particularly the sectoral bodies, were noted for their technical expertise. Indeed, UNICE had its own dialogue with one of its American counterparts, the National Association of Manufacturers (NAM) on transatlantic trade issues. The creators of TABD, however, believed the UNICE–NAM discussions were too bogged down in technical minutiae. They insisted that the TABD be a CEO-driven process with a broader political impetus.[24] Instead of associations, corporate CEOs would be responsible for meeting directly with senior government officials to facilitate change. TABD organisers (notably the Americans) were so determined to remove associations from the dialogue that they accorded associations with merely 'observer' status at the Seville conference. While the schism between traditional associations and companies has since been mended, associations are still viewed as secondary players within the TABD.

The TABD's creation has also led to greater coordination between business and the European Commission on trade and regulatory matters. Commission officials were intricately involved in the group's formulation. However, European companies became frustrated early on when they could not find the appropriate government official to discuss specific TABD regulatory matters. The Commission responded by creating a special point-of-contact list in which a Commission official was identified for each TABD action item. Over the years, this arrangement has led to considerable dialogue between the firms and Commission itself – thus further strengthening the role of individual companies and the TABD in external trade matters.

The Global Business Dialogue on e-Commerce (GBDe) is another such business group that emerged in the late 1990s.[25] Whereas the TABD was initially American-led, the origins of the GBDe are linked to then Industry Commissioner Martin Bangemann. On 29 June 1998, Bangemann invited European business leaders to a roundtable discussion on global communications issues, and promoted the idea of a new business dialogue that would focus exclusively on e-commerce. To be sure, traditional industry groups such as UNICE were ill-equipped to address the new technology area. Most national associations, for example, were still largely focused on traditional manufacturing as opposed to service industries. And, whereas the TABD was a well-structured dialogue with a subgroup devoted to e-commerce issues, it could not cover e-commerce as broadly and conclusively as a separate organisation entirely devoted to the subject. Moreover, the fast-moving nature and explosion of the e-commerce industry posed particular problems. Simply put, governments could not keep up with e-commerce developments. Instead of a regulatory framework imposed by governments, Bangemann and others believed e-commerce required more self-regulation by the industry players themselves.[26] Moreover, given the nature of the industry, this self-regulation would require the participation of global participants. With the German communications giant Bertelsmann taking the lead, the GBDe took shape over the next six months. Interestingly, Japanese companies were the first to sign on to the European initiative, followed by the Americans – who initially expressed concern that the organisation would be too bureaucratic and too linked to the Commission itself. The 'process', as it is called, was formally launched with a meeting of key CEOs in New York City on 14 January 1999.

Officially, the GBDe describes itself as 'a world-wide, CEO-driven effort to develop policies that promote global electronic commerce for the benefit of business and consumers everywhere.' More specifically, the GBDe seeks to develop norms, rules, and principles to shape the global public policy framework for e-commerce. The goal is to create industry-led, market-driven solutions to e-commerce regulatory and public policy issues around the world. Through self-regulation or, as the case may be, co-regulation, GBDe companies want to avoid the creation of national or regional policies that might impede this global medium.[27]

The GBDe has followed the TABD's format in several respects.[28] The GBDe is CEO-driven, with business leaders from three regional areas: Europe/Africa, Asia/Oceania, and the Americas. Of course, the leadership is largely drawn from EU, Japanese, and American firms. Like the TABD, the group's timetable revolves around an annual conference, the first being in Paris in December 1999, the second in Miami in September 2000, the third in Tokyo in September 2001. The GBDe has a core set of issue groups that focus on specific topics such as consumer confidence, the digital divide, cyber security, and intellectual property rights.

Yet, the GBDE also differs from the TABD in important ways. First, it is more global in nature given the inclusion of Asian firms. Second, it focuses specifically on the e-commerce value chain – from service and media providers to equipment manufacturers – as opposed to trans-atlantic industry in general. Third, the GBDe interacts with governments in different ways. In the TABD, the companies look to the governments to provide 'the deliverables' – that is, the changes in regulatory policy. By contrast, the GBDe emphasises self-regulatory or co-regulatory approaches to policy-making. Therefore, the 'deliverables' are often-times company codes of conduct that must be provided by the firms themselves.

Interestingly, the creation of the GBDe did not result in the closure of the TABD's working group on e-commerce. If anything, the TABD's subgroup has been strengthened. TABD representatives suggest that one reason for this situation is the need for there to be multiple voices who can speak out coherently on e-commerce issues. Thus, there is considerable coordination between GBDe and TABD companies (many of whom are the same) on e-commerce issues. Yet another reason for the two groups is that the GBDe tends to represent the service, media and equipment providers of e-commerce, whereas the TABD currently tends to represent the interests of the e-commerce users. Thus, the two organ-isations will likely experience both cooperation and conflict on matters of e-commerce in the future.

Transformation and coexistence

As this chapter has indicated, large firms have played an important role in transforming traditional industry associations and, when necessary, creating their own business groups to address changing economic and political developments. In doing so, they have brought new players, new resources, and new politics to EU, transatlantic, and global policy-making. They have also brought on charges that they carry undue influence to the policy-making process, thus weakening the voice of more 'representative' traditional associations.

Yet the most important factor influencing the creation of these groups was the perceived inability of traditional business associations to effect-ively, proactively represent the interests of industry in Brussels policy-making. Reinforcing this view was the seeming reluctance of traditional EU groups – usually national associations themselves – to strengthen their EU organisation's resources, especially if this meant sending more Euros to Brussels and less to the national headquarters. Perhaps as a result, today there is sharing of responsibilities in Brussels business organisations such as CEFIC and the TABD, with large firms and their CEOs taking the lead on major issues, and associations playing a second-ary role by lending expertise and 'representativeness' to the process.

In the past decade, an additional factor has emerged behind the creation of big business organisations. Groups like the TABD and GBDe were created not merely due to traditional associations' short-comings, but also due to government officials' difficulties in grappling with globalisation and the new economy. In the future, as events at the Seattle WTO meeting illustrated, the real struggle in Brussels policy-making may not be between large firms and traditional industry associ-ations, but between the companies and other members of civil society. The Commission, of course, has tried to address this through its Trade Policy Society with Civil Society meetings whose 'stakeholders' include traditional umbrella organisations in Brussels such as UNICE. The Commission's demand for the other transatlantic dialogues – the Trans-atlantic Consumers Dialogue, the Transatlantic Environmental Dia-logue – should also be interpreted in this vein. Increasingly, US and EU officials have called on business leaders themselves to initiate dis-cussions and work more closely with other members of civil society.[29] Interestingly, the GBDe has recently developed an ongoing discussion with Consumers International (a global consumer umbrella group) and BEUC (the EU consumer umbrella organisation) in an effort to bring greater legitimacy to its consumer confidence initiatives.

Thus, perhaps we are witnessing yet another phase in the transforma-tion of business groups in Brussels.

Notes

1 Please cite as Cowles, Maria Green or Cowles, M. G.
2 This chapter is drawn from Maria Green Cowles, 'Evolving Governance, Changing Firms: Explaining the mobilization of large firms in Brussels policy-making' unpublished manuscript. This latter piece provides a broader theoretical frame-work for understanding the collective action of these companies over time.
3 Portions of this discussion as well as Table 6.1 can be found in Cowles, M. G. (1998) 'The changing architecture of big business', *Collective Action in the European Union: Interests and the new politics of associability*, Greenwood, J. and Aspinwall, M. (eds) (London: Routledge), p. 114.
4 For an overview of the period from the 1950s to 1995, see Cowles, M. G. (1994) 'The politics of big business in the European Community: setting the agenda for a new Europe', Ph.D. dissertation, American University. See also Coen, D.

(1997) 'The evolution of the large firm as a political actor in the European Union', *Journal of European Public Policy*, **4** (1 March), 97–108.

5 Cowles, M. G. (1994) 'The politics of big business in the European Community: setting the agenda for a new Europe', Ph.D. dissertation, American University, p. 111.

6 The original name was 'Union des industries de la Communauté Européene.' The name was changed in 1987. For an early history, see Hammerich, E. (1969) *L'Union des Industries de la Communauté Européenne dans le Marché Commun* (Stockholm: Fédération des Industries Suédoises).

7 Ehrmann, H. W. (1957) *Organised Business in France* (Princeton: Princeton University Press).

8 Quoted in Cowles, 1994 (see note 5), p. 117, n. 39.

9 See Averyt, W. (1975) 'Eurogroups, Clientela, and the European Community', *International Organisation*, **29**(4) (Autumn), 949–72.

10 Cowles, 1994 (see note 5), 131–2.

11 The EU Committee is still legally linked to the Belgian chamber. However, the former is considerably larger than its purported mother institution.

12 Cowles, M. G. (1996) 'The EU Committee of AmCham: The Powerful Voice of American Firms in Brussels', *Journal of European Public Policy*, 3(3), 339–58.

13 Ibid.

14 Cowles, M. G. (1997) 'Organising Industrial Coalitions', in Wallace, H. and Young, A. (eds) *Participation and Policymaking in the European Union* (London: Oxford University Press), pp. 116–40.

15 Sandholtz, W. (1992) *High-Tech Europe: the Politics of International Cooperation* (Berkeley and Los Angeles: University of California Press).

16 Cowles, M. G. (1995) 'Setting the agenda for a new Europe: The ERT and EC 1992', *Journal of Common Market Studies*, **33** (4 December), 501–26; and Cowles, M. G. (1995) 'The European Round Table of Industrialists: the strategic player in EU affairs', *European Business Alliances*, Greenwood, J. ed. (Herts, UK: Prentice-Hall), pp. 225–36.

17 Betts, P. (2001) 'Industrialists criticise governments over pace of EU reform', *Financial Times* (29 March).

18 This section is largely derived from Cowles, M. G. (1998) 'The changing architecture of big business,' *Collective Action in the European Union: Interests and the new politics of associability,' Greenwood, J. and Aspinwall, M. (eds) (London: Routledge).

19 The TABD maintains that it is not an 'organisation' but a 'process' (see www.tabd.org). The view is largely promoted by the American side which fears an organisation would render the TABD less dynamic. In general, European companies are less troubled by the 'organisation' appellation, perhaps given the historic role of associations in the member states.

20 See Pollack, M. A. and Shaffer, G. C. (2001) 'Introduction: transatlantic governance in historical and theoretical perspective', *Transatlantic Governance in a Global Economy*, Pollack, M. A. and Shaffer, G. C. (eds) (Lanham, MD: Rowman and Littlefield), p. 13.

21 For an historical overview of the TABD, see Cowles, M. G. (2001) 'Private firms and US–EU policy-making: the Transatlantic Business Dialogue', *Ever Closer Partnership: Policy-Making in US–EU Relations*, Philippart, E. and Winand, P. eds. (Brussels: P.I.E.-Peter Lang).

22   Collomb, B. (2000) 'Communicating – and failing to – across the atlantic: transatlantic business dialogue presses for more open markets', *European Affairs*, **1**(2) (spring), 30–1. Collomb was EU Chair of the TABD in 2000.

23   For more on this argument, see Cowles, M. G. (2001) 'The TABD and domestic business–government relations', *Transforming Europe: Europeanization and Domestic Change*, Cowles, M. G., Caporaso, J. and Risse, T. eds. (Ithaca, NY: Cornell University Press), pp. 159–79.

24   In addition to CEOs, TABD members often include senior members (usually the president) of the board of European companies.

25   Cowles, M. G. (2001) 'Who are the rule-makers of e-commerce?: A case study of the Global Business Dialogue on e-commerce (GBDe)', *AICGS Policy Paper* (Washington, DC: AICGS).

26   Interview with GBDe participant, Brussels, 18 September 2000.

27   Cowles, M. G. (2001) 'Who are the rule-makers of e-commerce?: A case study of the Global Business Dialogue on e-commerce (GBDe)', *AICGS Policy Paper* (Washington, DC: AICGS).

28   Interestingly, the European TABD secretariat office provided much of the initial coordination for GBDe matters in Europe.

29   This development already appears underway. In Lisbon, 7–8 June 2000, the first 'dialogue of dialogues' took place that included the TABD, TACD, and TAED. Other discussions between large firms and civil society have occurred in the Climate Change debate, with Shell Oil and British Petroleum (BP) splitting with other industry leaders and working with civil society groups. Of course, the fact that Shell is a major player in the 'renewables' (renewable energy) market and BP is the leader in solar energy were important factors in this development. Interview with consultant, Brussels, 17 September 2000.

7
Challenges and Opportunities for Business Associations: Autonomy and Trust

Rudolf Beger

The structure and philosophy of European business associations is widely characterised by corporatism. As a result of this, generally, representatives of business associations do not represent their individual political will but act as members of associations who are fully integrated in and strictly bound and controlled by arrangements. These arrangements, which constitute the foundation and rationale of such associations, include, amongst others, the dominance of the association members' political will over the (political) expertise of associations.

What association members typically expect from their associations is not self-motivated initiative, value-added thinking, or (political) vision but the strict representation and execution of their collective interest. Therefore, quite typically, association representatives' power normally relate more to the power collectively represented by the association membership rather than to the attractiveness of their own, individual political analysis and goals which they could produce in the well-understood interest of the industry.

One can therefore say that it is the organisation which constitutes the basis for their activities. This organisation uses as a method internal consensus to create political influence. Most companies know that their individual position on a certain issue will not count in the political and legislative debate at European level unless it is bundled at least with the majority of other companies active in their specific sector. Therefore, and in order to secure their influence over the political debate, they are prepared to group with other companies in a business association.

By doing this, and sometimes even without being aware of it, they delegate with such moves something to an association which, quite frequently, they do not even possess themselves, political talent, insight and expertise.

It is in fact a paradox that representatives from an association's individual members:

- Normally insist on deciding on political issues, processes and procedures which they are normally not familiar with or, quite frequently, are not even interested in, on the one hand, and
- Are normally quite unwilling to assign more political responsibilities to their representative associations, on the other hand.

This is generally resulting in burdensome and painstaking consensus seeking efforts by the association management.

The agreements which are finally reached between an association's members are supposed to reflect their common interest which, because of the typical diversity of individual companies' interests, is typically expressed at the level of the lowest common denominator. The level of such lowest common denominator is typically the lowest in highly competitive industries which are commonly characterised by head-to-head rather than win–win competition.

There does not seem to be any doubt about the fact that in the era of globalisation and fallen national borders, most companies which enjoyed a comfortable win–win competition in the past, suddenly find themselves confronted with an uncomfortable head-to-head competition. Certainly, this new development has an important influence on the efficiency of their collective representation. As their *raison d'être* continues to be the resolution of problems between legislator and business interest by consensus and arrangement, their search for internal and external agreement on common positions is becoming increasingly subject to unsatisfactory compromises.

From an external, societal point of view, this process is dangerous because it will hamper, delay or even prevent progress from happening in a number of fields which are essential for the whole society (e.g. pollution). This is even more dangerous, as technological, economical and societal developments are getting faster and faster, leaving the political and legislative decision-makers rapidly behind. They continue to be entangled in their permanent struggle for consensus and balancing of powers.

The whining sporadic public complaints by high level industry representatives about slow political and legislative processes which they perceive as hampering their business seem phoney and hypocritical when one looks at the industry's own inability to modernise its representative structures and common decision-making processes.

At present, the painstaking search of business associations for credible political positions which:

- On the one hand, shall represent their members common interest; and
- On the other hand, shall match societal and political expectations;

is severely influenced by an (too) easy union between two deeply conservative forces (which should make the public actually uneasy, indeed):

- Associations representing their members' interests, on the one hand; and
- The administration and their bureaucracies' interest, on the other hand.

Their unholy alliance is detrimental to progress and supportive to conservatism, stagnation and/or marginal progress. The compromises found internally within business associations will rarely represent a true state-of-the-art position. In principle it will be protective (of the weakest or the least visionary member) rather than forward thinking, directing or even paving the way for leapfrog progress.

A good example for that dangerous practice is the current lengthy, burdensome and painstaking process in which the European bureaucracy is negotiating with the industry arrangements on internal combustion engine pollution control. The final agreement between the two parties typically reflect a number of major compromises.

The compromise found internally amongst the members of the negotiating industry association (generally reflecting the weakest, not the most advanced company's position), the compromise found in the discussions between industry experts (typically conservative, since they are not the final decision-makers but normally representing a rather defensive than offensive position), on the one hand, and European bureaucrats on the other hand.

The latter, because of their lack of own technical expertise, are generally fully dependent from the industry's technical know-how and input. The next compromise is then found at the political decision-making level which is normally characterised by egoistic national interests, absence of expertise and, quite frequently, political horse-trading which bears no relationship to the real issue in question.

This ultra-conservative system has led to the current legislators' stringency practice which, dictated by purely political considerations, imposes relatively short lead times on the industry for stepwise or partial improvements rather than stimulating and encouraging leapfrog change. Both parties in this conservative alliance seem to be happy with this system, although officially they claim in public:

- That, on the one hand, the industry could always do more than it is claiming it can do (the bureaucracy/governments); and

- That, on the other hand, the regulations imposed by the legislator are too stringent and are impeding the industry's competitiveness (the industry and their representations).

It is indeed questionable whether this permanent search for consensus within the industry and between the industry and the bureaucracy/legislator is or will continue to be in the general public interest. The question must be asked whether this system of compromise-oriented consensus is the best solution to achieve real break-through results in a world of growing challenges or whether it constitutes a barrier for maximum progress and for the full exploitation of the existing industry abilities to deliver more than presently done.

Currently, in the pollution control area, the governments short-term oriented approach (3–6 years) is leading to instability and costly and inefficient short term planning cycles in a long term oriented industry. In addition, it is missing a holistic approach which is required as many collaborating systems need to be analysed to come to maximum results. The current short term, narrow approach requires the industry to search for marginal improvements which are getting increasingly complex and costly but with diminishing results.

Therefore it cannot be surprising that there is well-founded suspicion that the industry (which is officially complaining about this approach) has in fact as part of its collaborative alliance with the other conservative force (the bureaucracy) tacitly agreed not to challenge that system.

It is clear, that a decision by the industry to dramatically change that relatively comfortable position, cancel their arrangements with the bureaucracy/governments and get engaged in a radical overhaul of their current, conservative approach towards real, marked progress, would rapidly lead to a number of break-throughs which would better match the current society's/environment's requirements.

The California air pollution control regulations can serve as a model. When the Government of California introduced its zero-emission approach a couple of years ago, it was first ridiculed by the industry. They felt, that this new approach could jeopardise their comfortable arrangements with the Government on 'reasonable and realistic' step-by-step improvements. But to everybody's surprise, later, the industry quietly changed its position and started to consider the avant-garde legislation of California as a catalyst for long-term oriented, radical change.

But neither the industry, continuously represented by its lowest common denominator-oriented associations, nor the bureaucracies/governments have understood, that the challenge will need even better, more radical responses. Their conservative alliance is unable to envision break-through change.

It is neither a conservative industry's, nor their associations', nor the bureaucracies', nor the governments' typical feature to stand for revolution, although revolutions are currently changing whole industries.

The typewriter industry, for instance, was still trying to save its future by introducing typewriters with memories, when personal computers and word processing programs were already hitting the shelves.

Conservative thinking, complacency and corporatist alliances with the goal to protect to the maximum the status quo, carry the risk of preventing the forward looking forces in the industry to adapt to the new challenges and the rapidly changing framework conditions. The result of alliances between deeply conservative forces such as business associations and government bureaucracies is an accelerating solidification of our society, stagnation, a slowing down of real progress and a growing inability to support and encourage 'flexibility and adaptability'.

Corporatism in business associations on the one hand, and lack of expertise, political vision, conservatism and tendencies to favour stagnation, on the other hand, must not replace market forces. The risk is that they will represent only narrow, special interest and ultimately work against the general (public) interest.

Max Weber, the well-known German Sociologist has said that each business association is 'a conspiracy against the public interest'.

This point of view can be supported when business associations are reactive, non-constructive, oriented by 'lowest common denominator' positions, in conspiracy with bureaucracies deeply suspicious about progress and therefore in effect, 'creating rigidity in the place of movement' (Ralf Dahrendorf).

As a result, these conservative forces, whether industry association or bureaucracy, are, 'robbing the constitution of liberty of its essence: the ability to bring about change without (*political*) revolution' (Ralf Dahrendorf, my emphasis).

What can and must be envisioned as a modern concept for a business association is an active, pro-active, credible, constructive, honest and innovative structure which defines its role not to solely defend its memberships' short term interest but, based on a common long term vision, represents a master plan for the long-term survival and prosperous development for the industry it represents.

It goes without saying, that under such a concept, short-term interests may become of low importance in favour of the implementation of long-term goals. This is in clear contrast to the farmers' success story, which is based on their associations' ability to 'turn a rumble into a revolution by getting the lads behind them over the weekend' (Michael Heseltine).

The European Union is suffering from its inefficient, costly and widely absurd Common Agricultural Policy which, in fact, is heavily influenced by conservatism on both sides.

In contrast to this traditional approach and orientation, a modern business association must be characterised by member pressure for progress and innovation, it must be long-term oriented and replace its typical inclination to react by pro-activity. The key words are 'management of rather than reaction to, innovation rather than status quo.'

A modern association management must lead its members rather than do what it perceives as what the member companies 'really want' or what they have been told by their members. They must feel responsible for bringing their members commercial goals into line with their own strategic political vision and with societal expectations. To be able to do this, a business association management must have the independence, the courage and the intellectual political abilities to do this difficult job. This requires strong personality and strength, credibility internally and externally, with the communication target groups and political vision.

In order to overcome the many challenges and barriers on the way towards a modern, forward looking business association, an association management must learn to re-define conflicts about issues into conflicts about methods. Pragmatism, not ideology, long-term goals rather than short-term protectionism, realistic political vision rather than narrow goals must characterise their activities.

It will be clear on the modern association management's mind that legislation is reflecting politics, politics is reflecting societal expectations and that business associations must respond to these expectations. Otherwise they will not become and cannot become a credible, constructive contributor and/or socially accepted business association. The modern business association envisioned here will be a partner and not a dull lobby, a contributor and not just an ambassador, and strategic in its approach and not just tactical.

'Lobbying lost its usefulness long ago' once said a German industrialist. He was seconded by a high level European politician who said that 'the old system of lobbying was not the most intelligent way of representing a sector's interest.'

8
The Changing Environment for Trade Associations and Strategies for Adaptation
Mark Boléat

Businesses are increasingly subject to a range of economic, technological and social factors which can force them to change drastically the goods and services they provide and/or the way that they provide them. Trade associations, however, for the most part have been sheltered from such forces. Broadly speaking they have needed only to make incremental changes to the services they provide or the way that they provide them. However, this is now changing as a result of a combination of factors.

The ideal trade association environment

It is helpful to identify the environment in which trade associations are most likely to flourish and to be effective. The ideal environment is one in which there is a discrete sector of the economy which is dominated by institutions which are nationally based and which are specialist in that sector. It is an added advantage, and one that could well influence the other factors, if there is a specific regulatory regime for the sector.

It is also helpful if there is a manageable number of members – say 100–400, with no firm having more than 5 per cent of the market and with a stable industry structure.

In such an industry there would be a substantial common interest, particularly in respect of the representative function. One or a small group of members would not dominate the association and the stable industry structure would help maintain continuity in the governance of the association and the subscription scale.

Few industries have ever presented such a favourable environment to a trade association. The building society industry in the UK in the 1970s came very close to it. Over 100 societies were in business and they dominated the mortgage market with a market share of over 90 per cent. They operated under special legislation which itself helped ensure that they were specialist institutions. However, the industry did have large members and a steady stream of mergers. At the opposite end of the spectrum are the global industries – airlines, computers and car manufacturing.

Generally, there is a move towards a far more difficult operating environment; in some sectors and industries the change is very rapid.

The changing environment – an overview

Five factors are changing the operating environment for trade associations. They apply in all countries and all sectors, although their relative strengths vary substantially from case to case. The factors are interrelated. In summary they are:

1 An increasing degree of concentration within industries as a result of take-overs and mergers.
2 Globalisation of business such that an increasing proportion of business is in the hands of foreign companies and domestic companies have an increasing share of their business in foreign markets.
3 The breaking down of barriers between markets and institutions.
4 Deregulation and privatisation combined with a gradual shifting of policy-making to the European or global level.
5 Information technology developments which should transform the way that trade associations work.

In general the threats provided by these developments outweigh the opportunities.

Increasing concentration

The structure of a sector is relevant to a trade association in two respects. First, the more that an association is dominated by a small number of members the more difficult it will be to manage the association. The large members may feel that the association merely serves to help their smaller competitors at their expense, and may seek to keep the association weak. The smaller members may feel that the association is dominated by the larger members and may want to set up their own association.

Second, most associations have subscription scales that are either capped or which taper or which are both tapering and capped. It follows that any merger of members will reduce subscription income. The larger the members involved in the merger the greater the effect on subscriptions. Members of an association will not easily understand being asked to pay a higher subscription not because they are getting a better service but rather because two other members have merged.

In those sectors where there has been merger activity and where the subscription scale is either or both of capped or tapering, so trade associations have suffered reductions in subscription income. Even where there has been no taper or cap the merged member may well question the subscription level thereby forcing the introducing of a cap or a taper. In some cases an informal arrangement will be made. In some associations, where membership is highly valued, it may be possible to extract higher subscriptions from the remaining members to compensate for the effects of merger activity, but even where this is possible there is likely to be adverse reaction from some members.

Normally however, associations have to react to this factor by reducing expenditure or seeking to increase revenue from other sources. This factor can itself also prompt mergers of trade associations where there are competing associations in a sector.

There are few sectors of industry and commerce, where there has not been a growing degree of concentration. In the banking industry there has been a mega-merger in France between BNP and Paribas, and in the UK NatWest has been purchased by Royal Bank of Scotland. In Germany there have been two attempts at mergers between the largest three banks but, as yet, these have failed. Other industries show a similar trend.

Globalisation

Globalisation is a special form of rationalisation, and involves one or both of two forces – increased foreign ownership of domestic institutions and increased trade such that a higher proportion of business is traded internationally. Recent examples of global mergers include:
- The Bass acquisition of Intercontinental in the hospitality industry. Bass now operates in 95 countries.
- The Daimler/Chrysler merger in the motor industry.
- The Vodafone/Airtouch/Mannesmann merger in the telecommunications industry.

The alliances between the airlines can be seen as a special form of globalisation.

While domestic mergers are invariably bad news for trade associations, globalisation may or may not be. A trade association would probably prefer the foreign acquisition of one of its large members to an acquisition by another larger domestic member. Foreign owned members are often good members for trade associations. Few international companies seem to discourage membership of national trade associations. Most leave the matter to the discretion of the country head.

However, globalisation often involves increased concentration at the national level and thereby affects trade associations. A good recent example of this is the acquisition of a French insurer, AGF, by a German insurer, Allianz, which led to a merger of their British subsidiaries. Taking the insurance sector again, the merger of two French companies, Axa and UAP, led to a merger of their British subsidiaries. The merged company has subsequently taken over one of the largest British companies, GRE, which has led to an increase in concentration in Britain and also rationalisation in other countries where both companies operated.

Where a significant part of a national market is controlled by international companies, particularly those based abroad, then management of the association may become difficult. The primary allegiance of foreign owned members is to their head office. The policies pursued by a trade association to which a subsidiary belongs may be at variance with those of the association of the parent company.

Breaking down of barriers between markets and companies

There has been an increasing trend for the boundaries between markets and institutions to become blurred. This is partly a consequence of deregulation and globalisation but also a reaction to market developments. The financial services market in Britain is a good example. Twenty years ago there were specialists banks, investment banks, stockbrokers, insurance companies and mortgage lenders. Now, the major financial institutions are in most or all of these markets as a result of creating subsidiaries or acquisitions. For example, one of the largest British banks, Lloyds TSB, has acquired two very large life companies, Abbey Life and Scottish Widows, and one of the largest building societies, Cheltenham and Gloucester. There has also been a blurring of the boundaries between products. In Britain unit trusts and life products have come to resemble each other. And there are now capital market instruments that look like reinsurance contracts.

The utilities are another example of this force. In Britain the gas, water and electricity companies can now sell each other's products and there have been mergers between the sectors. For example, Southern Water and Scottish Power are part of the same group, and in Wales the Hyder group provides water, electricity and a wide range of other services. A number of these utilities have moved into the telecommunications business.

Deregulation

Deregulation, in general, is partly a result of other trends yet it can accentuate those trends as well. While deregulation is often seen as a good thing in itself, governments are often encouraged to deregulate by market forces. Again, the financial services industry in Britain gives a good example of this. The method of implementing monetary policy in the 1950s became inappropriate because of market forces. As balance sheet controls of banks were lifted so they were more easily able to compete with the specialist mortgage lenders, the building societies. This contributed to the deregulation of building societies which allowed them to compete with banks in the deposit and retail loan markets. As the banks and building societies competed more strongly with each other so there have been mergers to create economies of scale. In effect, the building societies and the banks are now in the same industry rather than being in separate and distinct industries.

The utilities have similarly been deregulated. When there was a single national supplier of gas or water or electricity there was no need for a trade association. Privatisation generally meant the creation of a number of separate companies which have then needed to get together through a trade association. Further liberalisation has contributed to three of the other trends noted in this chapter – the breaking down of barriers between markets (the various companies now sell each other's products), increasing concentration and globalisation, with American and French companies buying British companies.

There has also been a trend away from specialist regulators and towards regulators covering a wide field. Again, taking a British example, the Financial Services Authority is being created to replace nine specialist regulators. As the specialist regulators for banks, building societies and insurance companies disappear so the need for specialist trade associations is reduced. Similarly, the gas and electricity regulators have merged.

In some sectors regulation is moving to the European or global level. The countries of the European Union have bound themselves to create a single market and much key decision making is now at the European level rather than the national level. Trade associations therefore increasingly have to operate at the European as well as the national level which they can do either directly or through European trade bodies or through a combination of the two.

In some markets where globalisation has been a major trend the decision taking is moving to the international level. For example, key decisions on banking regulation are now taken by the Basle Committee on Banking Supervision and there are similar bodies for the insurance and securities industries. Some issues, such as pollution and food safety, are increasingly being considered at the global level, if only informally, and the representative mechanism has to recognise this.

Conversely, in some countries there is a trend towards devolution with decision taking being shifted to smaller and smaller units. The former Yugoslavia and USSR have been broken up into a series of smaller units. Czechoslovakia has been split into two. In the UK Scotland, Wales and Northern Ireland now have their own parliaments (of sorts) with, in the case of Scotland in particular, considerable devolved powers.

Trade associations may therefore find themselves not only having to work at the traditional national level but also at the subnational level, the European or other regional level and the global level.

Information Technology (IT)

Technology has differing impacts on different industries. Some, like football, are relatively unaffected. Most use technology to make their administrative systems more efficient. Some are technology driven. Trade associations have largely been in the second category.

However, the Internet is capable of having a huge effect on the way that they do business, particularly when combined with the other factors covered in this chapter. Trade associations provide one or more of three core services:
- Representation.
- Provision of information, advice and guidance on best practice.
- A gateway for purchasers of the goods or services provided by members.

The balance between these three services is crucial to the impact of the Internet. Representation will be least affected. The main effect is to improve the efficiency with which information can be obtained – particularly from government and official bodies.

The provision of information and advice will be greatly affected. The Internet is surely the way in which all associations should be communicating with their members. Through the Internet instant access can be provided to all the information that the association has to all staff in all members. This removes an age-old problem that associations have had, that is that much of the information they provide does not get into the right hands in member companies.

However, the Internet has other implications. Most associations opt for a two-tier website – an open part accessible to anyone and a closed part which is password protected and accessible to members only – or so the theory goes. In practice, in many associations' passwords have a very short life. Staff in member organisations will happily pass on the password. At the same time many staff cannot remember (or are not given) the password and therefore do not access the site. Some associations recognise that they cannot keep part of their site closed and accordingly make the whole site open or at the least try to extract a fee for a subscription to the website.

This has important implications for membership of some trade associations, particularly those where most members do not actively participate in the affairs of the Association and join only for the information they obtain. Why should they pay for something which they can now obtain for nothing on exactly the same basis as those who pay the full fee? This is a major threat to many trade associations, particularly those with a large number of small members.

Most associations do not provide the third service – acting as a gateway for buyers – at all, either because it has been too difficult or because the sector they represent does not lend itself to it. There are some services in particular where buyers are infrequently in the market and a trade association is often the best access route. At present some of these access routes are wholly web-based, some are partly web-based – for example, a request can be made by Internet but a person decides which members should be put in touch with the enquirer, and some are entirely manual. In future such services will increasingly be totally web-based and the range of services provided in this way will increase. When small businesses in particular want to buy a one-off good or service the Internet will be their starting point. If the trade association is the portal to the providers that will be used; if a commercial portal is more efficient that will be used.

The key point is that the Internet opens the way, for the first time, for trade associations to face a competitive threat not from other trade associations but rather from completely new organisations unencumbered not only by the past but also by all of the problems which are inherent in membership based organisations. In the American trade association world all the talk is of the threat from vertical Internet portals.

One of the major software consultancies serving the trade association market in America, WEGO, summarises the position as follows:

> Hundreds of new Internet companies are launching specialised vertical portals that seek to capture the same audience that have historically turned to associations for education, news, events, networking, and the facilitation of trade.

WEGO goes on:

> The rapid rise of these types of 'vertical portals' poses a real threat to associations. As they become increasingly Internetsavvy, your membership will develop an affinity for the site that provides them with the information, services and on-line inter-activity they want and need. Though they would obviously prefer to get it from someone they trust (you) they will most certainly go elsewhere if they have to.

This threat is probably muted in Europe simply because the trade association market is much smaller and therefore the prizes for potential competitors are equally smaller. However, that does not mean that the threat is non-existent. Some vertical portals are already threatening associations' positions although most such portals, at least in Britain, have come from commercial publishing houses often based on trade journals rather than from venture capital backed start up companies.

The trade association response

How should trade associations respond to these powerful forces? The first essential is that an association should understand them and plan accordingly. This requires regular fundamental reviews of the association's market position and the way that it does business. The good associations already have a regular planning cycle but many associations do not – and as a result are likely to find themselves faced with a sudden crisis.

Restructuring

Many associations will need to engage in corporate restructuring to reflect the changing nature of the industries they represent. Rationalisations will lead to mergers of associations within the same sector as a response to falling subscription income. Where industries merge then there will be mergers of trade associations across sectors. This has already occurred and is likely to continue in the financial services sector as the boundaries between the banking, insurance and securities markets break down.

As policy making in some sectors shifts to the European or global level one would expect to see a shift in power away from national associations towards international groupings. In practice there is, as yet, little evidence of this. One problem is the inherent difficulty of running trade associations at regional or global level. In the past some of these associations have been badly run with membership of committees being seen as a reward and an opportunity for foreign travel rather than to make a contribution. And some people have been put on committees purely because of their linguistic abilities. It is also the case that even in the EU most decision taking relevant to trade associations is still at the national level, and national governments are also the most powerful means of influencing developments at the EU level. However, over the years globalisation is bound to increase the importance of international associations at the expense of national bodies.

There is the potential for a very worrying restructuring which could adversely affect national associations. In a number of industries (e.g. computers, car manufacturing, insurance and hotels) large international groups increasingly dominate the market. Very few look at their membership of trade associations in a strategic way. They do not actively consider whether they should be concentrating their resources on particular national associations or European or global associations. They do not consider whether they might be better pulling out of all national associations. Generally, decisions about trade association membership are left to operating units in each country.

It is possible however that some large international groups will decide to go it alone, particularly where policy-making is increasingly at the European or international level. In the hospitality industry McDonald's is one international company that has a policy of not becoming involved in national trade associations. Groups of large international companies may set up their own trade associations to concentrate specifically on lobbying and without having to worry about providing a service to thousands of members or democracy. In many sectors such bodies already exist at embryonic level. Most are talking shops but could easily develop into more formal groupings. National and international associations need to keep their big international members firmly 'onside' if they are to avoid such bodies taking off.

Using the Internet

Many trade associations are well aware of the importance of the Internet to them and have taken the necessary action to protect and enhance their position. Many others are not. In Britain the Trade Association Forum (www.martex.co.uk/taforum) is now the best portal for trade associations. If one is looking for an association covering a sector this is the site to use as one click gets from the directory to an association's home page. But over one third of the associations appear not to have websites – or if they have they have not told the TA Forum about them. Already those associations are missing out because they are less easy to contact than those which have websites.

And while some association websites are excellent others are very poor. Many have not been updated for weeks or months, whereas the best associations update their sites daily if necessary.

Every association should by now have undertaken a full assessment of the impact of the Internet on their business and the way that they deliver their services. The assessment will deal in particular with potential competitors and market opportunities.

Based on that assessment each association needs to have a strategy – recognising that there are different strategies for different associations. It is unlikely that such a strategy will include not having a website. Most associations should want their website to be the portal for their members wanting information relevant to their business. This will include having hotlinks to other relevant sites. Many associations will want their site to be the portal for potential purchasers of the goods or services provided by their members. If associations do not have their sites in order they will quickly find that their business is being stolen by other associations or commercial organisations, leading to a downward spiral. By contrast, a top quality website can enhance the value of membership of the association and may be a powerful tool in attracting new members, particularly where the association is the portal for new business opportunities.

So far most associations have simply seen the Internet as another method of communicating with members. But it is much more important than that. How to use the Internet is a crucial strategic decision. The wrong decision could be disastrous; taking no decision almost certainly will be. Even for those associations that get it right, having a good site may be simply a damage limitation exercise. The benefits of the Internet tend to lie with consumers and web-based companies rather than with traditional providers of goods and services.

Again the American experience is instructive about what might be on the way in Europe. Most American trade association sites are far better than British sites. Indeed for those goods and services where the market is global, American sites could well be a competitive threat to European trade associations. In America the leading software companies have now integrated their back office systems with websites and indeed now go one stage further through offering a whole IT package on an application service provider basis. That is, the trade association no longer has to worry about technology (something which many of them do and at great cost) but rather for a fixed monthly fee can outsource all of their in-house systems, membership database and website requirements to a specialist company. The problem in Britain at least is that no company is yet capable of providing those services, although some companies provide parts. Some of the American software companies are looking at the European market, although the experience so far is that their systems tend not to travel very well.

Outsourcing and the virtual trade association

Could the Internet and other developments described in this chapter lead to a fundamental change in the way that trade associations are organised and work? The traditional trade association is paper driven and employs a relatively large number of staff who sit in an office performing clerical and administrative functions. Technology has enabled much of the routine work to be mechanised and there has been a general trend, albeit slower than it should have been, for associations to employ fewer but better quality staff. Such staff do not need to be office based. They can work from anywhere, accessing the association's computer system from a laptop or PC in their home. All the papers they will ever need to see will be available to them anywhere in the world. They will need to use an office only for brainstorming with colleagues.

Newly established associations will increasingly look more and more like virtual associations. Instead of permanent staff a variety of consultants will be used on particular projects. All administrative functions will be outsourced. Serviced offices will be used rather than associations trying to manage (generally badly) their own buildings.

The permanent staff will be smaller in number but expert in everything they do and will concentrate on the representative and member services roles.

I suspect there will be increased use of association management companies. They are big business in the USA but underdeveloped almost everywhere else except Belgium and The Netherlands. Such companies can provide any level of service from a particular administrative function to a full service such that the association itself has no full time employees. They are particularly appropriate for smaller associations with a subscription income of under $1.5 million.

Governance

The governance of trade associations merits a book in itself. Associations are difficult organisations to govern. The members of the governing body, however they are chosen, are transient and often in strong competition with the other members. Officers are often chosen not for their ability but rather to secure the necessary balance, to appease a large member or, worst of all, because they have got plenty of time to do the job. Governing bodies frequently spend time discussing things that in their own companies they would not be allowed anywhere near.

There is the permanent danger of a poor quality governing body losing its few good members and finding that it could then attract only position seekers rather than good quality people. Many governing bodies are far too large to function effectively.

The forces outlined in this chapter have forced many associations to review their governance. Mergers have disrupted committee structures and globalisation makes it increasingly difficult to arrange meetings as many key people are out of the country at any one time. Many a chairman has been the victim of a merger of his company and has been faced with the choice of standing down quickly or hanging on in office but without a position in the industry. Busy people running big businesses will not commit themselves to serving on a trade association governing body if this requires monthly meetings for three years plus numerous special committees. Top people will not commit themselves to be nominated one September to serve two years as deputy chairman from the following April and then two years as chairman.

Reviews of governance generally lead to the same conclusions. The key one is that more should be delegated to the secretariat, with the chief executive being wholly responsible for the running of the association and also the principal representative and spokesman for the association. The chief executive should generally be in the lead at meetings with ministers and officials and should be the person who appears on radio and TV and who issues press statements. The Chairman's role should largely be managing the board and carrying out an agreed programme of ambassadorial and representative work.

Reviews of governance also conclude that there should be a cull of permanent committees with more use being made of *ad hoc* project groups. Time consuming liaison committees rarely survive a review.

These conclusions were borne out in the 1997 benchmarking exercise in the UK which concluded:

- Governing bodies should contain a cross-section of members, be of moderate size (12–25) and meet 4–6 times a year.
- Chairmen should be authoritative but not over-involved, limiting involvement to a maximum of five days a month.
- The use of time limited task forces/working parties is effective.

But delegation to the secretariat and the chief executive in particular will work only if the staff is of sufficient quality. In Britain, and in many other countries no doubt, there has been a huge change in the type of people who are chief executives. The traditional recruiting grounds – the sector and the armed forces – have largely been replaced by government agencies and management consultancies. The salaries of chief executives have risen very sharply and executive recruitment agencies are now finding good business in this area.

Most trade association governance structures are fair weather operations. Provided that good people are in place the system works fairly well. They tend not to work at all when poor people are in place. Only a tiny fraction of associations have a governance procedure in place that is capable of removing an ineffective chief executive in a timely way. The average time period between it being obvious that the chief executive is ineffective and removing him from office is probably around five years. More than one trade association chairman has found himself in the position of wishing to remove his chief executive but not even having a copy of the chief executive's contract or any details of his terms and conditions of employment. This is not a good starting point.

In putting the governance of trade associations on to a more professional basis it is vitally important that the role of and relationship between the chief elected officer and the chief executive officer are properly documented. Also, systems must be in place not only to ensure that the chief executive is allowed to manage but also that he or she is properly accountable to the governing body of the association and that if he or she is ineffective then they are likely to be removed from office in the usual way.

Trade associations are businesses but it is difficult to run them as businesses because there is no easily measurable output and governing bodies are transient. In the past a poor trade association could continue in business because no one could be bothered to do anything about it.

Now, the forces described in this chapter make it likely that a poor association will suffer a rapid loss of membership and will go out of business.

Managing a trade association is increasingly moving from being a very simple task – a sinecure in many cases – to a difficult and complex task which requires top quality people. The requirements of today are simply not compatible with old style governance arrangements and a bureaucratic method of working.

Conclusion

Trade associations today are being subjected to powerful forces which, as never before, will require decisive action to address them. In many sectors restructuring will be necessary to match changes in the industrial structure, either nationally or globally. Every association will need to have in place modern governance arrangements which unambiguously concentrate power on the chief executive. And the Internet must be at the centre of the association's communication system and its business generally.

Part II
Change Agents and Managing Change

9
The Impact of the CEFIC Reforms upon the Associational Sector

Jean-Marie Devos

Introduction

Today's industry associations are confronted with two considerable challenges, which affect the way in which they are conducting their mission. A first dimension is 'internal' and has to do with 'internal associations stakeholders'; the second one has to do with the surrounding world and external stakeholders with whom they have to operate.

The membership evolution

The first challenge is an internal one and is directly related with the evolution of the membership of associations. Companies are being more and more confronted with global competition and are focussing on their fields of excellence if they wish to respond to investors' growing expectations. This has some paradoxical consequences. Indeed, at a time when companies resources are under considerable pressure to achieve excellence, availability of such resources for 'common advocacy', for example, in regulatory and legislative activities, are diminishing. This adds to the pressure on industry and trade associations, which are expected to cover a growing number of areas (law, regulatory network). One example is curiously the area of international trade law in violent contrast with the necessity for companies to better understand the 'rules of the games' which are imposed on them.

The external world pressure

The world is changing. Sociocultural patterns are evolving, influencing trade and business patterns. Here again, Industry Associations have to anticipate changes and respond in a creative manner to new expectations. This implies a global analysis of these trends where political, legal, sociological, cultural and scientific factors are taken into account. More and more, a multidisciplinary approach is needed to prepare sound decisions. Such decisions should be non-defensive, confident, highly professional and communication minded.

Therefore, expectations are growing and Industry Associations have no option but to better manager advocacy and expertise while keeping their vital functions of 'ambassador' between the industry sector and public authorities. This also means a better coordination, or at least mutual information, between Industry Associations in order to build alliance and prevent duplications. This also implies more professionalism and capability to mobilise industry on strongly adhered objectives. The CEFIC experience is briefly outlined below. It is one of constant adaptation to these challenges to 'do better', to 'do more' often with tight resources.

CEFIC – an overview

CEFIC, the European Chemical Industry Council, is both the forum and the voice of the European chemical industry. It represents, directly or indirectly, about 40 000 large, medium and small chemical companies in Europe, which employ about 2 million people and account for more than 30 per cent of the world chemical production.

CEFIC is made up of the national chemical industry of 22 countries in Europe, including six Central European countries (Poland, Hungary, Czech Republic, Slovakia, Slovenia and Turkey). Large international companies are also direct members. Three countries benefit from the status of Associate Member Federations (Bulgaria, Lithuania, and Estonia). About 100 sector associations are affiliated to CEFIC.

CEFIC was incorporated in 1972 as an international association. CEFIC is regularly reviewing its priorities, its structures and its mode of operation in order to adapt itself to new challenges and to new patterns of its membership.

Role and purpose

The objective of CEFIC is to provide a mechanism for structured discussion of issues affecting chemical companies operating in Europe and to represent the industry's position on these issues in order to contribute to the legislative decision-taking process (Table 9.1).

In parallel to its links with official bodies, CEFIC has developed a wide range of relations with other organisations either public or private.

The issues addressed are those in which the European chemical industry has a common interest and which can be progressed most effectively at European and/or international level. They vary greatly in character from chemical legislation, production and products related issues, competition policy and fair competition, liabilities, intellectual property law, interna-

Table 9.1 CEFIC's main external contacts with public bodies/official organisations

Europe	Worldwide
The EU Institutions European Commission Council of Ministers European Parliament Economic and Social Committee The Council of Europe	UN Organs/Agencies/specialised Agencies UNCTAD, UNEP, FAO, ICAO, ILO, IMO, UNIDO, UNECE, WHO, WIPO International Organisations ICC, IEA, OECD, ISO, WTO

tional trade, protection of the environment, the distribution and safe transportation of chemicals, the consumption of energy, the supply of raw materials and other requirements.

Priorities change according to the needs of the industry and the external events and influences to which it is sensitive. CEFIC operates in accordance with issues driven programmes and is constantly adapting its action priorities in relation to changing circumstances.

CEFIC therefore serves the chemical industry to which it belongs and serves the society in which it operates. Its purpose is to make sure that progress is not impeded by misconceptions and that the substantial benefits which the chemical industry brings to the economy, the standard of living and the quality of life continue to be available without risk to health and the environment.

Other key functions

Authoritative information source

It is easier for the European Commission and other international policy-makers to rely on and respond to the authoritative voice of many companies and national federations than the individual or unrepresentative opinions of a few. CEFIC provides policy-makers with access to the collective expertise and opinion of the European chemical industry.

Gateway to decision-making process

CEFIC is the gateway for the European chemical industry to the decision-making processes of the EU and beyond.

Partnership

CEFIC enables the European chemical industry to become an active partner in the making of public policy in the EU and elsewhere at international level.

Early warning of problems and opportunities

Its intimate knowledge of the European legislative infrastructure enables CEFIC to gain early warning of policy strategy and direction, enabling members to prepare for and, thereby, minimise any adverse impact of EU and other international legislation. Equally, these sources provide an early warning of opportunities.

Advice

CEFIC's multidisciplinary team of experienced professional staff is available to support advocacy in dealing with legislative, regulatory and legal issues, which affect membership business.

Cross industry fertilisation

Through CEFIC, members' representatives are able to establish contact with their peers, generate cross-industry information and discuss with them their particular sectors of the European chemical industry.

Key priority areas

Competitiveness

A key priority of CEFIC is to help maintain the competitiveness of the European chemical industry in accordance with the rules of free enterprise and fair trade and the principles of Responsible Care, thus contributing to sustainable development.

In its drive to be a partner in the consultation process between authorities and industry on this issue of competitiveness, CEFIC works with other representative organisations such as ERT and UNICE.

Competitiveness has been high on the agenda of CEFIC. CEFIC produced two brochures entitled 'Focus on Competitiveness' – a presentation of some chemical industry initiatives within the framework of the European Communication on Industrial Competitive Policy. The work analysed the actions required by industry, the Commission and member-states to achieve the stated objectives.

CEFIC's contribution to the process of obtaining a Commission Communication specific to the chemical industry was recognised and a final document was approved in April 1996 entitled 'An Industrial Competitiveness Policy for the European Chemical Industry: An Example' (COM 96/187). High level Forum have reviewed the follow up process of the Communication in April 1997 and October 2000.

Specialist Working Groups have continued to meet to ensure effective follow through on the listed actions.

The impact of new regulatory trends on the competitiveness of the European chemical industry has been of special attention, especially in view of the Commission's plans to introduce drastic changes to the current product regulatory framework.

The Commission considers that the chemical industry in the EU which, as a whole, is among the most modern and competitive in the world, faces a set of challenges that must be met if it is to maintain and, if possible, strengthen, its international competitiveness. It is important to promote a level playing field, at least with the main OECD and newly industrialised competing countries, in terms of market access, environmental framework, competition rules, fiscal and social regulations. Effective competition requires that the unit prices for raw materials and energy inputs must not be distorted. It is important to ensure that health and environmental regulations are founded on a sound scientific basis and that their potential economic impact, including the international competitiveness of this industry, is fully taken into account.

Reputation through dialogue

Lack of effective communication with the public, authorities and opinion formers leads to the risk of loss of industry's license to operate and market its products. The overall objective of the industry's communications plan, therefore, is to help the European chemical industry gain acceptance at the community level, a first step which is prerequisite to the longer term goal of improving public perception and restoring trust in the chemical industry.

By orchestration from the centre, providing common themes, messages and guidelines, the aim is to implement the CEFIC strategic plan at national/community level taking into account local cultures. The objective is to close the gap between industry performance and the public's perception. All activities in this area are carried out under the chemical industry's voluntary initiative 'Responsible Care'.

Stakeholder dialogue

Key elements of stakeholder dialogue are:
• Dialogue with committed stakeholders (which may be handled differently for each separate component). Ways and means will have to be agreed between stakeholders.

- Communications with interested stakeholders through, for example, progress reports indicators of performance press briefing/conferences.
- Communications and the stakeholder dialogue will need to be handled at the national European and global level.

Product management and addressing future chemicals legislation

Another key commitment by CEFIC has been its initiatives in the area of chemicals risk management. It is a fact that the chemical industry has an impressive record of breakthrough inventions and, as a result, has brought great benefits to society, both in the past and today, and will continue to do so in the future.

Although not all the benefits are always immediately recognised, largely because of the invisibility of chemistry to the layman – it is without doubt that a world without chemicals is difficult to imagine. On the other hand, there are seen to be risks from chemicals to the health of people and to the environment.

During recent years there has been a noticeable shift in public concern about chemicals. Whereas, in the past, the concerns have been mainly about emissions and waste from processes, nowadays the concerns are increasingly about the long-term effects of chemicals on, particularly, human health.

Although there is a wide range of legal and voluntary instruments in place for the control of chemicals at national, European and international level, calls from political and environmental groups for restrictions or bans on chemicals suspected of harming health and/or the environment have become louder. Public confidence in chemicals has to be increased. The chemical industry has a responsibility and has taken a leading position in recognising and addressing such public concerns by trying to bring answers to the questions raised in the 'European Commission White Paper' on a 'Strategy for a future chemicals policy' of 13 February 2001.

Against this background, and in line with its commitment to Responsible Care, CEFIC has decided to enhance significantly and visibly its commitment to the responsible risk management of chemicals, using and improving at the same time the existing community regulatory framework and reinforcing the EU single market. A number of major industry initiatives at European and international level has been launched. Their ultimate aim is to achieve a high level of public confidence in chemicals by developing a more thorough process for their assessment and management in consultation with governmental and other stakeholders.

Evolving structures and better serving industry needs

CEFIC, as an umbrella organisation for advocacy in the policy and legal arena, has to adequately support both 'corporates' and 'specific business' concerns.

The structure aims at facilitating a better common advocacy on 'horizontal' issues (e.g. the communication on competitiveness, energy policy, competition policy, innovation policy, overall communication strategy, etc.) while fully supporting the branches and sectors to continue their activities in the best possible way in their specific business concerns.

To allow effective representation the CEFIC Board is made up on the basis of three constituencies. This means that in addition to the President, the Vice-President, the immediate past President, the Board is composed of a maximum of 21 members elected by the General Assembly, in the following manner:

- For one-third, on the basis of a list of candidates presented by the Consultative Assembly of Member Federations (AFEM);
- For one-third, on the basis of a list of candidates presented by the Consultative Assembly of Member Companies (ACOM);
- For one-third, on the basis of a list of candidates presented by the Consultative Assembly of Affiliated Groups (AFEG).

CEFIC is constantly looking at the most effective manner to integrate specific businesses concerns and to ensure their adequate representation. For example, business groups may operate within wider CEFIC programmes.

It should be observed that, from among the elected Board Members, representatives of AFEM, ACOM, and AFEG within the Executive Committee are also elected by the General Assembly.

International cooperation

The International Council of Chemical Associations (ICCA) is a council of leading industry associations representing chemical manufacturers associations worldwide.

The ICCA provides a forum for regular meetings of executives from the member associations to discuss policy issues of international interest to the chemical industry. In addition, the ICCA may make policy statements or develop programmes where consensus is reached among the member associations of the Council. The purpose of the ICCA is to exchange views among members, to coordinate action by Council members, and to present an international chemical industry view to international organisations. Such organisations would primarily be inter-governmental agencies (e.g. WTO, IMO, UNEP, OECD) and international private organisations (e.g. the International Organisation for Standardisation, ISO).

Policy issues of international significance to the chemical manufacturing industry form the agenda of the ICCA. Such issues include health, safety and the environment; international transport safety; intellectual property; trade policy; industry efforts to eliminate chemical weapons and diversion to illegal drugs. The ICCA does not deal with trade missions or business promotion activities.

ICCA promotes and coordinates Responsible Care and other voluntary chemical industry initiatives. Responsible Care is the registered trade/service mark, which denotes the chemical industry's international and voluntary commitment to continuous improvement of performance in health, safety and environmental protection.

The ICCA meets twice yearly. One meeting includes the chief executives of the Council's member associations. The second meeting includes the chief executives plus leading corporate executives from Council associations, usually the elected officers of the associations; ICCA meetings are hosted by Council members and held at various locations throughout the world. Administrative work to support the ICCA is performed by the Council Secretary, a responsibility that moves between associate members at year intervals.

10

The Case of EURELECTRIC: the Impact of Deregulation upon EU Business Associations

Paul Bulteel

The Electricity Industry is undergoing a revolution. The transition to a competitive environment demands new patterns of thought and flexibility, requiring companies to swiftly react to markets and competition. Liberalisation has led to unbundling and to new actors entering the market. A number of countries have established power pools or exchanges, and in many countries privatisation has transformed companies entirely. Additionally, in many markets both domestic and cross-border mergers and acquisitions are also taking place as a result of a growing interconnection of markets and changing strategies. These changes are summarised in the box below:

IN RECORD SPEED		
FROM REGULATED TO COMPETITIVE MARKETS		
Long-term Horizon	⇒	Commercial Approach
Predictable Returns	⇒	Greater Risks
Societal Drivers	⇒	Customer Orientation
Product Oriented	⇒	Service Oriented
Vertical Integration	⇒	Unbundling/Separation
National/Regional	⇒	European/World
Stable Players	⇒	New Players
Gradual Restructuring	⇒	Rapid Restructuring

An important driving force has of course been the European Internal Electricity Market Directive, which took effect in February 1999. The Directive aims to progressively create a single European electricity market – *as opposed to 15 liberalised markets* – with a minimum market opening of 26 per cent upon its entry into force. In reality, the average market opening across Europe was already 60 per cent by this date, according to European Commission estimates. Moreover, some countries had already gone much further ahead, opening their markets 100 per cent.

The Directive is of course not the only driving force; there are very important market forces that are also behind – our electricity companies in the first place. In addition, there is tremendous pressure from customers to create an open electricity market – and new proposals are currently on the table for accelerated liberalisation, both for electricity and for gas.

The potential consequences for international cooperation and association during such immense transition are huge:

- While continuing to respond efficiently to an ever-demanding customer and seeking to provide the best service, reduced resources coupled with increasing budget pressures means that greater attention must be paid by those at management level to the cost-effectiveness of the organisation and of the work performed.
- Companies focus more on their business – 'survival' is the name of the game – and those that were once colleagues, willing to share information and experiences, are now outright competitors.

This changed agenda brings with it added risks, notably that of lagging behind evolutions and going through a phase of destruction of cooperation, and poses a number of questions summarised below:

INTERNATIONAL COOPERATION QUESTIONED . . .

- Colleagues vs Competitors
- Disappearing Agenda?
- Changing Agenda
- Cost Reductions
- Disintegration?
- What Added Value?

The case of EURELECTRIC – how, as an association, it manages the transition from a regulated to a competitive industry

The mission and organisation of any national, or international trade association is affected by the globalisation of our economies and the rapidly changing business environment in which Industry is operating today. It is important therefore to be at the forefront of these evolutions

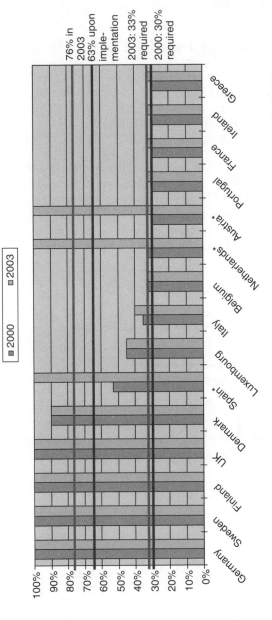

* Austria 100% from October 2001, Netherlands 100% from January 2003, Spain 100% from 2004

Figure 10.1 Percentage electricity market opening by member-state, 2000–2003.

in order to continue to create added value both for our members and for our 'partners in dialogue'.

THE CHALLENGE FOR EURELECTRIC

- Adapt
  ⇓
- Create Added Value
  ⇓
- Be at the Forefront

Professional management and the ability to continue to speak with one voice on behalf of the Industry; focusing primarily on strategic issues and involving CEOs more closely in our activities; adopting a more proactive style and a clear vision and agenda for the future are some key elements to assure a position at the forefront of the Industry. Some important elements to focus on are summarised below:

THE WAY FORWARD . . .

- Commitment from the Top
- Efficient Management of Resources
- An Adapted Agenda
- Members are Customers
- Top-Down Priorities
- Pro-Activeness

Structural and organisational elements, including the efficient use of resources are others – and must be reviewed on a regular basis. The trend in European Electricity associations is summarised in Table 10.1 and

Table 10.1   Organisational trends in the European electricity industry associations 1997–2000

	1997	1998–1999	2000
Associations	2	2	1
Secretariats	2	1	1
Staff	45	30	30
Groups (from Board to Task Force)	111	58	34
Decision steps	3	3	2 or 1

Figure 10.2, demonstrating the efficient management of resources with the total cost to members halved.

Dialogue and cooperation with our members and partners, and the ability to respond rapidly and adapt to changing market conditions is our motto for success. Our members are our customers – they determine and control our agenda. In view of the wide range of issues impacting on our business today, the agenda is now focussed on three strategic priorities, namely the Liberalisation Process, the Pan-European Context and Sustainable Development. These issues are summarised in the boxes that follow.

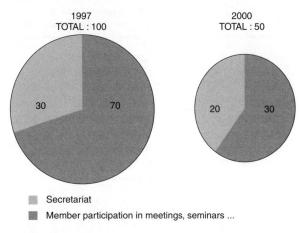

Figure 10.2 Member/Secretariat mix in the European Electricity industry associations, 1997–2000.

The total cost to members has been halved.

AN ADAPTED AGENDA
FOCUS...FOCUS...FOCUS
From: • Wide Technical, Strategic, Policy-Making Agenda and European/Worldwide Perspective
To: • Strategy and Policy-Making
• European Identity (including worldwide cooperation)
• Focus on Key Issues – Appropriate for international cooperation – Added value – Know-how not available elsewhere

TOP-DOWN PRIORITIES
Board defines key priorities and objectives:
1. Liberalisation Process Contribute to the creation of a pan-European energy market through harmonisation and industry action
2. Pan-European Context Contribute to a good business environment and to the integration of the Electricity Industry at international level
3. Sustainable Development Promote the role of electricity and electrotechnologies as 'part of the solution' to the global environmental problem; systematically integrate sustainable development policies in key strategies and actions

Some concrete examples:

LIBERALISATION OF ENERGY MARKETS
Decision of Board: 19 June 2000
• EURELECTRIC supports acceleration of liberalisation
• EURELECTRIC stresses the importance of accompanying the accelerated market opening with progress in related areas, such as:
market mechanisms for renewables, GATS negotiations, public procurement, environmental constraints, stranded costs, etc.

CREATION OF PAN-EUROPEAN MARKET
1998:
Support for accession countries
Creation of Accession Desk
Workshops
Bilateral visits
Traineeships
. . .
2000:
Accession countries – Full Members
Creation of Europe Desk
Creation of Mediterranean Desk

SUSTAINABLE DEVELOPMENT
Programme of Cooperation with DG TREN and DG Environment
– Energy Services Research Project
– Efficient Lighting Initiative
Energy Wisdom Programme
Greenhouse Gas and Electricity Trading Simulation (GETS)
Market Mechanisms for Supporting Renewable Energies: Tradable RES Certificates

Conclusion

We live in a globalised, competitive world with its obvious threats and also great opportunities. It is important therefore for an international business association to thoroughly analyse its business and to reflect on key questions, such as: What is my business definition? What added value can the association bring to its members? What are the key priorities? Can threats be turned into opportunities? Are we pro-active in our dialogue with stakeholders? Can we develop this further?

We all say we are pro-active, but are we really?

We all say we listen to the public, to policy-makers, to stakeholders – but do we really?

11
The Impact of Changing Sectoral Definition upon Associability: the Convergence of Business Interests in the Information and Communications Technology Sector in Europe
Oliver Blank

In the past there were big and powerful industry associations with large staff, huge facilities, complex structures and high fees. Their problem was that they have become so big that they no longer represented the interests of their members. Accordingly, they were perceived as slow and inflexible monster bodies, getting bigger and fat, creating more internal work rather than service to their members but with increasing demands to feed their structures financially, far from its members' needs, with no service mentality and unwilling to change.

The dinosaur age of associations is over. Industry associations of the twenty-first century need to be competitive, lean, flexible, open and ready for the changes that global markets bring. It is true that the new technologies have changed the pace, that is, in one Internet year as much happens as in seven calendar years. Industry associations today need structures that can cope with the challenges of the new e-Economy. If they do so, they are strong, powerful and important players, helping their members to get industry views across as well as helping policy-makers better understand the world for which those create the rules of the game.

History of EICTA

EICTA, the European Information and Communications Technology Industry Association, is a product of such a change of mind and of the convergence of ICT technologies. EICTA results from a merger of the former two European federations ECTEL (representing telecommunications manufacturers and professional electronics industries) and EUROBIT (representing information technology and computer manufacturers). It was founded on 16 November 1999, following some months of preparatory work by national associations and ICT companies with major operations in Europe who worked together to implement the convergence of the different sectors into one coherent industry representation at European level.

EICTA therefore has two kinds of members, national associations and ICT companies. Both constituencies are of equal weight if it comes to voting, but generally agreements on statements, positions and actions are achieved by a democratic consensus building involving all members.

Our 22 national associations represent 16 European countries and 10 000 company members: FEEI, Austria; AGORIA, Belgium; SPIS, Czech Republic; ITEK, Denmark; ITB, Denmark; SET, Finland; GITEP, France; SFIB, France; BITKOM, Germany; IVSZ, Hungary; ANIE, Italy; ASSINFORM, Italy; ICT, Ireland; NEDERLAND-ICT; IKT Norge, Norway; TBL-ITF, Norway; ANIEL, Spain; SEDISI, Spain; IT-Företagen, Sweden; SWICO, Switzerland; SWISSMEM, Switzerland; and FEI, United Kingdom.

In addition, there are 31 global players active in EICTA: Agilent, Alcatel, Apple, Bull, Cisco, Compaq, Ericsson, HP, IBM, ICL, Indra, Infineon, Intel, Italtel, Lucent, Marconi, Matsushita, Microsoft, Motorola, NCR, NEC, Nokia, Nortel, Olivettilexikon, Philips, Siemens, Sony, Sun, Thales, Thomson Multimedia, and Xerox.

The main work takes place in EICTA Main Committees, structured around seven broader policy areas:
- Information society and electronic commerce;
- Industry policy;
- Trade policy;
- Environmental policy;
- Research and Development and education policy;
- Legal affairs and consumer policy; and
- Radio and spectrum matters.

Around 500 experts from our industries are active in those committees and issue groups dealing with a large number of very specific topics such as the:
- European Commission's e-Europe initiative;
- Data protection and privacy;
- Copyrights and digital rights management replacing the levies system;

- Taxation of electronic commerce;
- Computer-related crime;
- Regulatory framework for communications;
- Environmental legislation and collection of waste;
- Framework programmes for R&D;
- Skills shortage in ICT;
- Trade disputes between the EU and US;
- Convergence of technologies; and
- Mobile communications.

EICTA's mission is:

- To work with European policymakers to ensure a fair and competitive legal environment for the development of the information society in Europe;
- To serve the common global interests of the ICT industry in Europe; and
- To promote the ICT industry as the key driver of competitiveness, growth and innovation.

EICTA experts meet regularly, mostly in Brussels. In addition, day-to-day issue work takes place by employing all electronic communication tools ICT can provide. Quick and easy exchange of ideas happens via listservs and the EICTA Extranet that is accessible for all members via the website.

In 2000/2001, EICTA has contributed to the ongoing policy debate with more than 60 statements and position papers. In its short time of existence EICTA has become a renowned partner of the European Commission, the Parliament and national governments. Our credo is to be different. We complain only if we know better, have possible solutions at hand and can effectively participate in the policy process. EICTA stands for a constructive dialogue with policy makers.

The convergence of business interests of different industry sectors into a joint EICTA happened because the environment in which we work changed. Globalisation of markets, the rapid technological change and the convergence of single technologies into network technologies are the basis. Those could be called 'Market and Product Factors'. In addition, the way how companies deal with policy issues, lobbying and communication has changed. We could describe these reasons as 'Management Factors'. Last but not least the recipient's side for political lobbying has also changed. European policymakers have an ever harder time catching up with technological changes and assuring that existing and planned legislation is in line with the speedy change of the global environment. We could call these reasons 'Policy Factors'.

Market and product factors

All ICT products and services compete on a global market. The products of the ICT industries include communications hardware – such as telephones, fax machines, PCs, keyboards, printers, scanners and CD-burners, and computer software. These are enhanced by hardware and software services and consulting.

Any producer selling on the global marketplace faces the challenge of different laws and regulations. Manufacturers of different products encounter similar problems and have an alike interest to find an international level playing field. Regulation needs to be harmonised over national boundaries, in order not to advantage or disadvantage certain regions or countries over others; it needs to be abolished where it hinders market development; it needs to be replaced by co-regulation with industry and other stakeholders where this leads to more flexibility.

This flexibility is needed because of rapid technological changes. Otherwise, once written into national law of the EU member-states, legislation would face the problem of being outdated by the time it is implemented. Furthermore, single technologies converge into network technologies. A mobile phone with the possibility to send and receive e-mails, to surf the Internet and download music and videos makes it difficult to distinguish between the different technologies involved. Should we call this mobile device a phone, PC, TV, video recorder or playstation? Information technology, telecommunications, consumer electronics, content and services have clearly merged on the product side. The fast development of electronic commerce applications and mobile communications will further foster this integration of formerly single technologies.

Management factors

The shortage of ICT-skilled people and technology experts is widening. According to recent statistics of the EITO – European Information Technology Observatory, Europe could have up to 4 million required jobs unfilled in 2003, representing 18 per cent of the total demand. Of these, 1.7 million are likely to be related to ICT professions and 2.2 million to e-business professions. The skills shortage estimates also include the so-called skills gap, that is the inability in present jobs to cover the required skills. Skills shortage in Europe could lead to an accumulated loss of some 3 per cent of potential GDP in 2003, hitting business productivity and the pace of Net Economy development.[1]

This shortage has implications for the dissemination of ICT expertise into the policy making as well. As fewer experts are available to spend time on lobbying and communications, the need to coordinate their time becomes more urgent. While in former years, company experts toured different associations and attended a high number of meetings, they do not have the resources nor the time anymore to do so and need to bundle their activities in a more efficient way. EICTA is a product of the need to bundle heterogenous interests and scarce human resources across single industry sectors.

Policy factors

In addition to the product, and management factors, we can observe a third kind of rationale underlying the convergence of business interests of the ICT industries in Europe. This evolution happens at the political decision-making level.

The way of policy-making has changed in Europe over the last years. In the EU we have seen a shift of coordination and regulation of network technologies beyond country boundaries and to the supranational level. The European Commission has the leading responsibility in Europe for proposing harmonisation policies among its member-states, to be approved by the European Parliament and the national governments represented in the European Council. Furthermore the European Commission has taken a more active role at the global level in order to foster worldwide harmonisation.

In accordance with this shift of policy-making from the national to the European level, European ICT industries have increased their direct representation in Brussels and Strasbourg gradually, addressing more frequently policy issues directly with the European policy-makers, rather than or in addition to their activities at national level.

For the ICT industry in Europe today, there is a choice of representation, between membership to national associations or by direct company membership of the European federation EICTA. The latter way was not possible for the ICT industry for a long time since the former European ICT federations allowed only national associations as members but no direct company membership. In the past, ICT companies in Europe were represented by the national associations to which they belonged, many of those associations representing broader industry sectors such as the electronics industries or manufacturing business. Traditionally, companies belonged to the industry associations of their sector in those countries where they had their major markets, operations, manufacturing and/or R&D facilities. National associations addressed mainly their own national governments, in addition to be active within their respective European networks, such as ECTEL and EUROBIT. ICT companies were only indirectly represented at the European level while their national associations had increasing problems coordinating the necessary expertise to address ICT policies at European level in the most skillful way.

But the dissemination of technology expertise into policy-making was urgently needed and repeatedly requested. Because of the complexity of policies related to information and communications technologies, political decision-makers became increasingly dependent on the expertise from the private sector. Who in the European Commission can foresee where the Internet is heading and what is needed in terms of regulation or deregulation in five years time? Only the experts from the private sector have at least a view and a vision.

In addition, political decision-makers have developed a keen interest to 'outsource' any coordination of sectorial views. The European Commission's review of the Convergence of IT, Telecommunications and the Media in 1998 has demonstrated the problem. More than 300 contributions from the private sector were submitted. Many of those statements from industry associations, consumer representatives and other stakeholders had conflictual and contradictory messages. How can one expect that policy-makers can evaluate who is right and who is wrong? The private sector has a better chance to be heard if forces are combined. With the creation of EICTA, ICT industries in Europe have recognised this need and taken up internally a coordination of their views between different sectors.

A vision for the future

The convergence process has not come to an end yet. Since technologies are getting further interdependent, the drive to align policy messages among the different sectors will continue, the need for cooperation with other industry sector will remain. In addition, the enlargement of the EU will call for further harmonisation. This will keep ICT industries in Europe and EICTA busy. In terms of future representation, EICTA has two objectives:

1   To explore deeper cooperation with other industry sector representations and eventually merge activities with other associations; and
2   To expand our activities into the EU accession countries.

The first objective is about to be met. Negotiations between EICTA and EACEM, the European Consumer Electronics Association, continue in a very good and constructive spirit. It is most likely that the two associations will join forces very soon. Issue-specific cooperation with other sector organisations such as telecoms operators, the software and content industry is increasing.

In relation to the enlargement of the European Union, EICTA carries out a project within the European Commission's PHARE Business Support Programme for Central, and Eastern European Countries. We help national ICT associations in the accession countries to develop an organisational structure and to understand the 'Acquis Communautaire', the legislative framework of the EU.

In addition, the role of European associations at the global level will become increasingly important in order to achieve harmonisation of policies and market conditions. No one knows where the convergence of business interests will lead and how future structures will look like. But one thing is sure that this will be a challenging and exciting process.

Note

1 EITO Report, Frankfurt/Germany, 2001. For further information, see http://www.eito.com.

12

The Impact of Sector Change upon EU Business Associations

Jan J. F. Timmerman

This impact is of course directly related to the characteristics of the business sector. There may be few business sectors which affect directly or indirectly so many other sectors or citizens either as energy user or consumer of products derived from oil.

- Oil and gas account for 70 per cent of the EU energy supply.
- The industry provides employment (directly or indirectly) for some 2 million EU citizens.
- Contributes to 155 billion through taxation to EU treasuries.
- The sector is directly affected by developments and trends changes taking place in society in the world.
- Globalisation, liberalisation, privatisation.
- Geo-political changes.
- The emergence of NGOs and the 'Civil Society' concept.
- Environmental concerns and the sustainable developments philosophy.
- Internally concentration (mergers and acquisitions) and rationalisation.
- Information Technology, the knowledge society and society's changing values and life styles.

What I would like to do is to briefly illustrate what, I believe, are some key success factors contributing to the effectiveness of a European business association, against the background of existing EU Institutions, Treaties and Legislation, that is, where consultation of business sectors in the legislative process is not a clearly established integral part, as I strongly believe it should be (as it is for example in the US), and where as a consequence industry contributions largely depend on either the goodwill of the EU Institutions' individual initiatives, as well as the effectiveness and importance, methods and strength of the sector – think about the power of street action from truck drivers, taxis, farmers as opposed to the influence of large global business sectors and industry in general.

Reflecting on recent events, where Nations' legislative action is triggered and forced through by sectors' street actions outside the law, I believe these developments would deserve a structured analysis and debate to evaluate whether these events signal fundamental changes in behaviour and values in our society and their consequence on the functioning of Western Democracies, and their parliaments' role in interaction with civil society.

The effectiveness of a business association should indeed been measured in relative terms that is, in the context of a competition with other forces. I believe only the inclusion of a clear, structured legal framework for industry consultation in the EU legislative process would guarantee the respect of the basic principles for a democratic functioning of a modern civil society.

Let me now come back to some internal business sector key success factors and questions:

- Professional structured design and management of our association are essential to obtain members confidence.
- Homogeneity and degree of common interest at national, EU and global level.
- Intensity of legislative activity and potential financial impact on the business sector as a whole.
- Specific sector or cross-sector impact of legislations defines the role of the association.
- The nature of consultation process decided by the legislator (illustrated by Auto-Oil).
- Changing roles and relationship between national and international associations.
- The increasing 'globalisation' of issues (e.g. climate change).
- Member own resources and communication strategy.
- Reputation means – credibility and influence.

Business process management

Business managers will more easily identify with the association activity if they are familiar with the methodology, management style and the organisation culture and semantics.

A structured process involving senior member company staff to identify the associations mission, objectives, activity plan and communication plan based on the analysis of threats and opportunities and business impact evaluation of legislative activity should create a sense of ownership, evaluating success (post-mortem) and effectiveness on a regular basis. A small secretariat managing the process of working groups for different activities staffed by experts from companies is working effectively for EUROPIA. Company experts together with secretariat staff offer credible technical input to EU institutions and are less prone to the 'ivory tower' syndrome.

Characteristics of the sector

Homogeneity and perception of common interest is essential. Mergers and acquisition naturally change the structure of the sector; it reduces the number of smaller local players and could potentially lead towards more homogeneity.

Critical factors are:

- The association's capacity to canvass the large company resources to contribute to identify and support the 'common good';
- To ensure that individual company initiatives are perceived by legislators to reinforce and support association views;
- Avoid 'lowest common denominator positions' but offer legislators constructive voluntary pro-active alternatives;
- A sufficiently large number of member companies representing close to 100 per cent of the industry is essential to justify common action and representativity;
- Involve national industry associations to support action *vis-à-vis* national governments in the EU Council;
- European and national associations have a complementary role as long as they manage to cooperate effectively harmonise positions and clarify roles;
- Overcoming cultural North/South, large/small, European/American, linguistic differences, different management styles, is a continuous challenge, especially for example on environmental and broader societal issues and geopolitical aspects. Nevertheless large multinational corporations are used to manage these diversities on a day-to-day basis which helps.

The EU legislative process

Interaction with all EU institutions is necessary but should be different in communication style, content (more or less technical) language, etc.

Finding common interest with the legislators is the biggest challenge but a critical success factor.

There is a strong need for a structured framework of principles for a transparent dialogue with stakeholders before legislative proposals are being put forward by EU institutions; this should include independent cost/benefit, macro and microeconomic impact evaluation.

Better informed legislation will be more practical to implement, be more effective, better understood and accepted by citizens and stakeholders alike.

For a business sector, the success of a European business association depends on its reputation (as a sector, or company as an association) which generates credibility and, in turn, legitimates influence on the legislation process.

The challenge for the association is to add value for both legislators and members, finding a 'win–win' on every issue is the key to success.

13
New Models of Large Firm Collective Action

Christophe Lécureuil and Simon Ward

It is perhaps generally recognised that companies need trade associations. Collective action is simply more likely to be effective, and should certainly be cheaper than uncoordinative individual action. Or is it?

Unfortunately, trade associations often prove more bureaucratic and less cost effective than the members would wish. When this happens the members should invariably blame themselves. Cumbersome decision-making processes and endless arguments over the nuances of policy positions are not usually originated by the staff, but by the members. Costs mushroom and members and staff become more dissatisfied.

The purpose of this section is not to offer up solutions to this conundrum, but to describe an alternative model. This is a model that exists in practice, and not merely in theory.

We shall describe the inception and workings of an organisation called The European Modern Restaurants Association, (EMRA), in order to illustrate the model.

First, a thumbnail sketch of EMRA as it exists today. The membership comprises nine companies each trading in at least two member-states of the EU. All member companies operate in the branded chain restaurant sector. For the record, the members are Autogrill, Bass, BurgerKing Europe, Goodys, McDonald's Europe, Nordsee, Quick Restaurants, Tricon Restaurants International, and Whitbread. Some members operate more than one brand.

The collective scale of the member companies is formidable. Together we trade in all 15 member-states, through some 8000 restaurants, employing well over 500 000 staff. We serve about 10 million customers every day. Franchising is an important way of doing business for some members, and between us we have some 1500 franchise partners, most of them SMEs.

EMRA is a relatively young organisation, having been formed in 1995. It was born out of necessity. At the time when the Social Partners were negotiating the Commission proposal on part-time work, one or two companies in our sector felt that the sector's interests were not receiving the attention that they should. Too many of the participants in the Social Dialogue, including the Commission and business groups, were using as their frame of reference a large manufacturing plant failing to understand, as many still do today, that the service sector now predominates. The peculiarities of the entire service sector, never mind foodservice were being neglected in the dialogue.

Now, part-time work is in many ways the norm in the foodservice sector. How revealing that in Commission-speak it is included within a bundle of working styles termed 'atypical work'. The Companies that were becoming frustrated by the absence of an effective voice compared notes on this issue and decided to form a loose grouping that became EMRA.

This initiative soon proved timely for it enabled the sector to achieve proper representation during the Commission's work on franchising which quickly followed.

In order to ensure proper governance, the Association agreed a written constitution which remains today. Like most effective organisations we have rarely, if ever, had to refer to it.

Formally, the mission of EMRA is 'to enhance the dialogue with policy makers and opinion leaders at a European and, if appropriate, national level on matters affecting the modern restaurant industry as a whole.' More specifically the aims are:

- To increase awareness of the EU's modern restaurant industry as a vital engine for economic growth and job creation.
- To establish a fact-based dialogue at the EU level regarding policy matters such as food quality and safety, franchising, employment and training standards and environmental responsibilities.
- To liaise with other business and interest groups on matters of joint interest.

Having set the scene by describing EMRA's birth and objectives, let us move on to consider how we work.

We manage our affairs through a steering committee with a chair selected by the consensus of the member companies. Each company is entitled to at least one seat on the Steering Committee but may, if it so wishes, send more representatives to a meeting. This happens from time to time depending on the meeting's agenda.

The Steering Committee meets quarterly in Brussels. Our meeting is preceded by an informal dinner, usually with an invited guest from a relevant organisation such as the Parliament, the Commission or another trade association. The meetings themselves are informal and again often feature an external input.

The members of the steering group, by accident rather than design, tend to have different professional backgrounds. For example, at present the Committee includes members whose jobs are in operational management, law, marketing and government relations. This makes for an excellent blend of experience and opinion when we come to consider a particular issue. Moreover it means that the conversation is not dominated by the government relations experts which can happen in similar circumstances, and can be non-productive.

EMRA has no staff. Moreover it has no membership fee or levy. Our principal resource is the time, energy, and ideas of its member company representatives. This constraint imposes a wonderful discipline on the organisation. It requires us to be utterly focused on a limited number of agreed issues. In practice this means that at any given time we try to interest ourselves in no more than two or three issues. Today, for example, our primary focus is on food safety and hygiene and on employment law. This unity of purpose is vital – and it is far too easy for conventional trade associations, often pushed by the membership, to fall into the trap of trying to do too much.

Having no membership fee does not mean that we are never prepared to spend money. There are times when we judge this necessary. A good example would be in commissioning research which helps us to present our case, which we have done before in, for example, examining the effect of sales taxes on our sector.

Of course, there are invariably more than two or three issues that interest our members at any given time. But the limited nature of our resources has obliged us to let other organisations take a lead in presenting a common position. For example, the introduction of the Euro and the general view of retailers that this will not be successful unless there is greater front-loading by the authorities of cash certainly concerns our members. However other groups are campaigning vigorously about this. There is limited value in EMRA trying to present its case separately, so we lend our support to those at the forefront rather than seeking to become directly engaged.

Another advantage, which we have over most conventional trade associations, is that, having only nine members (and by the way we are not looking for more), we can reach rapid decisions. Either at meetings, or more usually by e-mail, we can get unanimity on a proposed position in a matter of days or, if necessary, hours. That is beyond the wildest dreams of the average trade association, which typically has a complex and time-consuming decision making process, particularly when it operates in a fragmented industry such as our own.

Having few, rather than many, members also means that the policy positions we reach are sharp and uncontaminated by meaningless consensus. We rarely need to descend to the lowest common denominator that typifies many trade association policies. Officials and politicians prefer to hear straightforward policy statements undiluted by compromise. Even if they do not agree with the policy, they can see plainly what it is. They also like the fact that when they meet us they are talking face to face with business people – not trade association staff, and definitely not hired consultants. We select a delegation from member companies to represent the Association. No member would ever be excluded from the delegation if it wished to be present.

From time to time the steering group has set up smaller expert groups with member company staff to provide a more technical input into our deliberations. Franchising was a case in point a few years ago, and food safety is a contemporary example, where a degree of specialist knowledge is needed as a precursor to establishing policy.

How effective is EMRA? Assessing the effectiveness of any organisation engaged in public affairs is very difficult. EMRA is no exception. Nonetheless an attempt must be made.

One comforting factor is that, in the six years since its creation, EMRA has seen none of its member companies resign. Indeed attendance at our meetings is good. But does this merely indicate that we are an engaging talking shop, but not achieving our objectives?

Fortunately, the evidence does suggest a degree of effectiveness. We do achieve access to key target audiences, giving us the opportunity at least to present our position. Officials and others respond to our invitations to present their positions to us.

We have achieved dialogue. More promisingly, the European institutions have progressively come to EMRA inviting us to make an input in wider discussion groups.

For example, in 1999, when the Commission was reviewing franchising regulation, EMRA was invited to represent the industry position at a public hearing. In 2000 the Commission invited us to join a Consultative Committee on food which was in the process of getting established. Then early in 2001 EMRA accepted an invitation to speak at a public hearing in the European Parliament on the subject of the Commission's proposals on food safety. In each case the EMRA intervention was made by someone from one or other of our member companies.

A clear conclusion is that EMRA is recognised as a relevant actor in European public affairs. Achieving this status is a necessary pre-condition to getting results. Participating in dialogue does not guarantee results, but unless you get a hearing, then you will certainly fail.

On this evidence, we judge EMRA to be a success. There is no reason why this success should not continue and indeed grow.

It would be foolish to claim that the EMRA model is the only effective model. But it is perhaps worth concluding by enumerating the critical factors that make it a valid model – no staff, few members, a small number of agreed priorities, and rapid decision-making processes. It is this simplicity that makes for success.

14
EU Business Associations: Meeting the needs of Europe's Service Sectors?

Irina Michalowitz

Introduction

Services are presently faster growing and changing than any other sector – but this development is not reflected in their political influence. In the following, the needs and means of the services sector in terms of associational interest representation at the European level will be assessed. It will be argued that associations in the services sector are indeed necessary – but due to several reasons, the way the existing organisations are meeting the needs of services is suboptimal. The source of problems is not mainly the individual association itself, but its members who lack sufficient participation.

Analysing European interest representation involves multiple levels, and the services sector consists of a multitude of subsectors. Therefore, a selection has to be made in order to highlight the effectiveness of services associations. Tourism, which constitutes a so-called 'modern' sector, and financial services as a 'traditional' sector will be covered in detail, with some comparative illustrations. The additional focus alongside the European perspective on Germany as an example for developments at the member-state level enables the inclusion of impacts caused by national developments.

While each step will be started out at the national level and then moved to the European situation, first, the overall importance of tourism and its associational structure will be assessed. Second, a rather new phenomenon will be explained – the cross-sectoral representation of services. This also has implications on the overall structure and needs of services with regards to associations.

The third step will consist of a short return to a special service sector on the side of traditional services, the financial services sector, which will enable a comparison of the two major strands of services and will strengthen the conclusions drawn from the structure of cross-sectoral services representation.

Differentiation of services and the importance of tourism

In order to draw an adequate picture of the sector, services have to be divided into traditional and into newly developing or growth sectors. Traditional services are, for instance, the banking sector, transport services, or distribution and retail services, while modern services are those which have changed very much due to liberalisation and globalisation or technical developments, like computer/IT services, telecommunications or the tourism industry. They organise on a specific basis and cross-sectorally within services.

The vastly changing growth sectors already stumble into their largest problems on the question of how to achieve associability. To a large extent, they do not manage to organise sufficiently. Traditional services have generally well-established trade associations but run the risk of being dominated by single, powerful firms.

Definitions of services are very incongruent and often leave out a large number of related services. According to a 1997-Trade Policy Review of the World Trade Organisation (WTO), the share of services in total world trade accounts for one-fifth of the overall Gross Domestic Product (WTO, 1997: 2). In Germany, the share of the industrial sector on the German Gross National Product of 30 per cent in 1991 had decreased to 24 per cent in 1998, while the share of services related to industry and preliminary services for industry has continuously increased.[1]

Tourism

Within the services sector, the tourism industry is the leading branch of growth in the EU. According to the World Travel and Tourism Council (WTTC), the tourism sector is contributing about 22 million workplaces – which is more than one-tenth – to the employment market. It contributes 5.5 per cent to the EU's Gross Domestic Product, which is more than the share of the building/construction and the fuel/power industries, and nearly three times more than the contribution of the agricultural sector (ETOA, ETC/CET, ETAG, WTTC, 2000). Nonetheless, its representation on the political level is rather weak.

Associability of a sector is very much dependent on the structure of the business. Due to major market changes in the entire tourism sector, associations are either non-existent or only being formed at the moment. The situation in the nation-states affects associability at the European level. The tourism sector in Germany is an interesting example because four of the major tourism companies of Europe are from this country.

Tourism in Germany

For a long time, tourism in Germany used to consist of many small- and medium-sized enterprises, but this has recently changed.

Out of a period of mergers, three major companies arose in the 1990s: (i) the former raw materials and technology enterprise Preussag acquired TUI and with it, Hapag-Lloyd and became the largest German tourism company; (ii) Condor and Neckermann joined and became second largest; and (iii) the supermarket chain Rewe entered the tourism market by taking over the German railroad company DER and most recently, the air carrier LTU (Frank *et al.*, 2001: 204).

A look at Preussag gives a hint at the changes that have taken place. The market leader Preussag was founded in 1923 and is still rather known for its history as a coal and steel company. In the late 1990s, mainly during the past two years, a major portfolio change has taken place. It is now the largest tourism company in Europe and also world wide, with the acquisition of Hapag-Lloyd, TUI, First, Thomson Travel and Nouvelles Frontières. Two-thirds of the turnover of the company now come from the tourism section (Preussag, 2001). Ironically, this means that in the tourism industry, a former industrial company and a supermarket are amongst the top three.

Due to this restructuring, the basis for membership of specialised or umbrella business associations and activities of CEO of all companies changed substantially. Associations have now to be analysed anew with regard to the most effective way of representation, and they now have to meet the needs of an industry rather than of small- and medium-sized enterprises. No association for large enterprises of the tourism sector existed, until the development of a tourism industry took place – because there were no large companies.

Also, there was no general tourism umbrella association, because interests of the sector were seen as too heterogeneous, the branch 'hotels and restaurants' faces different problems than 'modes of transport' – and within 'modes of transport', air carriers have different interests than bus operators. Small travel agencies do not necessarily agree with the interests of large tour operators like TUI. Electronic commerce has different impacts on the diverse sections. The individual interests were only partially covered by specific associations, and those organisations did not see the need to join in order to establish an overarching umbrella association.

The hotel and restaurants association DEHOGA recognised the lack of a national umbrella association for the now emerged tourism industry. It therefore founded the federation of German tourism business, BTW,[2] in 1997. The BTW consists of 17 membership-firms and associations of the different tourism subsectors. Management and presidency are identical with the DEHOGA personnel – which is by some members seen as problematic. This association only focuses on two subjects, namely marketing and European affairs (Bundesverband der Deutschen Tourismuswirtschaft, 1999).

Tourism in Europe and at the global level

At the European level, the BTW is represented by one single person, its senior manager.[3] There is no European umbrella organisation the BTW could get associated to, which is a fact that might be regarded as one of the reasons why the BTW does not have a large amount of power in Brussels. Compared to other national tourism associations and with regard to what it is aimed at – which is strictly marketing of tourism – the BTW-lobbying is very successful, but in terms of influence on policy issues, it barely plays a role.

The different associations operating at EU level only loosely cooperate and coordinate. So far, interest representation on policies is only carried out by the affected companies themselves, or by European specific tourism associations like, for instance, the International Air Carriers Association (IACA) or the European Tour Operators' Association (ETOA) or the Association of Hotels, Restaurants and Cafés in Europe (HOTREC).

Global associability plays a smaller role with concern to the representation that is covered here. Although the global level is the most obvious one in terms of publicity, the world organisations WTTC and World Tourism Organisation cannot be regarded as associations in the sense that is applied here. In the WTTC, only Chief Executive Officials (CEO) meet; this is a very personal forum that aims at networking. The World

Tourism Organisation is an intergovernmental organisation also offering membership to the operating sector. This is also rather a large forum for discussion.

Problems: why not stick to the national associations?

With regard to the described situation, the thought arises that, since a European Tourism Association does not exist, it is perhaps not even needed, because the representation of the sector by national associations is sufficient.

A lot of companies actually do not see the need of a European Tourism Association. It is widely believed that issues create their associations – which mainly means that the incentive comes from the governmental side. EU institutions create their organisations when they need them. Industry partially prefers to wait for this governmental action to happen, partially single companies do not manage to advance by themselves on a single important issue. As long as something does not seem to have to be covered or is not urgent enough, nothing happens. So companies mainly react instead of act in response to needs of the institutions.

In the tourism sector, institutional interests – mainly those of the European Commission – and industrial interests do not even necessarily meet. To put it into simple terms, the commission mainly worries about how to get Japanese and US-American tourists to travel to Europe, the European Tourism industry tries to get Europeans to travel out of Europe.

The position of the companies is not surprising. A large obstacle for any association being established and maintained, but especially for associations of growth sectors, is the time that has to be invested.

In growth sectors, companies first worry about maintaining and improving their market position. Active participation in associations is not a prior issue, because economic problems are seen to be more important – political framework conditions are only considered after having reached a secure position with regard to the competitors.

The same is true for sectors like telecommunications, within which new companies have joined and the products have changed. The prior development of the telecommunications sector in Germany is comparable to what is currently happening in the tourism sector. Since large firms like Mannesmann and Viag had changed their portfolio, they wanted to leave their German umbrella association VDMA. The VDMA therefore employed staff at the costs of those two firms within the BDI to construct a platform for the telecommunications sector. Out of this platform, a new organisation was developed namely the Bitcom. At the European level, the association ETNO exists for the telecommunications sector, but it has large problems to adapt to the new needs of its members due to developments like mobile phones and Internet. Some active members are making efforts to improve the association.

That means that in the modern services sector, an association may already exist, but it does not manage to adapt to the changed needs of its members, as long as they do not give their input. Some manage to actually redirect the organisation, others fail because their priorities lie in meeting their economic needs first. But reliance on national associations is nonetheless by no means sufficient. It leads to the consequence that the institutions not only create organisations as issues arise, but they generally search for their own lobby, apart from the associations. This leads to the exclusion of companies the institutions do not deem adequately able to produce the information they seek, because they are not asked to take part in the consultation.

An example for such a development is the effort of the European Commission of generating employment in tourism. Because of the lack of a European voice of tourism, the Commission founded a High-Level Group consisting of 23 CEOs of all EU member-states in 1998 who worked out proposals for the creation of employment growth in tourism. The Commission would very much appreciate the creation of a European tourism association, and the BTW is also engaged in dialogues with other national associations in order to found one, but this only seems possible after the market has consolidated.

Services

Although large differences between the different service sectors make it impossible to generalise, services are in some respects seen as a whole, and there are efforts to represent them as such. Parallel and interacting developments take place at the national as well as at the European level.

Services in Germany

With the rise of the new market and with the major changes of business due to globalisation, the German business association BDI[4] ran the risk of losing some of its most potent members. Some of the largest firms that had formerly been engaged in different industrial branches had totally changed their portfolio and entered into the services sector – the most striking examples being Preussag (from raw materials and technology to tourism), and Mannesmann (formerly steel, now telecommunications).

In order to keep companies with such a portfolio change at least associated with the BDI, and because of the acknowledged fact that industrial companies were suddenly not only demanders, but also suppliers of services, the BDI started in 2000 to intensify its activities in the services sector, mainly targeting on market liberalisation. It therefore created two working groups – one on international trade with services, and one on the tourism industry,[5] thereby acknowledging the importance of the tourism sector as well as the fact that services because of their growing size now face the same problems industry faces.

Services in Europe

At the European level, services are represented via the Union of Industrial and Employers' Confederations of Europe (UNICE), of which the BDI is a member. Service activities of UNICE focus on the negotiations concerning the General Agreement on Trade in Services (GATS) of the WTO, because action is needed on a global level, and the commission is the main European negotiator.

A general problem is the question of who is covering other European services concerns. The sectoral associations only cover the interests of their members, and have a view that is too narrow to have significant weight. But there is no association with a broader scope such as UNICE covering overall European services interests and representing the entire services sector.

The process of advising on liberalisation issues is actively accompanied by the BDI and most of its equivalents in fellow EU member-states. They send delegates to the International Chamber of Commerce in Paris, to an UNICE working group on WTO services, and via this group to a network with the name European Services Forum (ESF) in Brussels.

The ESF is the typical case of an issue creating an association. With ESF, the commission created its own lobby. Upon request of the European Commission and on the initiative of Sir Leon Brittan, UNICE created in 1998 the European Services Network (ESN), now renamed European Services Forum (ESF), which supports the European Commission during the GATS-2000 negotiations. It is only intended to exist for this period of time until December 2003. UNICE leaves its activities on services to ESF – which means that, as of yet, this is the sole European platform representing services (ESF, 2001).

Administered by a small secretariat with office space provided by UNICE and headed by a secretary general, ESF consists of two different bodies, namely the 'European Services Leader Group' and the 'Policy Committee'. The European Services Leader Group joins about 40 CEOs from international services companies. The Policy Committee consists of delegates of European business associations such as the BDI, and a subworking group of UNICE (ESF, 2001). The BDI is represented by the UNICE WTO Services Working Group, which sends a delegate to the Policy Committee.

Two major problems exist with ESF:

1 The ESF also contains member firms that are owned by US-American companies. Therefore, the danger of American interests becoming ESF interests has to be watched. The case of a delegate has occurred, who served both as a European delegate to ESF and as the US-American delegate to another network, and in both networks he was responsible for drafts on the same subject. On the world market and especially when negotiating on the liberalisation of trade with services in the GATS, however, the United States and Europe are not always of the same opinion.

2 ESF consists of services like insurance companies, banks, architects and many more. To a large extent, they do not have a European umbrella association – this is not a peculiarity of the tourism sector. It leads to a latent presence of the question of separating from UNICE and establishing ESF as the European services association. UNICE does not appreciate these considerations, and a common set of principles has been worked out, which clearly states the interdependencies of the two associations.

Despite these weaknesses, the example of ESF makes clear that there are efforts to establish a common platform and representative forum by using the means that are already there.

The above stated problems within ESF give evidence for the fact that, as soon as an alliance or even an association has been established, lobbying also takes place within the forum. This can render an association inefficient, if individual members manage to dominate. That way, the platform may be useful for one member, but absolutely ineffective for all others.

Problems of this kind are more obvious in traditional services that have managed to build an association and are not undergoing major changes, as will now be clarified by a look at the financial services sector.

The financial services sector

Unlike the fast changing and very heterogeneous tourism sector, financial services have well-established national and European associations. Despite a high competition between the members, interests concerning legislation seem to be homogeneous enough to enable cooperation. Mergers and other structural changes have not substantially changed the character of the sector.

Business banks as well as most cooperative and regional banks are organised via their national umbrella associations in the European Banking Federation (or under its French name and abbreviation: Fédération Banquaire Européen, FBE) – which only accepts national umbrella associations as members. Only the cooperative and regional banks of Germany, France and Spain are not organised in the FBE because they have strictly regional interests and therefore cannot find a platform within the FBE[6] (European Banking Federation, 2001).

The FBE was formed in 1960. Problems mainly arise out of management; large banks are occupying certain topics by taking formal lead posts for their national association but also in their own interest, and the FBE lacks sufficient coordination with lobbying-offices of banking companies in Brussels. The *raison d'être* for some of the banking company-offices in Brussels seems to be the need to react to internal competition between the members of FBE. Public affairs offices must do their own lobbying in order to prevent another bank from:

a   Being informed in advance;

b   On that basis forming an opinion ahead of others;

c   Finally occupying this topic with the bank's opinion as a delegate of the national banking association within the FBE.

Also due to these conflicts in terms of competition, the FBE often only arrives at the common lowest denominator. Sometimes, negotiations are being blocked out of national interests – maybe a certain state has not advanced on e-commerce as far as another one, and by blocking the FBE, it can gain time. Banks try to find coalitions within the federation to impose their interests – which is of course difficult with the filter of national associations. Also, most banks have established their own public affairs office in Brussels. If necessary, they build alliances with other banks and bypass the association.

With certain topics, specific associations have therefore formed out of single banking companies. A recently established example is an association of members of company strictly dealing with the introduction of the Euro, called Euro Banking Association (EBA) (Euro Banking

Association, 2000). Nonetheless, the umbrella association does seem to serve the needs of the sector – in case of its non-existence, it would certainly be formed, because interests of the individual national associations are homogeneous enough to make a joint effort worthwhile. But this gives way to internal competition. The dominance of certain members weakens the overall effectiveness.

Reasons for problems of associability

Why do services run into the problems they run with their associations?

Reasons for the dissatisfying situation are found in the history of the service sectors as well as in legislative conditions, but they are mainly linked to the members of the association. Harmonisation may facilitate the building of associations, but the new development of a sector – like the turning of the tourism sector into an industry – with all economic problems to go with it, makes it very hard. Also, vast changes in a sector can turn a formerly rather well working association into an inefficient organ, because members do not manage to put enough time and resources into the restructuring of their association.

In tourism, the heterogeneity of the sector makes it very difficult to imagine joint forces on the national level as well as on the European level. One of the reasons of the perceived success of the BTW can be seen in the fact that it only tries to promote tourism as a major part of the economy. It will be more difficult to find common views on more substantial subjects. Since tourism is divided into many different special services that do not have common interests, the creation of a European umbrella association is seen sceptically. Personal problems also play a role.

A major obstacle for the European level is the fact that national legislation in the tourism sector has not been harmonised yet, and differs from the focus of the tourism industry.

A common view amongst involved interests is therefore, that homework first has to be done in the member states, before the European level can be tackled. As long as what has to be done at the national level is not solved, a European tourism association does not seem to add any value. Currently, only topics like liberalisation can find broad support. It means, that under the conditions of a typical growth sector, enough incentives to engage in an association can only be found, if this association already exists, like in the telecommunications or electricity market.

The employment of resources is a major reason especially for the modern sectors not to engage in the establishment and improvement of associations, since the impact that political conditions have on economic developments is often not understood in its scope. Since this problem does not only occur in the tourism sector but all modern services, they are also unlikely to put efforts into establishing further cross-sectoral representations. But do European services sectors really need business associations?

Conclusion: what do Europe's service sectors need?

Having stated a large amount of problems with the associability of services, the conclusion is now aimed at explaining the nonetheless overall positive view of services associations, with the pledge that is directed at the members of the association of improving weaknesses.

The European institutions prefer receiving an unfiltered view directly from companies. A European association cannot provide that. But the institutions also search for a European view and do not want to talk to a vast number of firms. A European association has a much higher impact than single companies or national associations can have, as it represents most member-states and many member companies. But it needs sufficient personal and financial support of its members and only makes sense, if interests are homogeneous enough to find satisfying compromises.

A large problem is the fact that, as long as something does not exist, its need and the profit from it cannot really be estimated. It cannot really be said if a business association can improve lobbying in the tourism sector. The established service association ESF under the roof of UNICE currently seems to be the most feasible solution of associability within the service sector, an established forum within a stable association covering single big issues which involve the entire sector can be efficient enough because of its simultaneous tight focus and broad subject. Also, the weight of such an association is larger than that of a single sector.

Possibly, the structure of associations in the service sector will get a different hierarchy. On the one hand, especially on the European level, single sectors like the tourism sector or even the financial services sector do not possess enough weight to get heard without the broader background of the entire service sector. On the other hand, it seems to be easier to find coalitions on a few very large issues, such as the negotiations within the WTO on the GATS, than it is to create a general European umbrella association. It seems probable that either *ad hoc* networks or temporary organisations will be created for covering especially important needs, or the scope of ESF will be widened with the end of the GATS-2000 negotiations.

To sum it up, the existing associations are useful and necessary, because if nothing else, they at least symbolise the presence, size and interest of the sector. But the needs of European Services go beyond that, and efficient associations can meet them. Therefore, improvement is needed. To practically achieve it, an approach is necessary, which is possibly too idealistic. Companies first have to realise that their associations only become effective by the input of all members, and they have to manage to find subjects that can be worked on together without getting into competitive questions. Sectors with a rather low overall importance in European policy-making will have to join forces, which makes associability even harder for them.

Notes

1   These figures come from an assessment of the German Industrial Association BDI (Bundesverband der Deutschen Industrie).
2   Bundesverband der Deutschen Tourismuswirtschaft
3   The current senior manager, Klaus-Heiner Lehne, happens to be a member of European Parliament at the same time.
4   The BDI is the leading organisation of German industry with 35 industrial specific associations – membership of single firms is not possible. Within Germany, it is a very powerful organisation and covers diverse industrial sectors. With the rise of the new market and with the major changes of business due to globalisation, the BDI has to rethink its scope (BDI, 2001).
5   The working group 'International Trade with Services' serves as a so-called cross-sectoral working group in order to work out topics of the services society. As of yet, tourism industry does not play a major role within the BDI, but because of the growing importance of this branch and the fact that tourism in Germany has turned into an industry – and therefore has to face problems an industrial sector faces – the BDI has now established a second working group that occupies itself mainly with the implication of industry and tourism under the name 'Industrial Tourism'. Members of this working group can also join the working group on international trade with services.
6   Those of Germany, France and Spain do their own lobbying, because the German savings banks, for instance, only have strictly regional interests and therefore cannot find a platform within the FBE.

15

Association Management Companies as Change Agents

Alfons Westgeest and Bruno Alves

In recent years associations increasingly felt the impact of the challenges that cause corporations to rapidly review and change their strategy, business planning or operation. The main drivers are international trade, technology and new management models. We argue that associations need to analyse and act upon several internal factors (friction or conflict) and external factors (environment). They also need to understand the governance issues that are typical for their organisation, how shall the Board take its responsibility for strategy? How can communication with the staff about division of roles with the Board be best organised? Throughout the years, the management of associations has significantly varied according to new political, economical and social developments. From the stage of defining objectives to the measurement of performance, several tools must be created in order to allow the association to continuously reassess the relevance of its management model. The establishment of Association Management Companies (AMCs) and creation of specialised consulting firms have contributed to new ways of reaching optimal organisational performance.

The need for change

Industries, markets and sector representations face the challenge of change on an unprecedented scale. Almost a decade ago, government and business leaders set the first steps towards the Transatlantic Business Dialogue. At the time, it was evident that trade issues would soon assume an international scope, and that representation of interests would surpass any geographical boundaries. Today, international trade is broadly recognised as a key catalyst for global economic growth.

International trade causes increased concerns

With the expansion of trade issues to worldwide dimensions came the need to thoroughly consider the existence of other legitimate transnational interests. Today, labour unions, environmental action groups and consumer organisations are an integral part of international trade politics. In December 1999, when representatives of the 134 member countries of the WTO met in Seattle to define the future of world trade, this could not have been more evident. Disagreements on setting agenda and heavy opposition from Third World countries, NGOs and action groups led to a failure of the Seattle Summit.

Technology drives new sectors and alliances

Technology has played a significant role in the creation of a new trade environment. Broadband communications and electronic commerce, to name but two of the main twenty-first century buzzwords, allows for industries to challenge traditional geographical limitations and reinvent production and distribution in their sector. New industry sectors are born, and with it, the need for representation and influence. The attempt to tackle this new trade environment with contemporary regulations results in the rapid creation of *ad hoc* industry alliances, which until a few years ago were unforeseen. In Europe, national governments and EU politicians have proposed Directives governing 'Electronic Commerce' and 'Copyright in the Information Society'. These proposals were among the most lobbied pieces of legislation ever discussed in the history of the European Union. 'Internet' is the common denominator in both regulations. Together with other technological developments, the Internet triggered a whole new organisational pattern in the world of business associations. As business grows to new services and faster communications, associations must adapt to new demands from companies (members) and consumers alike.

Government leaders are trying to keep the pace with this 'everyday' new environment. However, what are associations, federations and interest groups doing to respond to the new needs of their members and the decision-makers they want to influence? Governance and organisational issues together with management models and staff structures are central to ensure the effectiveness of the association and guarantee its future survival in an environment of rapid political and socioeconomical change. Next sections describes how associations can address these issues.

More options appear to assist business associations

The first international federations emerged about a century ago. While many of them still serve key functions in their sector of industry, the above changes (international trade and technology), however, caused a rethink of strategy and organisation. AMCs now play an important role assisting and successfully guiding associations throughout this new changing environment. The origin of AMCs in Europe (back in the 1940s), resulted from the same political and economic needs which prompted companies to organise into trade groups. At that time, many associations sprang up with a traditional volunteer structure, which in many cases lacked specialised management skills and staff resources. Hence, associations started progressively seeking external help to assist them in fulfilling their objectives. Soon after, the increasing liberalisation of trade resulted in a thorough revision of traditional organisational patterns, and in many cases, entrepreneurs who started off providing business advice to associations, gradually took on more of a management role and eventually established their own AMC.

The objective was mostly to tackle new challenges in the management models of associations, and prepare them for new realities. European Federations consisting merely of national associations, for example, have seen their existence challenged by larger companies forming interest groups on a European sector level. Industry sectors seem to generate new products and services every day, creating new challenges and, with it, new operating models for associations. It is estimated that well over a thousand European associations and interest groups are representing European business sectors. In addition, several *ad hoc* alliances and single-issue groups come and go. Several of these no longer require an organisation with many full time staff in a building that the association owns or leases. The emerging AMCs as well as support services provided by consulting firms increases the levels of flexibility and professionalism in all associations.

Organisational issues

Both internal and external factors can trigger change in the structure, functioning and overall existence of associations. In most cases, the difference between a threat and an opportunity will be in one's reading of a certain situation. The association's flexibility to react is as important as its capacity to pro-actively act. In both cases, a thorough understanding of the factors affecting the present and future states of the association can dictate its success.

Internal factors (friction and conflict)

In many models, conflict is considered a catalyst for change. Associations may well apply this concept to enhance their existence. Internally, the rummaging around, looking for areas of agreement amongst members, board, and staff is part of the day-to-day management of the association. Nevertheless, the energy spent in identifying these areas sometimes hinders a more thorough analysis and discussion of the areas of disagreement. Strategic planning is one of the concepts that comes from the corporate world and fits the need to adapt to changes. However, in times of severe internal conflict this may not suffice and associations must go back to basics; generate activity from areas of agreement and invest time resolving the areas of disagreement. The association cannot look for the best way to survive an existing conflict. Instead, it must manage this conflict and transform it into an opportunity.

Three important qualities dictate the outcome of a situation of conflict:

Timing: The association will not change in one day. The assessment of the best time to tackle the areas of disagreement must be made:
- The recognition that a certain conflict is jeopardising the existence and/or future development of the association (are members voting with 'their feet'?);
- The will to act upon this conflict and resolve it (who can take the lead and how soon).

Different bodies of the association may have different approaches to the same conflict. The members may recognise the existence of a dangerous conflict, but the board may overlook the need to act upon this conflict and resolve it. Moreover, even when everyone agrees on the need to resolve a conflict, the interests surrounding its discussion are different between members, board and staff. Associations are generally slower in making decisions than corporations because of the need to composite interests.

Negotiation skills: The acceptance of one defined objective for the association, above any sectoral interests is necessary if the association is to effectively manage a conflict. The forces involved in the dispute, are often led by:
- Individual interests imposed on the association's objectives;
- Disagreement on the best way to reach the association's objectives.

The latter implies the acceptance of one defined and commonly accepted objective, but different approaches on how to *reach* this objective, whereas the first implies an undefined or unshared objective. In any of the two situations, the objectives of the association will have to be further defined and discussed. Most importantly, all or a majority of parties of the association must reach consensus about these objectives.

Neutrality: The different parties involved in the dispute will naturally elect a moderator for this conflict. The moderator will have to be broadly recognised as neutral, and capable of transforming this conflict into a win–win situation. While some staff or Board members may be very well suited to fulfil this role, very often the will to have the best acceptable result leads the association to hire an external service provider. Such an 'outsider' would be able to independently guide the group towards successful outcomes for all stakeholders. The neutrality principle is not always an exclusive feature of an outsider. Some European associations gather in their advisory bodies the position of 'President d'honneur', or a collective group of high representatives of the industry that can potentially mediate successfully the resolution of a conflict. In all cases it is important that relevant background knowledge and analyses will be gathered beforehand by the moderator together with staff.

External factors (environmental changes)

It is not only internal conflicts that constitute opportunities for the association. The external environment of the corporation is very well described in general management literature. The association has increasingly to face similar challenges, including:
- What other organisations serve the same sector or business interest?
- How to define the border lines between competing associations (products and services are not stable for long).
- What is the role of commercial organisations in your industry? Note that trade show organisers, 'Messes' and publishers compete for the revenue 'euros' from corporations.
- Which revenues exist other than membership dues or can be created?

Scanning the environment

The complex environment in which associations operate makes it more and more appropriate to develop regular environmental scanning programmes. The search for information about events and relationships outside the association that can affect its future activities is a core function of associations. However, is this search a proactive and regular mechanism, or simply a matter of chance?

The identification of a fixed set of data sources, periodically visited and monitored, will not obstruct the association from obtaining unsolicited or casual information from other sources. It will nevertheless enrich the range of information that the decision-making bodies will have at their disposal when the time has come to plan the next step of the organisation. Moreover, the whole concept of environmental scanning is based on the associations' capacity to interpret the information obtained. This implies a permanent use of this information, together with a detailed analysis of the impact that a certain issue will have in the present and future state of the association.

Responsibility of management

Therefore, the environmental scanning programme can provide an important tool to support tactical decisions on the present state of the association. For example, when preparing a political argument on behalf of a certain industry sector, the presentation or simple consideration of quantitative market indicators is often essential to the success of the operation. Finally, one level above in the decision-making pyramid, these indicators will be reused when discussing the strategic planning and the development of the association.

According to the first American Society of Association Executives (ASAE) Foundation 'New Horizons Think Tank' held in June 1997, in the near future, the association executive with management responsibility is expected to devote one-fifth of his or her time to be involved in or supervise environmental scanning. In other words, associations are realising the importance of creating information systems able to effectively scan the environment surrounding the association. The objective is simple – improve activities and operations, facilitate strategic decisions, and increase the overall effectiveness of the association.

Governance issues

Associations are often, if not always, under immense pressure from industry interests and policy bodies on which, and with whom, they operate. Strategic decisions on the future of the industry must be taken rapidly and effectively.

The involvement of core stakeholders decides the outcome

The board, the membership and the management staff of the association all play complementary roles in this process. The good relationship between board, working groups and staff is very important to the sound existence of the association. The board holds the latent duty to decide on the strategic objectives of the organisation. This decision must nevertheless consider both the needs of its members and the operational capacity of its staff structure. Any strategic decision that fails to involve one of these core stakeholders is likely to result in failure.

Delegation and the responsibility of management

Although superficially simple, the roles of board (as delegator) and staff (taking operational responsibility) very often conflict, either through overlapping, or where they do not recognise the Board's legitimacy. While the division of responsibilities between board and staff are for the most part clear and virtually unchallenged, there are also areas that are fiercely challenged by both staff and board. The dimension of this area must be reduced. To reduce these areas to a minimum, boards and staff have to continuously communicate and negotiate their positions, and find adequate and shared solutions. The strategic component of the association is the side inevitably affected by the lack of definition of areas of responsibility.

Three important pitfalls

- *Micromanagement*: When the board of the association invades the operational area of responsibility allocated to its staff, we run into a system of micromanagement that can potentially damage the whole functioning of the association. The strategic component necessary to the development of the organisation will be overlooked, and the staff will feel mistrusted and thereby frustrated when pursuing its operational role.
- *Disengagement*: When staff of the association are carrying out most of the work, in operational and strategic terms, the board may feel disinterested and thereby considerably reduce its involvement in the association. The isolation between staff and industry input will seriously reduce the effectiveness of the association, challenging its legitimacy to represent common interests.

- *Miscommunication*: Adding to the difficult balance that must be reached between operational capacity and membership demand, the board of the association is deemed to cope with scarce time resources. Time constraints intensify the necessity to clarify the goals of the association and clearly communicate these goals to the board, staff and members of the association. Well-planned communication and information channels are key elements to foster the relationship between the different bodies of the association, and cannot be overlooked. The definition of effective goals will greatly depend on the capacity of listening to membership needs and understanding what the operational structure is able to offer. A conflict between these two factors will easily provoke a conflict of powers – yet, this conflict is usually the first indication that change is needed in the structure of the organisation. Internal frictions are only one of many factors that can impose a new organisational model to the association. Seizing a conflict to the benefit of the association is difficult, but it is the only way forward.

Management issues

Management patterns of associations have always varied significantly according to new political, economical and social developments. The management structures of associations are particularly affected by new ways of facing internal and external factors of the organisation discussed above. For the purpose of this article 'management' includes the board, staff and possibly key working groups (or so-called standing committees). In order to become more effective, associations also have to constantly reassess the relevance of their management models. This article identifies three important phases. From the stage of definition of objectives to the measurement of performance, several tools must be created in order to allow the association to continuously reassess the relevance of its management model. These are the definition phase, the implementation phase, and the evaluation phase, and are considered in turn below.

Definition phase

- *Inventory of resources available*: The first task in managing the association is to define and verify the resources currently available within the organisation. The process of defining operational capacity will determine the possibility for obtaining from the board additional internal or external resources to achieve the objectives of the association. Similarly, a thorough knowledge of the resources of the association by the board and the feedback from its working groups (committees or task forces), will reduce the danger of setting up strategic objectives impossible to fulfil at operational level. The resources of the association cannot be limited to the concept of 'how many staff serving how many members'. It can include alliance partners as well as law, accounting and consulting firms. An accurate analysis will thoroughly assess the knowledge, information and technical means that are or can be made available to the association.

- *Strategic guidelines translated into an activity plan*: The management of the association is expected to define an operational plan, following the strategic guidelines provided by the board. The matching of strategic guidelines with operational capacity of current resources is of extreme importance. It will support any decision of obtaining additional resources, or revisiting the strategic objectives set previously. The activity plan is also a key tool for the definition of 'who manages what'. As was suggested earlier, it must be aimed at establishing the correct balance of governance powers and responsibilities, and will impede the association from running into 'micromanagement' and 'disengagement' spirals.

Implementation phase

- *Business planning and measurement*: Once defined, the activity or business plan is intended to guide the association all the way through to the achievement of its goals and further on to its strategic objectives. The implementation of the plan will not release board or members from further responsibilities. On the contrary, the operations carried out by the association will inevitably be measured against the final goals established previously. The Board, working groups and members must remain informed on the progress of the association towards its objectives, and if need be, should be involved in any revision of previous decisions concerning the strategy of the association.
- *Participation and buy-in*: This involvement will be essential for the creation of a 'buying-in' concept that will encourage active participation, and therefore result in the availability of extra resources by adding revenues or reallocation of the budget. Nevertheless, efforts to achieve the highest possible participation of members in the life of the association can easily penalise the decision-making structures. It is important to clarify that active participation means additional

input to assist the decision-making bodies and management in the implementation of the association's activities. It cannot allow for the substitution of decision-makers who were elected or nominated to carry out this mission.

Evaluation phase

The final stage of the process can be described as the evaluation phase. Although tools are used in the implementation phase to monitor the progress towards the goals of the association, there is a need for a clear assessment on whether or not goals were missed or achieved. This will naturally result in a continuous evaluation process.

- *Victory*: Membership will perceive the achievement of the associations' objectives as a justification for their past and future investment (of time, resources, etc.). Thus, the board and management structures will capitalise on their authority to lead the association to success. Overall, the association will build on the legitimacy for its existence, and demonstrate sound performance of its structures. The process of sharing the victories of the association is usually as complicated as blaming for failure. The occasion is nevertheless a unique opportunity to propose future activities, develop the association, and most importantly to unite its different players.

- *Defeat*: When evidence is produced indicating failure to attain an objective of the association, members rarely accept any responsibility. The management of the association are sometimes put under the natural scrutiny of the 'unsatisfied customer' with rights and without obligations. The staff of the association is in the difficult position of justifying the failure of the association to the board and directly to its members. The board is under pressure from the members of the association, and often shifts responsibility to management. The worst possible outcome of this crisis is when staff and the board of the association lead separate efforts to determine the reasons for failure. The efforts to assess the reasons for the failure of the association must allow for an open discussion involving all players.

Again, the association as a whole will have to identify the reasons for the failure. The only way forward is revising governance, management and organisational issues, and identifying the impact of each of these groups in the performance of the association. This exercise can be the only, but vital positive outcome from not achieving the objective of the association.

- *A balanced outcome*: Obviously the margin of error between calling a victory and failure can be very small. The purpose of the above is to sharpen the management's understanding of both the importance of involvement of all stakeholders as well as the constant measurement and evaluation process.

Can design and management make a difference?

Associations have different needs from the corporations and other organisations that they represent. Indeed, the management of associations cannot rely exclusively on the vast industry experience of volunteers, nor in the acumen of external management expertise in the corporate sector. Nowadays, associations and other similar groups can be formed 'virtually', and a range of alliances built following models. This does not necessarily imply that new models of associations are more effective than older, traditional models. Instead, it stimulates entirely new thinking on how to reach the most effective management and organisation of any given association.

The structure and management of the association must be flexible and prepared to accommodate external changes, and to benefit from the opportunities arising from conflict situations. The staff, working groups and board of the association must create the necessary tools to operate successfully and develop new levels of effectiveness. The matrix of factors (governance, organisational and management) affecting the association will not always immediately dictate the effectiveness of the association. These factors will essentially shape the model of the association. It will be up to all stakeholders to revisit them continuously and creatively generate new models that can ensure the development of the organisation.

Can associational management and design make a difference when environmental factors seem to predict associational effectiveness? The answer is Yes. Effectiveness of the association will greatly depend on your capacity to analyse environmental factors and respond by projecting an adequate structure and management tools.

Part III

Cross Sectoral and Employers Organisations

16
Employer vs. Product Market Associations: Different Dynamics in Associational Governance?
Franz Traxler

Business is present in manifold markets, with a correspondingly wide range of interests to be pursued there. This raises the question of whether and how this multiplicity of interests translates into differing problems of associational governance. If such differences indeed exist, business associations have to synchronize very carefully the scope of interests represented with their governance capacities, when it comes to ensuring the effectiveness of their activities.

The following analysis addresses this relationship between differential interests and associational governance. Its first part discusses the preconditions for and dimensions of effective associational governance. The argument is that business associations face two fundamental governance problems: (i) the management of interests; and (ii) the dual logic of associational action. Second, the chapter examines how distinct interest categories of business interests relate to these governance problems. This brings us to the distinction between employer interests and product market interests. These two interest categories contrast in terms of their requirements for associational governance. The chapter concludes by providing empirical evidence of how Europe's business associations cope with these problems.

The problems of associational governance

The effectiveness of business associations is here understood in the broad sense. This means that they must not only be able to exert actual influence upon the interlocutors but also to secure legitimacy of their action in relation to both their members and interlocutors. Any kind of such associational action creates a *governance* problem, that is, a problem of overcoming opportunist behaviour. This is for two main reasons. First, the self-interest of the (potential) members differs from their collective interest (Olson, 1965). Second, when realizing their goals, associations have to take account of the interests of those whose decisions and actions they seek to influence (Traxler and Schmitter, 1995). As a consequence, associational governance implies intermediating between the members' individual and collective interests on the one hand and between member interests and their interlocutors' interests on the other hand.

One can differentiate between two dimensions of this governance problem (Table 16.1). The first dimension refers to the management of interests. Given a multiplicity of business interests, associations have to deliberately demarcate their interest domain which defines the scope of interests advanced on behalf of their constituency. An associational domain can be demarcated in terms of issues and/or membership. Issues refer to the range of market interests covered and the number of interlocutors addressed. For example, an association may concentrate on matters of foreign trade represented *vis-à-vis* the authorities. Furthermore, interest domains may be demarcated by defining what businesses are eligible for membership. To narrow down the complexity of interests covered, specification of either issues or membership is sufficient. For instance, a business association specialized in creditor's claims is rather narrow although any type of business can join. The same holds true for an association highly specialized in terms of membership (e.g. suppliers

Table 16.1   The problems of associational governance

Dimension	Conflict
The management of interests	*Complexity of interests*
Domain demarcation	Problems of aggregating interests and
Internal decision-making	formulating common goals
The logics of associational action	*Balancing member demand and external imperatives*
Logic of membership: member recruitment and member compliance	
Logic of influence: exerting influence on interlocutors	

in the car industry) even when the range of issues covered remains unspecified and general.

For the sake of manageable interests, it would thus be reasonable to establish rather narrow interest domains. However, this may conflict with the requirements for effectiveness which result from interactions of an association with its interlocutors. They normally prefer dealing with that business association which is most representative within the relevant policy field. At Community level, representativity has become an important issue, because distinct Euro-associations often compete for influence and participation in policy-making. The Commission has placed special emphasis on representativity as a basic criterion for resolving such conflicts. Encompassing associations are widely regarded as more representative than narrow associations.[1] Therefore, the demand for representativity induces associations to demarcate their interest domain in rather broad terms.

This brings us to the second dimension of the governance problem, the dual logic of collective action. Interest associations have to face in two directions at once, towards those whose interests they claim to represent; and towards those whose decisions and actions they want to influence. This gives rise to two conflicting logics, a logic of membership and a logic of influence (Weitbrecht, 1969; Schmitter and Streeck, 1981). The logic of membership refers to an association's ability to attract members. Above all, this means recruiting members and ensuring their support and compliance.[2] The logic of influence concerns an association's capacity for strategic action *vis-à-vis* its interlocutors. These logics conflict with each other in that they impose competing demands upon associations. The members expect associations to realize their interests as authentically as possible. Exerting influence – at least on a recurrent basis – is bound to strategic exchange (Pizzorno, 1978) relying on mutual concessions of the actors involved. This forces associations to find and sustain a precarious balance between these logics. If an association makes too much concession, this tends to undermine its membership base. Conversely, an association risks its recognition as an interest representative, when it proves unable to reach compromises with its interlocutors and to bind its members accordingly.

These problems of associational governance apply not only to business associations but also to any kind of interest association. It is, however, important to note that their manifestation and magnitude varies with the kind of association. For example, there are significant differences between business associations and trade unions that result in corresponding differences in domain demarcation, associability and internal structures (Traxler, 1993). The following section analyses whether such differential effects are also at work within the business class in that distinct business interests give rise to rather differing governance problems.

The differing requirements for governing employer and product market interests

Differences in associational governance become more pronounced the more diverse business interests are. In this respect, the main divide is between employer interests originating in the labour market and those interests ensuing from other markets that will be designated here as product markets. In organisational terms, this divide reflects the distinction between employer associations which represent business' labour market interests and trade associations which organize product market interests. The governance problems of these two categories of business interests are mirror-inverted. The management of interests creates much more problems regarding product market interests, compared to labour market interests. Conversely, the representation of labour market interests is much more burdened with the conflict between the logic of membership and the logic of influence than the representation of product market interests (Table 16.2).

The management of interest is more difficult in the case of product market interests because they are more complex than labour market interests. Interests in product markets are more complex because businesses have two roles there. On the one hand, they buy resources such as raw materials and intermediate goods from other businesses; on the other hand, they supply other businesses or consumers with their own goods. Exchange relations between buyers and suppliers always involve interest conflicts over the terms of trade. This conflict becomes manifest not only in individual exchange relations but also in cleavages in collective interests.

Table 16.2 The relationship between associational governance and interest categories

Interest category	Association	Main problem of governance
Product market interests	Product market associations	The management of interests
Labour market interests	Employer associations	The logics of associational action

For example, the chocolate industry which uses powdered milk as raw material probably prefers more liberalized imports of this product than the manufacturers of powdered milk do. It is evident from this that the collective product market interests of business differ *qualitatively* along the distinct chains of production. As a consequence, representing product market interests of one certain business group often requires advancing these interests in relation to and in conflict with another business group. This means that the product market interests of distinct business groups often need representation via separate associational channels. Concerning the management of interests, this implies rather *narrow* demarcations of an association's interest domain.

Compared to product market interests, the labour market interests of business are much less divisive. In the labour market, all businesses have only the role of buyers, that is, employers. Hence, the main conflict of interest is external to the business class. Employer interests must be advanced *vis-à-vis* labour and its representatives, the trade unions. This is not to say that conflicts are completely absent among employers. Employers compete for labour, something which provokes conflicts within business, especially when labour markets are tight. Conflicts are most likely to emerge between labour- and capital-intensive businesses because the former can offer less concessions to labour than the latter can. Likewise, the employer interests of small and large firms also differ since unionization rates normally increase with firm size. All these differences in interests, however, are *gradual* in contrast to the *qualitative* cleavages in the case of product market interests. Regarding employer interests, there exists a clearly defined common denominator to which each single employer can subscribe, that is, those terms of employment which even the marginal enterprise can afford.

For all these reasons, employer associations can demarcate their domain in broad terms and even have to do so in particular when being confronted with an encompassing domain of their union counterparts. This is because employers have to control as many segments of the labour market as the trade union does. Otherwise, they run the risk of being played off against each other.

Turning from the management of interests to the dual logic of associational action, one finds the reverse relationship between interests and governance. Employer associations face more serious problems than trade associations do. This ensues from differing modes for interest representation.

In the case of employers, collective bargaining is a key mechanism of processing interests. Collective bargaining creates delicate problems of compromising. To maintain both the support from its members and its reputation as a reliable bargaining party, an employer association has to reach collective agreements which well balance member interests and union demands. Moreover, when engaging in collective bargaining, employer associations act as a (private) government *vis-à-vis* their members in that they impose binding decisions on them. This is not a very popular activity, seen from the members' perspective.

In comparison with labour market interests, the dual logic of associational action provokes less conflicts in the case of product market interests, since the usual mode of pursuing the latter is lobbying the authorities. This brings about no need to formally accept compromises and to commit one's members to a formal agreement. Under these circumstances, effective associational governance rests simply on the ability to ensure the (potential) members' willingness to join, to pay their subscriptions and to participate in the association's goal formation. Narrow trade associations rarely require member support beyond these activities, such that they can be run by a very small staff or even by professional public relations agencies.

There are, nevertheless, notable exceptions to this standard pattern of processing product market interests. In most cases, this involves activities aimed at ensuring certain levels of product safety and quality on a voluntary, associational basis. In a few sectors, where these issues are seen as particularly important and sensitive, such arrangements have become an essential element of regulation. The pharmaceutical industry which relies on associational self-regulation at the national, European and international level has traditionally been among these sectors. At all these levels, the industry's associations managed to establish voluntary codes of practices for the promotion of medicines. Its European voice, the European Federation of Pharmaceutical Industry Association (EFPIA) has also worked as a vehicle of European integration in that it helped standardize the national codes (Greenwood and Ronit 1992). When formulating and implementing such standards, trade associations indeed assume the role of a private interest government in a way analogous to those employer associations which are engaged in collective bargaining. As Greenwood and Ronit (1992: 80) note with regard to the European case, 'Of importance here was the ability of EFPIA to be able to deliver the promise to the Commission of securing compliance of its members over the negotiated settlement, and in the proposal to act as an agent of policy implementation....' Under these circumstances, the conflict inherent in the dual, associational logic of membership and influence is much more accentuated than in the case of lobbying.

Nevertheless, private interest government of employer interests tends to be more demanding than such arrangements covering product market interests. Collective agreements and related compromises on labour market interests must be renegotiated on a recurrent, institutionalized basis, something which seldom applies to product market interests. Furthermore, collective bargaining always takes places under the threat of industrial action, in stark contrast to negotiations over self-regulation of product market interests. It goes without saying that member compliance in the course of a labour conflict (i.e. a strike or lockout) is especially difficult to secure.

Regardless of whether labour market interests or product market interests are at issue, imposing binding decisions on members is the biggest challenge an association can face. This especially applies to voluntary associations whose members can respond simply by leaving the association. However, for reasons of legitimacy, even such business associations as the chambers which are privileged by compulsory membership tend to refrain from disciplining their members. To bind their members, associations thus strongly need external support, namely support from the state, in particular when it comes to performing public-order functions.

Regarding product market interests, the threat to impose state regulation is an important means of stimulating the establishment of and compliance with associational self-regulation. Such threat paved the way for all the above-mentioned codes of practices for the pharmaceutical industry (Greenwood and Ronit, 1992). In the case of employer associations, a comparable, state-provided means is the statutory provision for extending the purview of a collective agreement to non-affiliated companies. While such measures are explicitly devised to ensure compliance, they also back an association's ability to recruit members. If their association is empowered by the state to fulfil public-order functions, businesses have a strong incentive to join so as to be entitled to participate in the decision-making process the outcome of which may affect them in any case.[3]

Practices and trends

The above differences between employer interests and product market interests in the requirements for associational governance have given rise to functional differentiation of business associations. There are three types of business associations established in Europe. First, pure trade associations exclusively deal with product market interests.

Second, pure employer associations are specialized in organizing labour market interests. Third, 'mixed' associations combine the representation of both interest categories.

In each member-state as well as at Community level one finds pure trade associations which are highly specialized in terms of tasks and/or membership. As a result of this high degree of specialization, they are usually so numerous that it is impossible to give reliable figures on their total number. At any rate, they significantly outnumber pure employer associations. Empirical evidence from a comparative study of seven comparable sectors in nine countries for 1980 shows that there were three pure trade associations to one pure employer association on average (Traxler, 1993). In comparison to employer associations, the higher number of trade associations within one and the same representational space indicates narrower interest domains. Closer consideration of the range of distinct business activities covered by each of these associations supports this assumption; the pure trade associations operating in any combination of the seven sectors and nine countries embrace a significantly narrower range of business activities than pure employer associations do (Traxler, 1993). This narrower interest domain of trade associations indicates that product market interests are much more divisive than labour market interests.

At the European level, the frequency distribution by type of business association is even more asymmetrical than at the national level. More than 900 EU business associations are estimated to exist (Greenwood, 2000) the vast majority of which is sector-related. However, only 17 of them have embarked on sectoral social dialogue with the unions (Keller and Sörries, 1999). This clear predominance of pure trade associations not only reflects higher diversity of product market interests but also more progress in European regulation of product markets, compared to a rather underdeveloped 'social dimension'.

The functional differentiation of business associations is less visible at the cross-sectoral level. Comparable figures on cross-sectoral business associations for 15 countries of Western Europe reveal that in the late 1990s pure employer associations were in operation only in Denmark, Sweden, Germany, Switzerland, Spain and Italy. The standard pattern of cross-sectoral coverage is mixed association. One may also understand Italy as case of this pattern, since only one minor association (i.e. the Confederazione Autonoma Sindicati Artigiani for the artisan sector) is a pure employer organisation while all the other cross-sectoral associations including the principal business voice, Confindustria, are mixed.

However, this suggests a higher degree of unity than actually exists. This is because many pure sector-specific trade associations are not affiliated to a higher level, cross-sectoral association. This configuration is even more pronounced at European level, where a multiplicity of sectoral trade associations operates outside the umbrella of the cross-sectoral peak organisations. Most importantly in this respect, the sectoral dimension of business interests is formally excluded from the domain of UNICE, the principal cross-sectoral business association at the European level. The non-affiliation of sectoral trade associations underscores the fact that product market interests, in particular when narrowly defined in associational terms are so idiosyncratic that any effort to aggregate them across sectors becomes pointless. This suggests that mixed peak organisations are more engaged in coordinating employer interests than they are with regard to product market interests. Regardless of this, mixed associations numerically prevail over any pure type of association at most representational levels. As regards the national level, this applies to the cross-sectoral associations, as already noted. According to the comparative study of seven sectors in nine countries cited above, this also holds true for sectoral associations. Of the total number of associations covered by this study, 6 per cent were pure employer associations, 18 per cent were pure trade associations and 76 per cent were mixed associations (Traxler, 1993). Likewise, mixed domains are most widespread among cross-sectoral Eurobusiness associations. The exception to this pattern is the pan-European representation of sectoral business interests. The overwhelming majority of this type of interest organization are pure trade associations in that they refuse to enter any negotiations with the unions.

On balance, the above findings show that the management of interests is more difficult for product market interests than for labour market interests. The standard response to this problem is to narrow down the associational scope of product market interests so much that they become as homogenous as possible. Furthermore, they are often processed separately from and independently of both labour market interests and other product market interests.

Turning from the management of interest to the dual logics of associational action, one also finds practices that confirm the differences between product market interests and labour market interests, when it comes to reconciling the requirements for membership and influence. The representation of labour market interests faces more problems than product market interests in this respect, since the former – in contrast to the latter – usually requires making the members comply with compromises concluded with the association's inter-locutors.

Employer associations strongly differ in how they cope with this conflict. At one extreme, one finds the Nordic employer associations which have given clear priority to the logic of influence, by deliberately strengthening their authority *vis-à-vis* their members. For instance, Sweden's SAF managed to establish high fines to ensure compliance with its bargaining strategy and did not shrink from imposing them on defecting members. This was possible since the union movements are very strong there, as is the case in the other Nordic countries as well. The price the Nordic employer associations have to pay for prioritizing influence so clearly is a relatively low density rate in comparison to other European countries (Traxler, 2000; Traxler *et al.*, 2001). It is thus no mere coincidence that in the other countries employer associations tend to orient themselves primarily towards the logic of membership. This priority is most pronounced when they offer the special member-ship status of a 'non-conforming member' who is not subject to col-lective agreements signed by the association. This arrangement is widespread in the UK. In Germany, it was introduced by a few affiliates of the Bundesvereinigung der Deutschen Arbeitgeberverbände (BDA) in the 1990s. In some cases, this membership status is obtainable only for new members for a limited time period (Müller-Jentsch, 1998). The non-conforming membership status is unusual for trade associations since their requirements for member compliance are normally much less demanding.

Another strategy of employer associations that is devised to tackle the conflicting dual logic of associational action is narrowing down the range of issues covered by collective agreements, such that as many aspects of the employment terms as possible are left to the discretion of the firms. Manifestations of these tendencies are the so-called 'taboo catalogues' as adopted by the German employer associations (Jacobi *et al.*, 1998). They list all issues the employers definitely refuse to negotiate.

Given the problems of binding employers, one may wonder why their associations should not better disengage from collective bargaining and limit their activities to lobbying the state. However, this is done at the risk of becoming irrelevant. If they fail to replace the bargaining tasks with other, attracting activities, they will lose members and political power. A case in point is again the UK, the only country, where single-employer bargaining has indeed supplanted associational, multi-employer bargaining. In the course of the shift from multi-employer to single-employer bargaining during the 1980s, density of employer associations dropped by around half (Millward *et al.*, 1992). Although it has become fashionable among employers to struggle for single-employer bargaining in a situation of slack labour markets, single-employer bargaining is risky also for the employers themselves. In comparison to multi-employer bargaining, single-employer bargaining tends to increase the firms' transaction costs and makes them more vulnerable to whipsawing union tactics, aimed at confronting the employers individually.

Despite the differing requirements for governing labour market interests and product market interests there has been a tendency to fuse their representation, by merging employer associations and trade associations. One can observe this tendency at both the cross-sectoral and sectoral level (Traxler, 1998). At cross-sectoral level, the principal employer peak associations of Norway and Ireland each amalgamated with their trade association counterpart in 1989 and 1993, respectively. In the mid-1980s, the Confederacao da Indústria Portuguesa transformed itself from a pure to a mixed organisation as a consequence for its incorporating regional trade associations. In 1991, Dansk Industri, a larger trade association, became an affiliate of the principal employer peak, Dansk Arbeijdsgiverforenining. Amalgamations of trade associations and employer associations at the sectoral level occurred frequently in Sweden.

These amalgamations have been driven by two reasons. First, the representation of product market interests and labour market interests have become more interdependent at national and EU levels. Second, mergers can help economize on resources and avoid duplication of efforts in interest representation. Since the 1980s, the member firms have increasingly put pressure upon business associations to do so, in response to intensified market competition which forces firms to curb costs.

As a result, mixed associations which have traditionally been most frequent have even more expanded during the last decade. This is remarkable because they organise the differing requirements for governing product market interests and labour market interests under one single umbrella. Coping with both interest categories relies mainly on three mechanisms.

The first one is the provision of selective incentives which may be positive or negative. Positive incentives reward members, whereas negative incentives punish non-members. Selective incentives thus induce potential members to join and comply independently of any matter of interest representation. This makes it also easier for mixed associations to process both product market interests and labour market interests. Typically, services – such as representation of a member in court proceedings or advise on matters related to collective interest representation – work as selective incentives if they are provided exclusively for members. Examples of negative selective incentives are legally-based compulsory membership and statutory extension procedures for collective agreements (see p. 163).

Another mechanism refers to the principle of subsidiarity. Accordingly, representational functions are carried out as close a level as possible to the individual companies affected. Under these circumstances, higher-level associations leave to lower-level associations responsibility for all issues relating to their respective interests, while the higher level itself concentrates on interests which extend beyond the specific areas of responsibility. The subsidiarity principle relieves higher-level associations of dealing with divisive forms of product market interests. This approach requires a very complex, multi-layered associational system. As cross-national evidence shows (Traxler *et al.*, 2001), peak-level business associations usually cover more hierarchical levels of interest aggregation than the corresponding union confederations.

Finally, an association may disconnect the decision-making procedures regarding labour market interests from those related to product market interests. An example is Austria's Wirtschaftskammer Österreich (WKÖ) which is a mixed association covering almost all parts of the business sector. When aggregating business interests at cross-sectoral level, the WKÖ's procedures for employer interests completely differ from those for product market interests.

Conclusions

The requirements for governing product market interests and labour market interests differ structurally, such that they constitute specific modes of interest representation. Regardless of this, their practical implications vary with circumstances. Leaving aside cyclical changes, there is a clear trend towards associational governance becoming ever more complex. This is due to such developments as growing interdependence of policy fields, specialization of firms, intensified market competition, and expanding inter- and intra-sector trade.

These processes make business interests even more heterogeneous. At the same time, they create a strong need for concertation. This in turn exacerbates the conflict between the logic of membership and influence.

Since these tendencies are difficult to reconcile within one and the same associational framework, they stimulate two contrasting responses. The first one is a proliferation of highly specialized pure trade associations. The very narrow range of interests covered enables them either to ignore the interdependences of policy fields or to selectively consider them without generating too much problems of unifying heterogeneous interests. Structurally, these associations travel light, with a very small, possibly subcontracted staff. As highly special interests are rather volatile, these associations are rather flexible and even unstable, all the more since informal alliances among businesses might offer an alternative to this pattern. The second pattern is the mixed association embracing a broader membership domain than that characterizing the first pattern. Mixed associations are well suited to deal with externalities and policy interdependences. Although the pattern places special emphasis on the logic of influence, this does not necessarily mean extending the scope of decisions that bind members. In industrial relations, the trend towards mixed associations has been accompanied by delegating certain bargaining tasks to the company level, within a framework of organized decentralization in almost all European countries (Traxler, 1995). However, since coping with externalities is a constituent goal of this pattern, the capacity to bind members will continue to be one of its essential properties. Furthermore, such capacity is a competitive edge in relation to the narrow associations of the first pattern, when it comes to negotiating over product market interests and competing for representational privileges.

The upshot is that the associational system of business is likely to polarize along these two patterns. What pattern will prevail in interest representation, crucially depends on the interlocutors' preferences.

Notes

1 Another criterion for the representativity of business associations is membership density, measured as the ratio of actual to potential members or, alternatively, the ratio of employees working in member firms to the total number of employees within the association's domain. However, data on density are difficult to collect (Traxler, 2000). This especially applies to associations whose membership demarcation crosscuts conventional statistical classifications.

2 Recruitment and compliance create distinct problems for governance. The willingness to join does not necessarily imply conforming to an association's goals and rules (e.g. dues payment) and vice versa (Traxler, 1993).

3 As a result, state-provided support for member compliance tends to blur the formal distinction between voluntary and compulsory membership. This is

most evident when associations use such support also for acquiring financial resources. In several countries (e.g. Belgium, The Netherlands), sectoral multi-employer collective agreements impose certain charges on firms which – via the statutory extension mechanism – also those firms not affiliated to the signatory voluntary employer association are obliged to pay (Traxler, 2000).

17
National Members and their EU Associations

Zygmunt Tyszkiewicz[1]

From the outset I must make clear, based on 30 years experience in business and over 12 as Secretary General of UNICE, that I have the greatest respect for business associations, whether at the national or the EU level. With minimal resources, they consistently perform miracles on behalf of their members and provide valuable services to the political authorities with which they are in contact.

UNICE, with its tiny staff (less than half the numbers of the equivalent Trade Union organisation) is well respected by, and has built up a constructive partnership with the European Institutions. It successfully defends and promotes its members' interests at EU level. One only has to look at the current work programme of the Commission to see that the agenda is a 'UNICE' agenda, pursuing competitiveness and innovation, the need for which was brought out so graphically in the benchmarking studies published by UNICE over the last three years.

As for the sectoral associations, on the whole they are well organised and provide essential professional expertise, often of a highly technical nature, to politicians and civil servants who could not do their work without them.

However, the theme and purpose of this conference is to discuss 'The Effectiveness of EU Business Associations.' So, we are not here simply to applaud what is right but rather to see what is still wrong and could be improved.

Most of the points I shall develop in this chapter are aimed less at the sectoral associations than at the 'horizontal' or multi-sectoral organisations such as UNICE and its national members, where the need for restructuring is, in my view, the greatest.

'Hypocrisy is a tribute which vice pays to virtue'

When the Duc de la Rochefoucauld wrote this in 1678, he must have had a premonition as to the future attitude of political authorities to the business associations which surround them.

Much hypocritical nonsense is spoken and written about business associations. I remember Jacques Delors, former President of the European Commission, when UNICE came out with position papers firmly supporting Commission policies, proudly declaring, '... and our policy has the support of UNICE, the strongest and most respected business organisation in Europe.' Yet, when UNICE opposed or criticised Commission initiatives, he would sometimes be heard to ask, 'UNICE?? ... Who is UNICE?'

In his speech of 6 April 2000 entitled 'Towards a European Civil Society' delivered at the second European Social Week in Bad Honnef, the current Commission President, Romano Prodi, said:

> ... if civil society is to play an effective part in European governance, we have to ensure that European policy initiatives are debated in Europe-wide fora. The media must be involved, obviously, but also trade unions, business associations, churches and all the various non-governmental groupings which make up civil society.
>
> An important question arises at this point: to what extent does civil society actually exist at European level? Are there Europe-wide trade unions, business associations and churches?
>
> *The ETUC and UNICE certainly exist, but they are federal groupings of national groupings and do not directly consult the grassroots membership they aim to represent.*
>
> Europe therefore needs much more wideranging and representative fora, and a system for using those fora effectively.

Such a statement indicates either extreme cynicism or inexcusable ignorance. I lean towards the former explanation. President Prodi knows perfectly well that organisations such as ETUC and UNICE are the closest Europe can ever get to a genuine voice for trade unions and companies at the EU level. It is only through such organisations that information about Europe is systematically communicated to the grassroots membership, where it is debated and analysed and the resultant feedback, democratically arrived at, is passed to the Commission. That's exactly what President Prodi probably fears. Such organisations cannot be ignored.

How much easier for the Commission to deal with some vast, amorphous and unstructured 'European Forum' which would provide the illusion of consultation without the need for the Commission to take any real notice of the opinions expressed. The fact is that most governments, including the European authorities, have always preferred to deal with weak and pliable business associations. They therefore seek ways to weaken associations that are strong, coherent and representative. The old seventeenth century maxim 'Divide and Rule' is still widely and cynically practised.

Associations of course know this and are realistic enough to accept that it will never change. The challenge for them is to resist politicians' efforts to divide and rule by becoming ever more united, well organised and thereby strong. I much regret to have to admit, however, that human nature being what it is, divide and rule tactics too frequently succeed, especially as regards business organisations which foolishly, often choose to compete rather than cooperate.

Characteristics of business associations

National business associations tend to be venerable, 'traditional' bodies. Most of them, whether sectoral or 'horizontal' (i.e. multi-sectoral) were created around the end of the nineteenth century. Some still preserve a bias towards manufacturing industry which at that time was the dominant economic force and by far the biggest employer outside the agricultural sector. Today, of course, that is far from the truth, with the Services sector now dominant in all modern economies.

President Prodi is right that many national organisations are indeed 'federal groupings' (though wrong when he says they do not consult their grass-roots membership), with individual companies joining together in sectoral associations representing the interests of their members on strictly sectoral issues. The sectoral associations, in turn create one or several national multi-sectoral associations to defend the general or 'horizontal' interests of business. In a few cases, these multi-sectoral associations also allow direct company membership, though the majority are composed only of associations.

The national sectoral bodies have formed their own European sectoral federations, while the national multi-sectoral associations have created the European horizontal bodies such as UNICE, UEAPME (SMEs), and CEEP.

Thus, we have national organisations over a century old as 'owners' of EU organisations created in the 1960s and 1970s. It is hardly surprising that relations between the two levels are still evolving, while the problems between them, to some extent, are similar to the problems between the EU institutions and the member-states, involving questions of sovereignty and resources.

The national associations are deeply rooted in their own local environment, where their Presidents, Directors General and senior officers are respected national figures, part of their country's 'Establishment', featuring prominently in the local media. They have close relationships with their national authorities, to whom they have privileged access.

Such people, who are well-known national personalities in their local environment, are rather anonymous on the EU stage and this, understandably, makes them reluctant to play a role at that level or to devote as much attention as they should to EU issues. Instead they tend to delegate such matters to more junior people who become highly competent specialists, but have insufficient authority or high level support to influence policy within their own organisation.

It is thus not surprising that many national associations tend to be inward-looking, highly resistant to change and reluctant to make the adjustments required in order to adapt to the new situation in Europe and in the world.

Finally, in a number of European countries the horizontal business associations are fragmented, with separate, often rival organisations representing, for example, – Industry, Employers, SMEs, Commerce, Services, State-owned companies, Chambers, Company Directors, etc., reflecting the historical divisions and rivalries on the national business scene, no doubt resulting from decades of successful 'divide and rule' tactics by the local authorities.

To their credit, several national associations have restructured in the last ten years thus improving their productivity and representativeness. However among UNICE's members there are still those who do not represent, for example, Services, or State companies, or Commerce, or whose representation of SMEs is challenged. In other cases, the old division between 'Industry' and 'Employers' still exists, leading to duplication and sometimes to harmful conflict. All this naturally weakens UNICE's claim to be the 'Voice of European Business', even though it is of course far and away the most representative horizontal organisation at EU level.

The new environment

Though I have no statistics to prove it, my guess is that Jacques Delors' prediction, made in 1985, that soon 80 per cent of the laws, regulations and policies affecting companies would be designed, debated and decided not nationally but at the EU level, has now come true. The single market and single currency are the main cause, but there is also a growing realisation that concerted EU action at world level is more effective than individual action by member-states.

More and more initiatives affecting companies are therefore now being taken not nationally but in Brussels. Furthermore, negotiation of binding agreements between Employers and Trade Unions now takes place at that level. Logically therefore, business associations ought to equip themselves so that their ability to influence the EU decision process and their capacity to negotiate with Trade Unions are at least as effective in Brussels as nationally.

Unfortunately they have been slow and reluctant to do this. Most EU business associations remain chronically under-resourced and thus ill equipped to perform the tasks demanded of them. Some, especially in the SME sector, have become unhealthily dependent on funding from EU budget sources, which calls into question their impartiality.

As decision-making power continues to shift away from the national to the EU level, it would be logical to see the national associations redeploying existing resources to enable their EU organisations to cope with the increased load of work at that level. That has not happened to the required extent.

Here I must stress that I am not advocating the replacement of national business associations by those at EU level. Far from it. Both remain essential for the effective defence and promotion of company interests. That can be illustrated by the simplified description of the EU decision-making process which follows.

The EU decision-making process

The commission stage

The process begins within the Commission which, under the Treaty, has the exclusive right of initiative. A civil servant is charged with the task of preparing the first outline of a Directive, a Regulation, a Policy or some other document. Confidential drafts begin to circulate within the Commission services.

It is worth mentioning here that in Europe, unlike in the USA, very few civil servants and politicians have any first-hand experience of business. Words such as 'competitiveness' have no real meaning for them. They are therefore quite likely, when drafting legislation, unwittingly to make serious mistakes which could be very damaging to companies and to the economy.

However, EU business organisations which are doing their job properly ensure they get invited, in confidence, to give their views and advice to the Commission already at this early stage. To earn that privilege, business associations must be seen by the Commission to be useful partners, able to help the legislators make better legislation, and not as negative forces bent only on preventing any legislation from being passed. They must also be seen to be fully representative, putting forward views that are shared and supported by their membership.

Earning that reputation is not simple. Business associations of course must cultivate close personal relations with key Commission officials. But they must also be well organised internally, so that they can respond in time and convincingly to the Commission's request for views. That can be most challenging, especially when, as is often the case, there are conflicting views within the organisation. Indeed, it is its ability to bring to the Commission a 'business solution' to a conflictual problem that establishes an association's reputation as a useful partner.

In addition, the association must earn a reputation for high quality, original research that supports the views it expresses. The capacity to carry out this type of pro-active work, which does so much to add substance to an association's views, is still sadly lacking at the EU level although almost all national associations have high powered research organisations working either for them or closely with them. (By contrast, the trade unions have a fully fledged research institute (ETUI) supporting their work in Brussels.)

This early stage in the legislative process is the most fruitful for business associations. Matters remain technical, in the hands of technicians. Issues are confidential and low-profile. Drafts can be amended with no loss of face and no political fallout. Business views are readily taken on board provided they are well argued, carefully presented and kept confidential.

Action at this stage is taken mainly at the Brussels level by the EU business associations, whose task it is to find out what is being prepared, to inform their members and mobilise them so that a common position is developed for transmission in good time to the Commission. All that sounds fairly easy, yet takes enormous effort and absorbs scarce resources.

The council stage

Once the College of Commissioners has approved a draft legislative or other instrument, the document is made public and sent to the Council of Ministers, which in turn directs it to the European Parliament, the Economic and Social Committee, the Committee of the Regions and most importantly to the Committee of Permanent Representatives 'COREPER', whose task is to work towards a final document for approval by the Council, mostly in codecision with parliament. The matter now becomes a subject for public debate, often of a highly sensitive and political nature.

At this stage, for EU business associations, the main focus of attention is on the Parliament and on COREPER. Both these organisations have the ability to introduce far-reaching changes to the Commission's original proposals. Yet they present two major problems for interest groups – COREPER works confidentially behind closed doors, so business associations cannot (officially) know what it is up to, while the Parliament is so vast, it is impossible for the average sized EU business association to cover it adequately.

That is a serious weakness because the Parliament's role in the decision-making process took on added importance following the Treaty amendments approved at Amsterdam in 1997. These greatly extended the list of subjects on which the Parliament has rights of codecision and thereby, is able to exert strong influence over the final content of legislation.

Action in this second stage must be taken both in Brussels by the EU associations and nationally by the local organisations.

The main tasks for the EU associations in this stage are to discover what is being prepared in COREPER, and especially what 'alliances' are being formed among member states, in favour of, or against the legislative proposals under discussion.

They must also contact and work closely with the relevant parliamentary Committee and its Rapporteur and mobilise their member federations in order to devise common positions and prepare an action plan on the issues under discussion. Finally, they must ensure that their views are communicated to the media, especially those most widely seen and read at the EU level.

The tasks for the national associations are to meet with their own Ministers, Civil Servants, Permanent Representatives and Euro-Parliamentarians, to lobby them on the basis of the common position defined in their EU level organisation, while drawing media attention to that position. Most importantly, all this must be done strictly within the time frame of the EU legislative process. Views expressed too late are of no value whatever.

The national associations play an absolutely vital role at this stage in the process, because only they and not the EU associations, have any political clout in their own country *vis-à-vis* their national Ministers, Europarliamentarians and civil servants. People often reproach UNICE because its name is virtually unknown at national level. Yet that is as it should be. The national organisations' names should be household words at national level, while the name of UNICE should be very well known in the EU Institutions.

The timing and coordination of actions at EU and national level is crucial for success but this is another weakness requiring attention. The reasons are that national priorities are very different from those of the EU organisations. Also at national level there is still insufficient understanding of the EU legislative process. EU associations have no authority over their national members. It is therefore very difficult to get their members to act in concert *vis-à-vis* their national Ministers, prior to a crucial Council of Ministers' meeting in Brussels where some decision of great importance to business is about to be taken. This is a failure to mobilise the potentially enormous political influence that associations could exert, if they acted together at the right time, on EU issues important for their members.

The future

As the European Union expands, so the need for more sharply focused, more widely representative and better resourced business organisations will become even more acute. This is not only because the tactic of divide and rule will be so much easier to employ when there are more member-states, each with its set of interest groups seeking the attention of the EU authorities.

That is important enough, but there is a more mundane reason. There are already so many organisations treading the corridors of power in Brussels that it is becoming a physical impossibility for the EU Institutions to give them all a proper hearing. The situation will worsen after enlargement. Nobody wants to create business association 'monopolies', but the need for consolidation, broader representativeness and avoidance of costly duplication is manifest.

Pressure for such change must come from companies. They finance the whole structure and often needlessly pay several times for more or less the same services. Without company pressure, national business associations will find it impossible to overcome the internal resistance and inertia that have hitherto delayed or prevented the required restructuring.

Actions required

Restructuring of national multi-sectoral associations

Ideally, while there can be as many sectoral associations as there are sectors, there should be only one multi-sectoral business organisation per member-state, speaking on 'horizontal' business issues on behalf of all economic actors in that state. With enlargement of the EU, this will become even more essential.

Where separate associations still exist, representing 'Employers' and 'Industries', these should be merged. The national multi-sectoral associations must be put in a position to represent the collective views of Industry, Services, Commerce, SMEs and of companies with State participation (provided these are subject to the same laws as private companies). They must be capable of reconciling internal differences, for example, between the users and the providers of services, and be mandated to act at the EU level, for instance within UNICE or in negotiations with the Unions.

Such broad based horizontal organisations already exist in a number of countries and have proved their strength and credibility at EU level.

Strengthening the EU level associations

With one or two rare exceptions, the EU level sectoral and multi-sectoral associations are too weak in terms of staff and finances to be capable of meeting the growing demands put on them by their members, by the EU institutions and by the continuing shift of policy and decision-making away from the national level towards Brussels.

The EU legislative programme is admittedly less heavy today than it was some years ago, when 300 single market directives were being put through the system. However, UNICE as well as various sectoral associations are now deeply involved in the 'management' of the single market and of other EU programmes. This means sitting on numerous committees or participating in activities covering a very wide range of issues where competent business representation must be assured. UNICE, in addition, must also handle EU level union negotiations.

What is needed is a quantum increase in the size of the budgets of EU associations, commensurate with the quantum shift of work that has moved from the national to the EU level. Till now, national associations have either ignored this problem or have only tinkered at its edges.

The EU level associations must also be given the capacity to carry out serious research in support of the policies their members wish them to

promote and to conduct other pro-active initiatives, such as conferences, seminars and publication of studies, through which business
views can be made better known, understood and accepted.

Having said all that, I hasten to add that I do not advocate increasing
the total amount of money that companies make available to finance
the thousands of business associations that exist today throughout
Europe. I firmly believe that the additional resources needed at EU
level can be found in two ways:

1 By redeploying money and people from the national to the EU level,
  in line with the shift of decision and policy-making power from
  member-state level towards Brussels. At first sight such an idea strikes
  fear into the hearts of national associations, but in practice, the shift
  of resources per association would not be huge, since the effort will be
  spread throughout the membership.

2 By restructuring and rationalising certain national and EU associations where there is still a great deal of avoidable and costly
  duplication.

However, such ideas will continue to be ignored unless companies
take matters into their own hands and demand action from the associations for which they pay.

One way to get things moving would be for a number of companies to
join together and retain a competent Consultant, whose task would be
to show how their money is presently spent, how much unnecessary
duplication exists, what savings could result from rationalisation and
how much should be reallocated from the national to the EU level.

Modifying the command structures

In the system that exists today, the EU organisations have no authority
to trigger action at national level. As discussed earlier, this leads to
frequent failure by national associations to act on time on EU issues
vis-à-vis their political authorities, because if national priorities get in
the way, action is either not taken at all, or is taken too late to be
effective. Ignorance of the EU decision-making process is also a factor.

Understandably, national associations do not want their EU organisations to become 'the tail that wags the dog'. However, just as member-
states have delegated certain authorities to the European Institutions, so
there must sooner or later be some change in the command structures of
business associations, allowing the EU level organisations, with the
consent of the national association Directors and Presidents, to impose
a timetable of actions at national level on major issues of vital concern
for companies.

It would also be helpful if the senior managers of national associations could be given short courses explaining how the EU prepares and takes its decisions, and why timely action at national level *vis-à-vis* Ministers, civil servants, Euro Parliamentarians and the media is so crucial to the final result.

Conclusion

National members and their EU associations, the subject of this talk, do a surprisingly good job, with minimum resources, in the defence and promotion of company interests at the level of the European Union.

However, much of their success is precarious, relying to a dangerous extent on *ad hoc* measures that cannot be guaranteed for the future. Much essential work is left undone and the political potential of concerted and timely action at national level is left unexploited.

It is now up to companies to press their national associations so that action is taken to restructure the national multi-sectoral associations, to strengthen the EU level organisations and to modify the command structures, so that the voice of business is consistently heard, understood and supported in the expanding European Union.

Note

1   The views expressed are the author's own and do not necessarily reflect those of UNICE.

18
How SMEs can Influence the Effectiveness of European Business

Hans-Werner Müller

Much has been written and said about the influence of associations and their representatives on political protagonists during the opinion-forming phase and during the legislation process.

This chapter, which is the extended version of a speech made in September 2000, however, aims to give an idea of how the European Organisation for craft and SMEs, based in Brussels, attempts to follow the European legislation process.

The importance of knowing both sides of the coin

The following description is mainly based on my political experiences in the national and European circles. My credentials in the political field are based on almost 20 years service as a representative in the German Parliament, as well as three years as a member of the European Parliament. In these functions I was always consignee of lobbyists' efforts, especially in charge of working in the extremely important field of the budgetary committee of the German Parliament.

As general secretary of the UEAPME at Brussels, the 'Union Européenne de l'artisanat et des petites et moyennes entreprises', I practically changed sides. Now I try to influence the different authorities of the European Community in order to support the legitimate interests of the enterprises that I have to represent.

General attitude towards lobbyist work

Many might have an emotional prejudice against lobbyist work, although the opinion and the comprehension of this term varies from country to country.

In my opinion the lobbyist efforts can be a valuable factor in the political decision-making process as long as the generally applicable ethical principles are being respected.

As it has often been underlined, lobby work is always a tightrope walk between having influence on the political decision-makers in a legitimate way and undue exertion of influence. Of course it is legitimate for the lobbyist to fight for my ideas and to present corresponding proposals, on the other hand it is and should remain legitimate not to take these proposals into consideration.

The necessary tools

The institutions of the European Community are a large and complex system. Therefore not only the knowledge of the decision-making processes is important for a successful lobby work at Brussels, but even more important is the personal contact. Everybody working within the area of Brussels has their own personal circle of qualified contacts that has to be build up in months if not even in years.

The secret of success in Brussels, as well as in most other aspects of life, is having the right contacts.

The role of SME policy in the European Union

SMEs' position in the international game

Concerning the SMEs, there are some structural exceptions that have to be mentioned in a fundamental discussion.

The organisation that unites the national horizontal organisations of craft and SMEs in Brussels, the UEAPME, has to be clearly distinguished from other organisations dealing with similar topics on the European level. On the one hand there are the representations of big industry interests' and on the other hand the European organised trade unions, who fight for the interests of the employees. Certainly there are often common positions, that is, with the consumers' organisations, but sometimes they differ completely.

At this point it should be remembered, that the big industry organisation has been involved in European affairs right from the beginning, as one big sector, the war industry, was the reason for the creation of the European Community of Coal and Steel in 1952. This was the foundation stone of the European community. And even the trade unions have always had an international importance, as their ideas have not been limited to national borders.

The small enterprises however, as their field of activity by nature is normally limited to a smaller area, discovered the opportunities and the importance of the European Community quite late.

To understand this it might be useful to describe the role of craft trades and SMEs in today's Europe, as SMEs are now the most dynamic economic actors and creators of employment of all.

The economic importance of SMEs

Of the 18.6 million enterprises in the European Union today, 99.7 per cent are SMEs. There are only 35 000 enterprises with more than 250 employees, but 18 million enterprises employ less than ten people – the microenterprises. The average European enterprise provides employment for six people, including the owner-manager. In the last decade SMEs were the creators of new jobs, while, on average, big industries have reduced their employment. SMEs are, thus, the most dynamic force within our economy.

The growth of SMEs was largely export-led as a result of the gradual increase of SMEs fulfilling their desire to trade abroad and of the expanding service sector, respectively. Turnover growth in SMEs between 1988 and 1998 has proved greater than in large enterprises. In general, 10 per cent of total SME turnover comes from outside national boundaries. Many SMEs are also acting as 'intermediate exporters', through their role of supplier of intermediate goods and services.

The reduction of inflation, and, moreover, economic convergence (particularly with the introduction of the Euro) have contributed to making business better for SMEs. Between 1988 and 1998 there has been a 15 per cent growth in the number of enterprises in Europe. Since 1993, microenterprises have also begun to recover from recession, and are growing at a faster rate than all other enterprise size bands.

The future of the European economy, as in the fields of electronic commerce, the information society, subcontracting, outsourcing and cross-border service provision, depends largely on the development of SMEs. SMEs are an important connecting link in the economy and to customers. Therefore, they are essential for the functioning of the economy and the local supply of the people. That is why the critical role of SMEs in European economic development and structural changes must never be underestimated.

The responsibility of being involved in the 'European Social Model'

SMEs could also be called the crucial actors for the success of the European Social Model. They have not only an important role in the economy, but also in society, and are at the nucleus of the so-called European Social Model. Owner-managers of these enterprises are, in general, more interested in the long-term development of their local economy, while shareholders and management are primarily concerned with short-term profit and boosting turnover. In general, SMEs are more responsible towards their employees and more integrated into local society. They play an important role in stabilising society and have a bridge-building function between workers and capital/equity owners. Therefore, many EU member-states have created a regulatory framework, which tries to secure continuity and quality among SMEs, as well as special schemes for vocational training and rules for access to certain professions. Other countries are trying to reach a similar goal through standardisation and certification.

For healthy and sustainable economic and social development, the right balance must be found between structural changes and dynamism, on the one side, and a certain degree of security for the actors in the economy on the other. Concurrently, modern economic societies need a sustainable combination of short-term market efficiency and favourable conditions for long term investments in capital, qualification and infrastructure. For this reason, the institutional settings and the regulatory framework play an essential role for the capacity to modernise an economy and to stabilise society. SMEs are affected to a greater extent by economic and social tensions and are therefore traditionally more sensitive to changes in society than big industry and capital owners.

SMEs as contributors to European cultural values and human skills

The role of craft, trades and SMEs as the pacemakers for stable and gradual cultural development in Europe for the last two Millennia should not be underestimated. That role in pacing sustainable change and preserving heritage and values attached to it must be encouraged and fostered in the new Millennium. Through flexibility, plurality, entrepreneurial thinking, ingenuity and inventiveness craft enterprises and trades, in particular, have helped create clear lines of cooperation and understanding as well as appreciation between different groups within society – races, nationalities, classes, sexes, young and old, and so on. The preservation of yesterday's culture as today's heritage and the building of tomorrow's heritage are the sole preserves of our enterprises.

Nevertheless until the creation of the Single Market, SMEs were not greatly affected by EU developments. It was a game for big industry and their representatives who were the key players in building up the European economic framework. Especially with the introduction of free movement of services and freedom of establishment, major steps in harmonisation and mutual recognition (e.g. in the areas of qualifications and standardisation), as well as the establishment of a common legal framework in the whole business area, EU developments and policies began to directly affect SMEs. As there was then no powerful representation for SMEs, the interests of big industry, employees and different member-states dominated economic and structural policies, but not principally according to the needs of SMEs. Since then, however, UEAPME has become the European 'voice' of SMEs and stressing their crucial role for the economy of the EU, for its competitiveness, growth and potential to create employment. This is widely recognised by policy-makers all over Europe.

Historical development of SMEs' status

If we come back now to the historic development the role of craft, trades and small enterprises took, it is obvious that their power was certainly underestimated during the period of economic expansion that followed the end of the Second World War.

The economic theories current during the 1950s and 1960s were all predicated on the virtues of the large enterprise, as already said above. It was not until the onset of the oil crises of 1973 and the resultant recession that it was again realised how vital the creation of small businesses was for the renewal of the economic fabric, and attention began to refocus on the many resources and aptitudes that are their strength. Notable among these is the speed at which they are able to adapt their production processes and a generally more placid industrial relations climate than that commonly found in the big corporations.

Although the Treaty of Rome made no provision for a Community enterprise policy, the 1980s were marked by a series of initiatives in the context of the 'Single Market' (White Paper on Community policies, creation of SME task forces in 1986 and adoption of an action programme for SMEs following the Council Resolution of 3 November 1986) aimed at establishing an environment favourable to Community enterprises, while promoting equality of opportunity for SMEs. The first action programme, in particular, established the legal and financial basis for the Community drive to promote small- and medium-sized businesses.

The possible starting points for an effective exertion of influence

There are of course many different political fields that are relevant representing the interest of SMEs. Over and above that in each of these fields there are varied processes moving on simultaneously. Because of that the possible initiatives taking place in order to influence are spread horizontal as well as vertical, concerning different political fields and different stages of development.

To give an example of the variety of activity fields within one political sector a quick presentation of the relevant enterprise policy of UEAPME could be informative. In 1999 a new European Commission was installed. Following this major upheaval, UEAPME participated in a round table meeting between EU businessmen and Commissioner Erkii Liikanen, who is responsible for enterprise policy.

For UEAPME, the new institutional structure of the Commission, especially the merger of DG XXIII with DG III, forming a new DG Enterprise seemed to be an opportunity for a new and better policy approach for crafts, trades and SMEs. At least it looked as if enterprise policy would now be positioned on the same level as industrial policy.

According to tradition, UEAPME's activity in the enterprise policy concentrated on what should be the core elements of EU Enterprise Policy. Examples are the access to finance for SMEs, the reduction of the VAT rate for labour-intensive services, the reduction of red tape both at European and member-states levels, stimulating the adoption of information and communication technologies as well as electronic commerce, the promotion of entrepreneurship throughout the EU, improving innovation, research and development, stimulating the internationalisation of European businesses, and improving the access to the Internal Market, which for most SMEs is not a reality.

UEAPME concentrated much of its resources in monitoring the developments of the fourth multiannual Programme for SMEs, Craft and Trades from the beginning and participated actively in the hearings organised by the Commission on this issue.

In the field of public procurement, UEAPME participated actively in the Advisory Committee on Public Procurement and was involved in the preparation of a Commission Communication on public procurement.

That should suffice as an overview of the varied themes which can be important and can be influenced by the representatives of interest groups such as ours.

The reader might ask himself at this point which political fields are the most important gain involvement, in order to structure effective lobbying work. The first answer is, that any policy area can become important, without exception. This is one of the reasons the work for the SME lobby is so interesting and varied.

But regarding the specific needs of SME representation, the most influential decisions are certainly taken within the economic and fiscal, the social, the legal and the vocational training fields

Can a definition of SME be found?

One of the biggest difficulties in talking about SMEs is that there is no common denominator for which enterprise should be considered small- or medium-sized.

The European Commission comes to a similar conclusion, trying to give a definition of SMEs in a report to the council in April 1992 (Doc.SEC(92)351):

> There can be no absolute definition of SME. The question of the appropriate definition of SMEs is meaningful only in the context of a specific measure for which is considered necessary to separate one category of enterprises from others for reasons of the 'size'. The criteria adopted for making this distinction necessarily depend on the aim pursued.

In consequence and in order to handle this problem and to make the term SME more tangible and comprehensible a list of a certain number of characteristic criteria has been developed.

As clues to identifying a SME, helpful criteria might be:

- Business that is owned and managed by the same person or persons;
- Close links between family and business;
- Personal involvement of the head of the firm in production;
- High input of skilled labour;
- Production structure with a strong labour bias, frequently associated with use of advanced technology, low capital intensity, financed

mainly from own resources in view of the difficulty of obtaining loan finance or risk capital funding;
- Preponderance of unit production or work to order.

The role of UEAPME in Brussels

As the result of the amalgamation of various European trade associations and organisations of medium-sized enterprises the UEAPME was formed in 1979. The full members which it represents are national trade guilds and SME organisations from all over Europe. More than that there are several associated members such as trade associations and support providing organisations within the European countries as well as, and this is playing a very important role for the integration of the candidate states, in the eastern European countries.

Since then the main objectives of UEAPME have become:
- To inform its members about development in European policy;
- To promote joint action on the part of the national organisations at European level;
- To ensure that the interest and views of its members are understood and reflected by the institutions of the European Community.

In this context, UEAPME tries to encourage its members to collaborate directly in its policy committees and facilitates the placement of national experts in events and meetings organised by the EU.

Up until now almost the totality of SME organisations of the 15 member-states and the 11 candidate states are members of the organisation and therefore UEAPME has become the perfect example of what is called an umbrella organisation.

Verified figures show us that we represent 10 million enterprises within nearly 50 million employees in Europe. If you consider that the EU has 370 million inhabitants and 18.44 million enterprises you see the importance and the representativeness of this organisation.

Problems to solve

Of course the European enterprises we represent have deficits. As SMEs they naturally have problems related to their size. They are often lacking in progress owing to the role of the owner-manager who is not only responsible for finance but also for personnel, for production and everything that is involved in running a business.

That is one of the reasons why they need somebody who acts as an intermediary, as a kind of mediator to compensate for these deficits.

This intermediary has to be available during the whole life cycle of the enterprise – helping in the phase of creation, known in technical jargon as 'start-up', assisting during the difficult periods and giving support initiating transfer steps.

The economic situation of a country, and that is same throughout Europe, could be compared to the health of a forest. A forest comprised only of a few large trees would be a sad picture. To have healthy forest, you need some young saplings and medium-growth shrubs. In an economy, just as in ecology, mono-cultures are doomed to extinction.

This brings us up to an important question. With the creation of the single market, having a common currency, which is already an economic fact, does the European Commission have to organise the enterprise policy, as such, for all enterprises, or has such as policy to take into account the specific need of a small enterprise?

In confronting ourselves with this question we come up against a huge current debate. Occasionally you can find the opinion that 'an enterprise is an enterprise' and so all enterprises should be treated equally. The UEAPME of course is arguing in a different way, as are the majority of politicians.

A small enterprise is not the Bonsai version of a big enterprise.

Daily lobbying and campaigning

A business organisation like UEAPME has to do lobbying and campaigning. For that it is necessary to be completely independent. It is not possible to attack the Commission for one or the other issue, decisions, and so on, and on the other hand ask for financial support. That does not exclude presenting projects concerning SMEs to EU institutions and realising these projects partially with money coming from the Commission. However, in general a lobby organisation has to be self-sufficient and self-supporting. When we speak about effectiveness we also have to speak about financial resources. Sometimes it is not easy to convince the national members that a European representation is useful and necessary. They cannot see either the added value or the possible output. In this respect there is a clear difference between an organisation with compulsory membership on national level and an organisation with voluntary membership.

Most things a small enterprise is able to do, a big enterprise can also do. Yet, the other way around it is not possible. That is the reason why in each European country after the Second World War, SME organisations have been created next to the organisations for bigger industries.

Of course, we have different forms of organisations in the different European countries due to tradition, history and so on.

Sometimes they are organised in chambers, sometimes in branch organisations or they find other forms of cooperation.

Nevertheless, all these organisations play an important role in the respective country as political-economic actors with each government, the Parliament and the other legislative and executive institutions.

In what way is it possible to influence the legislative process at European level, or, in other words, how do we ensure the effectiveness of this work?

The first issue is to find a common position about the different political themes concerning our enterprises, that is:

- From a legal perspective;
- In questions of environment;
- Concerning vocational training, public procurement, social issues and so on.

This work is done in the different committees and working groups as there are legal affairs, social affairs, vocational training, environment, taxation and more.

The next task is to set up common positions for our enterprises coming from Portugal, Iceland, France or Finland and all over Europe. In the further process we try to introduce our own ideas. It is our duty to provide the necessary information, as the civil servants of the Commission cannot know everything.

In Brussels there are currently around 350 advisory committees at different levels. UEAPME has identified some 50 of them that are having an importance in daily cooperation. Our staff have to be present when important decisions are taken and the role of our national organisations is to organise the impact within these committees. In the national organisations you find the necessary experience and know-how, as our secretariat at Brussels with about 20 employees cannot be more than a clearing institution.

However, it is fundamental not only to cooperate with existing organisations and structures, but more important is to close existing gaps concerning the representation of interest.

Speaking for the SMEs in particular two topics were urgent to address:

1 The first one concerned the interests of SMEs in European standardisation.

2 The second important gap seemed to be that there was no European organisation that occupied with research focussing on SMEs issues.

In order to unite the voices of the SMEs in these fields UEAPME supported the ambitious plans to found new organisations dealing with these topics, the NORMAPME for the first and the Academie Avignon for the second.

The NORMAPME

Because of their structure, and rare participation in the standardisation committees, craft and SMEs were rarely involved within the elaboration of standards.

As a consequence SMEs did not get the information concerning European standards until they were published as national standards in their own language, that is, long after their development had begun. This lead, inevitably, to disadvantages and to loss of market shares.

That is why the creation of NORMAPME, the European Office of crafts, trades and SMEs was necessary to concentrate and represent SMEs interest.

The Academie Avignon

As the experience showed, concept, content and realisation of an active craft and SME policy on European level also needed secure knowledge from the political decision makers as well as from the enterprises and their associations respectively.

With the establishment of the Academie Avignon the institutional framework for European cooperation in the field of research and transfer of knowledge in favour of craft and SMEs has been created.

The results of an effective lobby work

On European level UEAPME has become a strong institution, whose absence is now impossible to imagine. If the national organisations of SMEs are strong too, UEAPME can represent them in the most effective way. And conversely, if they are effective, UEAPME can even be stronger.

There are two considerations that should be kept in mind when working for a lobby at Brussels in general and for the lobby of SMEs in particular.

First of all a European business organisation has to have certain statutes. Such an organisation is composed of members, a General Assembly is convoked and a Board is elected.

This is the point at which the influence at national level is transposed onto the European level. In this way, the effectiveness of a European organisation is influenced. The second point is that policy at Brussels is highly influenced by social issues.

We have to be Social Partner to obtain access to the different consultative committees. If on national level our organisations play a role as social partner this will have an impact on European level. A recognised social partner has an optimal position in the consultative bodies.

UEAPME struggled long and hard to reach this position – the power to make this effort was taken from the knowledge that our SMEs needed help through and from an effective organisation.

19
The European Round Table of Industrialists: Still a Unique Player?
Bastiaan van Apeldoorn

Scholars who have written on the European Round Table of Industrialists (ERT) all argue that given its specific organisational features, this club of Chairmen and Chief Executive Officers (CEOs) of Europe's largest transnational corporations (TNCs) is quite a different animal from all established business associations (see, e.g., Cowles, 1995a; Greenwood, 1997: 110–13; van Apeldoorn, 2000). Still, 18 years since its formation, the ERT has become a very well-known and well-respected actor within Brussels, certainly an 'insider' within a number of important European policy areas. The question therefore arises whether over time the ERT has not become more of a 'normal' business group, whether it is indeed still a *unique* player.

This chapter will argue that the answer to this question has to be a qualified 'yes'. The ERT is still is a unique player in EU politics in several respects but it is less unique than it used to be for two reasons. First, activities of ERT, and its role *vis-à-vis* Brussels policy-makers, over the years have become more institutionalised, and with that more like that of established organisations. Second, and even more important, ERT's impressive success has to an extent made it into a model for both established business associations and for new organisations. The phenomenon of the Round Table is in fact, I maintain, a manifestation of a larger trend in which the evolving landscape of European business representation has become increasingly dominated by large, and increasingly global, firms and their CEOs.

This chapter is divided into three parts. The first part examines what in fact has made the ERT so unique. The second part analyses the institutional evolution of the Round Table. The third part discusses the rising dominance of large transnational firms within European interest representation and concludes that the ERT is in fact part of a broader transformation, which its own success has partly helped to bring about.

The ERT as a unique player: a policy-shaping forum for Europe's transnational business elite

I would consider the Round Table to be more than a lobby group as it helps to shape policies. The Round Table's relationship with Brussels is one of strong co-operation. It is a dialogue which often begins at a very early stage in the development of policies and directives.

Wisse Dekker, ERT Chairman 1988–1992 (*Europe 2000*, 1990: 18).

When European integration was at a low point in the early 1980s and many large European firms were increasingly exposed to growing global competition, leading members of Europe's business community began to perceive the need to for a European-level political initiative that was lacking from Europe's politicians. It was thus at the initiative of Pehr Gyllenhammar, the cosmopolitan CEO of Volvo, and with the support of Etienne Davignon, the energetic pro-business European Commissioner for Industry, that 17 industrialists of major European companies (such as Philips, Fiat, Olivetti, and Lafarge) came together in 1983 to found the Roundtable of European Industrialists (later ERT) with the self-proclaimed aim 'to revitalise European industry and make it competitive again, and to speed up the process of unification of the European market' (Wisse Dekker quoted in *Europe 2000*, 1990: 17).

Today, the ERT consists of 45 CEOs and Chairmen of Europe's most transnational and biggest industrial corporations, with members from all EU countries except Luxembourg as well as all major industrial sectors (from oil to multimedia).[1] The membership of the ERT is personal rather than corporate (and by invitation only), but the fact that its members together control such a significant part of the European private sector – a majority of the members' companies are Fortune 500 firms,[2] and a about half are amongst the 100 biggest TNCs of the world (United Nations, 1997) – of course helps to explain the large political influence that this group of people can command. Generally recognised to be one of the most powerful business groups in Europe (Gardner, 1991: 47–8), the ERT is in particular credited with bringing the completion of the internal market back onto the European agenda and thus with being one of the driving forces behind the relaunching of the European integration process (Cowles, 1995a; Fielder, 2000).

The ERT meets in a Plenary Session twice a year, but is led by a small Steering Committee of seven members, while its daily activities are coordinated through a small secretariat of Brussels. The Round Table seeks to provide an input into European policy-making through publishing reports, sending letters and communiqués to the European Council, but above all through face-to-face communication between the CEOs of the ERT and Europe's leading politicians and policy-makers.

Why the ERT is not an association

Although but one of many European business groups, the ERT indeed occupies a unique place within the EU's evolving landscape business groups in a number of respects. In particular, in terms of both its structure and its role, the ERT must be distinguished from other *cross-sectoral* European business groups, while at the same time also fundamentally differing from more sectoral, or individual (i.e. of single TNCs) business lobbies. As a *strategic* actor, the activities of the ERT transcend that of 'mere' lobbying, while at the same time it is also not an association of interest intermediation as is UNICE. Going beyond both the pluralist logic of lobbying and the more corporatist logic of interest *intermediation*, the role of the ERT is that of a forum in which the ideas and interests of an emergent European transnational business class are articulated into a coherent and long-term strategy (van Apeldoorn, 2000, forthcoming). Although the ERT is often put under the same heading as UNICE, namely that of the cross-sectoral business groups, the qualitative differences between the two organisations are striking indeed. Whereas UNICE is the official European federation of national employers' associations that as such has a public and formal ('corporatist') role to play *vis-à-vis* the Commission, and as a 'social partner' in the dialogue with the European trade union federation (ETUC), ERT is not an interest association at all. The ERT is a 'club of bosses', relatively small (to keep it that way there is a membership ceiling of 50) and with only little bureaucracy involved. In contrast to corporatist organisations, the ERT has no members either to represent or to discipline, in other words, it does not face the same kind of 'governance problems' that Franz Traxler discusses in this volume. As Vice-Chairman of the ERT, Gerhard Cromme, who formerly also had a leading position within UNICE, puts it:

> The European Round Table is a forum in which European business leaders meet (...) we are not an association, we are not an interest group (...) and we also do not engage in lobbying in that sense but

leave that to the relevant institutions (...) UNICE is an association of interest representation whereas ERT is not... [but is] a private gathering of people who discuss themes and then try to arrive at a common opinion.[3]

As many ERT members and associates emphasise (in interviews with the author), these organisational characteristics of the ERT give it a number of advantages over formal associations. First, compared to big cross-sectoral associations representing several 'constituencies', the Round Table has – lacking any formal responsibility to represent the whole or indeed even a particular part of European industry – less diverging interests to balance and can act with relative speed and flexibility. Consisting exclusively of heads of TNCs – the relative effectiveness of the ERT is thus in part a function of the relative (to other cross-sectoral groups) homogeneity of interests and the concomitant process of informal consensus formation on the basis of shared interests and a shared world view. Moreover, unlike UNICE which as the official cross-sectoral peak association has to react to the details of all proposed EU regulation, the ERT is free to 'set the political highlights' according to its preferences.[4] This freedom, or 'selectivity', is in fact an important justification for having an organisation like the ERT next to UNICE in the first place.[5] Within the ERT are the CEOs themselves who have the power to communicate what they would like to be put on the European agenda. As André Leysen, former ERT Vice-Chairman and formerly Vice-Chairman of UNICE, points out '[when it comes to] selling two or three points in a simple manner, a business leader can do a better job than someone who is mandated by hundreds of organisations and suborganisations, which is to say that he is in a "corset", whereas we just take the freedom to express our opinions'.[6]

Second, and following the former point, the fact that the members themselves *are* the Round Table, *and* that these members control Europe's biggest companies, gives the ERT a power that cannot be matched by any interest group in which that power is mediated through a bureaucracy of representation. The ERT has a privileged political access directly deriving from the power positions of its individual members, as is illustrated for instance by the following quotation from Peter Sutherland, now ERT member, but also a prominent former Commissioner (for competition) under the first Delors's Presidency:

I think that the importance of the ERT is not merely in the fact that it co-ordinates and creates a cohesive approach amongst major industries in Europe but because the persons who are member of it have to be at the highest level of companies and virtually all of them have unimpeded access to government leaders because of the position of their companies...That is exactly what makes it different [from other organisations]. The fact that it is at head of company level, and only the biggest companies in each country of the European Union are members of it. So, by definition each member of the ERT has access at the highest level to government.[7]

Third, and crucially, ERT's elite character allows it to play a more *strategic* and pro-active role, one that transcends lobbying or interest representation in a more restricted sense. The ERT does more than defending relatively clear-cut (narrow) corporate interests but rather seeks to define the *general* interests of transnational big business, that is, to formulate a relatively long-term and forward-looking strategy oriented towards the shaping of European socioeconomic public policies. As former ERT Vice Chairman, David Simon, explains, precisely because it brings together around '45 bosses who run businesses, they [the ERT members] will tend to take a more strategic view than an association...because after all that's what they're responsible for, they're responsible for direction and strategy. [The ERT thus] tries to concentrate on strategy and direction for the economy at large'.[8]

These three characteristics explain in part the *effectiveness* of the ERT in achieving its goals from the 1980s onwards. The influence of the ERT should above all be understood in terms of its *agenda-setting power* (Cowles, 1995a), or, at an even higher, more general level, in its capacity to shape the framework of ideas in which European policies are formulated. Next to the well-documented case of the internal market we can mention here ERT's more recent role in shaping the debates around European competitiveness, and indeed in making competitiveness the number one policy goal for European public policy, and in giving a certain content to that concept – linking it for instance to the promotion of labour market flexibility (see van Apeldoorn, 2000).

The institutionalisation of the ERT

When the ERT was formed in 1983, it was no more than a very informal club of businessmen engaged in a dialogue with the Commission about the future of European industry. In these first years, the Round Table was really in its 'experimental phase',[9] lacking any fixed procedures, and being run by part-time staff from the Paris office of Volvo. In 1988, under the leadership of the new Chairman, the then Philips CEO Wisse Dekker, ERT underwent a significant institutional transformation, marking the year 1988, in the words of a senior ERT official, as a 'watershed' in the development of the organisation.[10] First, as a testimony to the growing contacts between the ERT and the Commission, and the Round Table's desire to further develop these links, the secretariat moved to Brussels. Second, with this move the ERT also became a formal organisation – registered as an 'Association International avec un But Philantropique, Scientifique, et Pédagogique' under Belgian law, and was, moreover, from now on fully equipped with a professional full-time staff. The Round Table hired Keith Richardson for the new position of Secretary-General; a job which he held until the end of 1997, providing the organisation with a great deal of continuity that would otherwise be hard to maintain with a private club that has a relatively high turnover in membership. With Richardson as Secretary-General the ERT became a professional player within the policy networks of Brussels, developing regular contacts with the Commission as well as with other business groups (not in the last place with UNICE, through its then Secretary-General, Tyszkiewicz). Upon his departure Richardson was thus described by the *Financial Times* (8 April 1997) as 'the man credited with turning [the ERT] from something of a shadowy set-up into an effective lobbying force.'

Third, 1988 saw the 'merger' with another round table of European business leaders, the *Groupe des Présidents des Grandes Entreprises Européennes*. The *Groupe des Présidents* (GdP) had been founded in 1967 as a low-key discussion group of prominent industrialists from all EEC countries, and was regarded by the ERT as more of a 'dining club' than as a platform seeking to influence public policy. The merger, however, was important because of the resulting major expansion and *change of composition* of ERT's membership. The ERT from now on came to include many more 'global' (rather than primarily European) TNCs (such as Shell, Unilever, and later Bayer) whose CEOs also had a more global (and hence more economically liberal) world view, advocating a vision of a Europe well integrated into – rather than shielded from – the globalising world economy (on the further implications of this transformation, see van Apeldoorn, forthcoming). With this broadening of ERT's membership base, the Round Table also became much more representative of European transnational big business as a whole, rather than above all of those firms (especially from the car and electronic sectors) that were under heavy competitive pressures from Japan. This has most likely further enhanced its legitimacy *vis-à-vis* both the Commission and the national governments.

Finally, and partly as a result of the merger with the GdP, from the end of the 1980s onwards the ERT becomes more conscious of its role as a pro-active shaper of policies, self-confidently putting itself on the map of European interest representation (even if knowing itself to be different from other interest groups). As a former senior official of the ERT reflects on this redefinition of ERT's role in the wake of the merger with the GdP:

> I think it [the merger with the GdP] also led us to define more clearly our role, because the *Groupe des Présidents* discussed important issues, policy issues, but much more like a dining club, a good dining club [but] with the merger we sort of really thought: well let's define what the ERT should do, and we defined it really like an input into policy making, providing an input into those policies that are important to industry at European level. So it is *not* a dining club, we are there actually to influence what happens in the real world.[11]

The above quotation is illustrative for the fact that although the ERT on the one hand clearly distinguishes itself from interest associations like UNICE (and indeed, is correct to the extent that there is no interest *intermediation*), the ERT of course does speak for certain interests – namely those of globalising transnational business – and as such consciously seeks to shape policies. As such, into the 1990s, the ERT has transformed itself into an established player in Brussels, as well as in national capitals, maintaining regular and partly institutionalised contacts with Commissioners, national political leaders and with other business groups.

The ERT and the rise of a transnational business elite in the EU

The Round Table, as an organisation of CEOs of Europe's most globalised transnational corporations, can in my view be seen as exemplary of a growing trend in which TNCs, their leaders, and their organisations, have come to dominate the landscape of business interests in Europe. This rising dominance of the interests of TNCs has to be understood in the context of the sustained transnationalisation of capitalists production of the past 20 years. As this transnationalisation deepens we witness in particular the rise not only of TNCs as political actors in their own right and more broadly of what Stopford and Strange have called a 'privileged transnational business civilisation' (Stopford and Strange, 1991: 37; see also van der Pijl, 1998).

Within the field of organized interests, the logic behind the dominance of TNCs is an obvious one, they provide 'the resources, experience in political action, and status for collective structures' (Greenwood, 1997: 125). To this we may add the structural power of transnationally mobile capital itself. The globalisation process has enhanced the exit option of TNCs and thus their leverage over both governments and other socioeconomic interests such as trade unions. The phenomenon of regime shopping by holders of mobile assets is thus well described within the globalisation literature. Even if in reality (industrial) firms do not move across borders to the extent that some of that literature suggests, just the mere threat of exit can be sufficient for governments to try to create more favourable conditions for business. This structural power is also backed up by the sheer size of TNCs and their weight in the global economy, indicated for instance by the statistic that the 600 largest TNCs alone are producing more than one fifth of the world's real net output of industrial production, whereas about 40 per cent of employment in the industrialised world depends directly or indirectly on TNCs (United Nations, 1997). This clearly makes states and governments rather dependent on these firms and hence tends to induce competition (for investment) between them. The full extent of the power of transnational capital, however, can only be understood at a level that transcends that of individual lobbies, and is expressed in the collective strategies elaborated within organisations and forums of what can be called a transnational business elite, the members of which share a particular world view and in the pro-business climate of the 1980s and 1990s, have gained a prestige that carries far into the political sphere. Within the EU context, the political prestige that business leaders both enjoy and can confer upon policy-makers is for instance apparent in the frequency with which Commissioners cite the support (at press conferences) of groups like the ERT for their policy initiatives.

The ascendancy of TNCs and their leaders can be witnessed across the board of EU business groups. First, as has been documented by several studies (Mclaughlin *et al.*, 1993; Coen, 1997), the large (transnational) firm has increasingly become an actor in its own right within Brussels. Indeed, much of the lobbying now going on in Brussels consists of individual lobbies of Europe's large TNCs (according to Greenwood and Westgeest in this volume, at least 250 of them have public affairs offices in Brussels). Increasingly, formal business associations have also come to be penetrated by the interests of large global firms. In fact, the ERT was never the only cross-sectoral big business group active in Europe. The EU Committee of the American Chamber of Commerce (AmCham) – present in Brussels since the early days of the EEC – for instance has been very effective in representing the interests of its constituency of large US firms in Europe (Cowles, 1996). One important difference with the Round Table though is that AmCham is not a club of CEOs but of large firms represented through officials.

Significant also is the way UNICE has been transformed into a much more effective organisation, but at the same time one much more dominated by TNCs. As Maria Cowles has documented in her impressive study of European big business (Cowles, 1994: Chapter 4) UNICE's restructuring has been in particular carried out through the European Enterprise Group, an informal structure consisting of European-affairs directors from a number of European TNCs (partly the same as those in the ERT). The result has been that whereas in the early 1980s the top executives of Europe's largest firms regarded this peak association as slow, bureaucratic and not all capable of defending their interests (the frustration with which partly motivated the foundation of the ERT), they now view it a lobby force that although being fundamentally different from the pro-active ERT, still plays a very useful complementary role. Since 1990 large TNCs are directly represented in UNICE through the Advisory and Support Group while the chairs of its committees are also drawn from these ranks (Greenwood, 1997: 109). Indeed, in the 1990s several prominent ERT members have also served within UNICE. The most important sectoral organisations too have been transformed from 'Euro-groups comprised of national federations to organizations increasingly led by large firms' (Cowles, 1995b: 18). Thus, several among them are direct (firm) membership associations, such ACEA (Association des Constructeurs Européens d'Automobiles), whereas others – such as CEFIC (European Chemical Industry Council) – have a combined structure of national associations on the one hand and large companies being members in their own right on the other.

Maybe the most significant development in this context, however, has been the recent emergence of a number of less formal business groups modelled on the light structure of the ERT, with CEOs themselves being directly involved and exercising leadership based on their experience and prestige gained as members of a global power elite. The most prominent among these have been largely initiatives of ERT members. An early example is the Association for Monetary Union in Europe (AMUE). Amongst the core membership of AMUE we find many ERT companies such as Fiat, Philips, Siemens and Total, whereas prominent (former) ERT members such as former Vice-Chairman André Leysen, Giovanni Agnelli (Fiat), and Etienne Davignon are long-serving members of AMUE's governing board. A more recent initiative is the Transatlantic Business Dialogue (TABD), bringing together CEOs of leading TNCs from both sides of the Atlantic, mainly to discuss Atlantic trade relations with a view to promote further liberalisation. The ERT is itself not a participant in the TABD, but many ERT members are involved in its activities, and they are an important channel through which the ERT maintains its transatlantic links.[12] The TABD initiative has been welcomed and explicitly supported by both the US administration and the Commission, and the talks within the TABD have been credited with advancing transatlantic trade liberalisation over several difficult issues (Cowles, 2000). The most recent addition to the growing number of Round Table inspired forums is the European Round Table of Financial Services, consisting of the chairmen and CEOs of initially 12 European financial institutions (amongst which AEGON, Allianz, AXA, and Deutsche Bank) and headed by the first Chairman of the ERT, Pehr Gyllenhammar (see *Financial Times*, 2 March 2001). The proliferation of such groups, including even more informal and secretive ones, as well as the increasingly central role played by TNCs and their CEOs in more formal business groups, in my view clearly reflects the rise of a transnational business elite as a political actor within EU politics, a rise associated with that of the transnational corporation within the globalising world economy.

Conclusions

The ERT has always been regarded as unique amongst European business groups, and indeed, although representing certain interests, cannot be regarded as an interest *association* in the proper sense of the word. The ERT to a degree is still a unique player, in both the direct power it wields and in promoting the general interests of big transnational business at the level of the business leaders themselves. Although it has been said that the ERT has become somewhat less active in recent years, a recent front page opening of the *Financial Times* (20 March 2001) on ERT's letter of warnings and recommendations to Europe's government leaders on the eve of the Stockholm summit seems to indicate that the ERT is still a key player, working behind the scenes on a comprehensive strategy for the socioeconomic governance of the EU.

At the same time, 18 years after its founding, the ERT has become a very well established and institutionalised organisation, certainly no longer an outsider in Brussels. Moreover, through its very success, the ERT has functioned as a role model for both established and newly-founded business groups (of which some can be directly linked to the ERT). Business groups have thus increasingly centred their organisation and activities around large transnational firms and their CEOs, which have thus gained a leadership position in what increasingly is less a system of associational governance – that is, the representation of interests through (several layers of) formal organisations – and more a system of elite governance dominated by the interests of TNCs and their executives.

In this chapter, I have argued that all of this points to the rising political power of TNCs in general, which in turn must be linked to the ongoing globalisation process. To represent their interests, transnational big business need formal associations only to an extent. Often their interests are better served through more private forums like the ERT or through individual channels with CEOs representing huge economic interests communicating their positions directly at the highest levels of government. One may argue that formal associations in fact need the TNCs and their CEOs more than the other way around, they need their resources, their political power and prestige, the unique political access that executives and chairmen of these global giants have. Without their input and leadership, organisations like UNICE as well as sectoral groups would not nearly be so effective as they are today. No doubt then that the rise of large firms has enhanced the effectiveness of many European business groups. Groups like the ERT, UNICE, the Competitiveness Advisory Group (another ERT initiative, but one that also includes non-business representatives), as well as the TABD with respect to international trade, have still different but complementary roles and they all carry the same message, which is that of enhancing competitiveness through liberalisation and the freedom of enterprise. This is a message that was first formulated within and propagated by Europe's new transnational business class as organised early on within the ERT. It is this transnational business elite that has come to dominate the European landscape of business interest representation, reflecting a new logic of collective action. This has made the ERT less unique while at the same time being a testimony to its success.

From a critical perspective one may wonder, however, if business associations lose in representation what they gain in effectiveness as a result of being led by transnational corporations and Chief Executive

Officers. It is for instance questionable if UNICE is in effect capable of equally effectively representing the interest of SMEs as it does those of large firms. Finally, and although this is of course not the task of business associations nor the theme of this volume, I would like to end this chapter with the observation that the effectiveness and power of European *business* groups stand in stark contrast to that of labour and other societal interests. Almost all academic observers agree that from the mid-1908s onwards, the shaping of European policy-making by private interests has been rather one-sidedly dominated by business, whereas labour remains largely nationally fragmented. This could be regarded as another dimension of EU's so called democratic deficit, and thus as potentially undermining its legitimacy, and may thus endanger the interests of business groups like the ERT themselves.

Notes

1 For a list of current members, see ERT's website, http://www.ert.be.
2 *Fortune's* 1998 Global 500, see http://cgi.pathfinder.com/fortune/global500.
3 Interview, Essen, 4 September 1996.
4 Interview with senior German ERT associate, Brussels, 30 May 1996.
5 Ibid.
6 Interview, Antwerp, 21 May 1996.
7 Telephone interview, 27 January 1998.
8 Interview, London, 12 September 1996.
9 Interview with Etienne Davignon by Otto Holman and author, Brussels, 6 July 1993.
10 Interview, Brussels, 27 April 1993.
11 Interview, Brussels, 24 May 1996.
12 Interview with senior ERT official, Brussels, 24 May 1996.

Part IV
Conclusions

20
Globalisation and the Future of Associational Governance

William D. Coleman

This chapter examines the future of associational governance under the present conditions of economic and political globalisation and the growing internationalisation of policy-making. It begins by reflecting briefly on the meaning of associational governance and what is meant by globalisation. The analysis continues with an assessment of how globalisation is affecting the organisational development of associations. This assessment is based on answering two questions: (i) how is globalisation affecting the membership domains of associations? and (ii) how is it changing the environment in which associations operate? The chapter will then examine how the growing internationalisation of associations' policy environments is having an effect on how associations function. The chapter concludes by outlining six challenges that associations face, if they are to function effectively in these changed environments.

Associational governance

Governance may be defined broadly to include the totality of institutional arrangements that coordinate and regulate transactions inside and across the boundaries of economic sectors, including professions (Hollingsworth *et al.*, 1994: 5). Interest associations assume governance roles as intermediary organisations, a status that distinguishes associative action from other governing mechanisms like markets and states (Coleman, 1997). Associations act as governance mechanisms in the following kinds of ways:

- By defining and procuring public goods through organising and enforcing cooperative behaviour among their members (examples here might include arranging training schemes for members or setting up an educational facility or scanning for and compiling information).

- By engaging in collective contracts with other associations (examples might include setting up quality standards for products, collective bargaining).
- By securing delegations of state authority to be used to the advantage of their members (examples of this activity include various self-regulatory arrangements ranging from codes of conduct to designing standards, to certifying professional skills, to devising and enforcing rules for economic transactions).

In order to assume such a governance role, associations must reach a certain level of organisational development. A developed association is one that is capable of ordering and coordinating the complex range of information and activity that it is asked to assume by its members and by other organisations, particularly state bodies. Second, such an association is autonomous from its members and the state. It takes on a life of its own and is able to rise above the short-term, particularistic interests of its members. It can see what the long-term interests of its members might be and has the capacity to set up a plan to realise these interests over time. How then might the processes of globalisation affect the organisational development of associations and thereby their capacity to assume a governance role.

Globalisation

Central to the notion of globalisation is the idea of transcending of territorial boundaries, or of deterritorialisation (Scholte, 2000). It involves the growth of relations between people that are much less bound by territorial locations than in the past. In this respect, globalisation refers to *processes* whereby the boundaries and imagination of social relations become more autonomous from physical location, and time and distance become less of an obstacle to building human relationships in these new spaces. Individuals and the communities and organisations to which they belong become more *conscious* of the resulting changes in their social situation and place these changes in a global context. These globalising processes are economic to be sure, but also take political, ecological, military and cultural forms (Held *et al.*, 1999).

In the *economic* realm, we can think of some markets that seem to be truly global, with perhaps the most obvious example being currency markets. You can buy the Euro virtually anywhere on the globe, at any time of day or night, and all without leaving your place in front of your desktop computer. We are also familiar with corporations that organise themselves to compete in a global space. They view the entire world as a potential site for production and are willing not only to sell into any market, but also to produce at any site where the costs are right and the labour available is appropriately skilled. Politically, we can think of the WTO, particularly with its new binding disputes settlement mechanism, as a global actor whose political reach supersedes in some ways conventional territorial boundaries.

This capacity to transcend territory is linked intimately to the information and communications technologies revolution. As we are coming to understand, some rather special things began to happen in the realm of communications and information technologies in the early 1970s. The information and communication technologies revolution is centred on four key technologies that have gradually become more refined, more powerful and more interlinked: (i) the semiconductor transformed into the microprocessor; (ii) the computer; (iii) the move to digital transmission of information in telecommunications, facilitated by fibre optics; and (iv) biotechnology (Castells, 1996: Chapter 1). With these technologies, individuals and the communities and organisations to which they belong are much more highly likely to be able to transcend the constraints of space and time and thus are able to situate themselves more in a global context.

What is distinctive about these technologies, as the sociologist Castells (1996) reminds us, is that their raw materials are not iron, or petrochemicals, or grapes, but information. These are technologies that act on information. And because information is an integral part of all human activity, all processes of our individual and collective existence are affected to varying degrees by these technologies. For organisations like associations whose stock in trade is the gathering, organising, and exchanging of information, these technologies and their supraterritorial capacities are bound to be essential. In this way, the activities of associations may be more profoundly affected by these technologies than will their members, depending on what sectors are home to these members.

Globalisation and associational governance

In beginning to assess how globalising processes will affect associations, it is useful to remember that the organisation and activities of an intermediary body like an association depend on relations with its *membership* and with *key actors in its environment*. Schmitter and Streeck (1981, 1985b) have suggested two organising concepts for studying these relationships. First, they emphasise the importance of how an association defines its domain of potential members. This definition constrains the size of the association, the pattern of economic organisation and geographical location characteristic of its members, and its degree of sectoral specialisation. In short, the domain sets in motion a particular logic of organisation, the 'logic of membership'. Second, they take note of the environment within which an association acts on behalf of these members. Always complex, this environment is populated by various actors, of which the most important normally are state bodies. The characteristics of the state, including its own organisational capacity and its specific needs and objectives, have a further impact on the organisational characteristics of an interest association, an impact assimilated by Schmitter and Streeck under the concept of the 'logic of influence'.

As intermediary organisations, associations must accommodate the often competing demands of these two logics. Certainly, their assumption of governance roles in a sector is based on a set of conditions involving the balance between the logics of membership and influence and on the impact of this balance on internal structures for goal definition and implementation (Schmitter and Streeck, 1981; Streeck, 1989). What is evident nonetheless is that associations take on governance roles in the context of a broader institutional environment that favours dense social organisation around market allocations. Any assessment, therefore, of the fate of associations as governance instruments in the present era requires a consideration of the impact of increased global competition and its supporting neoliberal ideologies on such patterns of social organisation. Changes here, in turn, may affect the ability of associations to order and coordinate complex information and to maintain autonomy.

Globalisation and the 'logic of membership'

More international competition in global markets may alter the *logic of membership* in ways unfavourable to organisational development of associations. For example, it may encourage the rationalisation of production within the nation-state or larger economic regions leading to increased concentration of ownership and centralisation of production. Consequently, the number of firms eligible for membership in an association may diminish, the geographical distribution of production sites may change, and the very definition of the sector may broaden or narrow. Such revisions in the membership will have an impact on *the internal organisation of an association* and on *relations with other associations*. Members may see less need for collective action. Or mergers may follow, new information may need to be studied and learned, and internal procedures and structures may be redefined. These kinds of changes will also affect an association's resources including its funds, the quality of its staff, and its ability to draw on the expertise of its members. To the extent that these kinds of changes hamper the ability of an association to define collective interests, to coordinate with other associations, or to retain resources, associational governance becomes less likely.

Globalisation will affect an association's logic of membership still in another way. As noted above, the information technology revolution has had a profound impact on the accessibility and availability of information. It has also changed the nature of the information needed by many association members. As they situate themselves in a global space, and we must remember that there will be varying degrees in the extent to which this takes place across associations, their information needs expand and change as they develop a global perspective on what they want to do. Some information that associations used to provide to their members, such as government documents and other technical pieces, is now available readily on-line. Part of the old information gathering and processing function of associations would seem to be declining. In their place, members will require new sorts of information to permit them to function in a more global context. They will also face problems of information overload – there is too much information available and a surfeit of information can be paralysing. So associations may need to adapt by gathering new sorts of information and by sorting and organising information for their members.

Globalisation and the logic of influence

Globalised economic competition may have an impact on the *logic of influence* in ways that might also retard organisational development. The liberalisation of trade relations and financial markets has reduced the use of tariffs, quantitative barriers to trade, and controls on foreign exchange and interest rates. Domestic policy-makers find themselves with fewer policy instruments available for promoting or defending any given sector. Accordingly, individual states and regional bodies like the EU may be faced with very difficult questions about how to react to the rapid decline of a poorly competitive sector when the traditional remedy of higher tariffs is no longer available. Important for associations here is the fact that it has been in the definition and management of these kinds of distributive or regulatory instruments that government actors have often sought to involve interest associations. In other sectors, increased global competition may foster the emergence of supranational 'regimes' for managing the rules of the game. Not only must governments adopt new strategies for negotiating in these fora, but also associations must assimilate a new *definition of what governance entails*. The complexity of this new governance environment, in particular the diffusion of authority, may render more difficult the delegation of state authority that is often central to associational governance.

A revitalised commitment to neoliberal principles by state actors often accompanies the internationalisation of production relations and may bring attacks on associational governance. Such a commitment entails giving primacy to markets among governance mechanisms. Neoliberals have advocated less political intervention into markets and have attacked other governance structures whether associations, informal collusive practices, or excessive state regulation that restrain the 'freedom' of markets. These attacks extend, in many instances, to trade unions which are viewed as nefarious obstructions to the free development of labour markets. In short, the ideological changes among some national ruling classes that have accompanied globalised competition will affect the perceived legitimacy of associational governance. The general political environment may become considerably less hospitable to close working relationships between governments and associations and to cooperative behaviour within associations.

Generally speaking, this analysis would seem to suggest that the processes involved in the internationalisation of economic activity do not appear to favour associational governance. Rather, they promise to destabilise memberships, possibly to the point that the association may be forced into mergers or even defined out of existence. They favour developments in the policy process that may undermine cooperative behaviour between the state and collective interests. As cooperation decreases, associations will lose their access to some information, may cut back on their own policy research, and thus become less autonomous from members. Without this policy expertise and autonomy, they become less able to exercise a governance role.

The changing nature of policy environments

This apparently bleak future for associational governance does not take adequate account of the changing nature of policy environments. There is a future for associational governance, providing associations are able to understand how these environments are changing and the challenges they pose. Wolfgang Reinicke's (1998) work on global public policy provides an introductory look into the changes in these environments. He invokes the concept of internal sovereignty as his starting point. For Reinicke (1998: 56–7), internal sovereignty 'refers to the formulation, implementation, and maintenance of a legal, economic, political and social order that allows individuals to peacefully coexist and interact in a relatively predictable environment.' In today's modern democracy, it means 'the ability of a government to formulate, implement, and manage public policy.'

In his analysis of 'global public policy', Reinicke argues that globalising processes bring about a loss of 'internal sovereignty'. Traditionally, the operational capacity of governments to exercise internal sovereignty through public policy has depended on a considerable correspondence between the public and private spheres. Reinicke and many others have observed that as economic activity globalises, this correspondence is undermined. Political geography and economic geography increasingly fit together less well.

States can respond to the developing discontinuities between the political reach of nation-states and regional structures like the EU and thus their internal sovereignty on the one side, and economic and phenomena on the other in several different ways (Reinicke, 1998: 76–80). They can act *defensively* by maintaining or resurrecting barriers to globalisation through protective measures such as barriers to trade, capital controls, immigration restrictions, and various other regulatory measures. They can act *offensively* by striving to provide the most attractive environment possible for the strategies of global companies within their own territories or to lobby other countries on behalf of their own domestic corporations.

We should note, however, that the first of these strategies, defensive intervention, is increasingly difficult to pursue in a globalising context and can be very costly in all kinds of ways in the medium to long term. The second strategy can also be costly and does demand a particular kind of institutionalised relationship between the public and private sectors that is not available in many nation-states, and is difficult to develop at the regional level (Weiss, 1998: Chapter 2). In the face of these difficulties, we witness nation-states and regional organisations pursuing a third strategy of trying to *pool and collectively operationalise* internal sovereignty. Here Reinicke (1998: 73) suggests we are speaking of *competitive cooperation*, that is, a bargaining process ultimately resulting in cooperative agreements that define rules and procedures by which internal sovereignty is achieved and maintained on regional and global scales.

If we can agree to accept this argument for the time-being, namely that economic globalisation favours a globalising of public policy-making through attempts to pool and collectively operationalise internal sovereignty, then two other observations are in order.

First, the transformation of power and authority involved is leading to new centres of authority at the international and global levels that share some particular characteristics (Coleman and Porter, 2000). These centres of authority tend to rely heavily on *technical knowledge*, whether it be risk analysis in international finance, scientific and legal knowledge at the WTO, or macroeconomic theory at the G7. An important basis of power at these centres and a mechanism for including and excluding participants is this kind of technical knowledge. The possession of technical knowledge becomes a 'credential' for access to policy-making. In addition, in some of the emerging centres of authority, there are strong linkages with global private actors. Cutler *et al.* (1999) have recently edited a book on private authority in international affairs and noted the development of 'private regimes' as new centres of authority. Reinicke (1998: 89) uses the concept of 'horizontal subsidiarity' to capture the growth of these kinds of public–private relationships at the global level.

Second, consistent with this kind of structure and the strong presence of technical knowledge and expertise we find an overwhelming emphasis on 'effectiveness' in policy-making. If we want an analogy at the domestic level, it might be monetary policy and central banks. It is usually argued that monetary policy is too technical and too important to be left to politicians. Effectiveness must come first and hence the policy must be left in the hands of experts sheltered from the vicissitudes of the political realm. Similarly, then, when G8 Ministers of Finance speak of creating a new international financial architecture, their concerns are primarily in the realm of effectiveness and efficiency. This point is important because when effectiveness and efficiency are given overwhelming priority, then accountability and democratic responsiveness tend to be forgotten.

Working in internationalised policy environments

Two implications for associations follow from this analysis of changes in policy-making. First, associations will work less and less in a bilateral fashion with government departments and agencies and more in *policy networks*. By policy networks, I am referring to *a set of informal and formal interactions between a variety of usually collective public (state) and private actors, who have different, but interdependent interests. Operating in a more or less institutionalised setting, these actors are engaged in horizontal, relatively non-hierarchical discussions and negotiations to define policy alternatives, or formulate policies, or implement them.* Thus, more of associations' activity will take on this horizontal, negotiating character with various players. This policy style will be familiar to most associations working in the EU. It is gradually being reproduced at global levels.

Second, the policy environments in which associations will work will be *internationalised*. 'Internationalised' policy environments refer to those where at least some part of policy-making takes place at a more encompassing level than the nation-state or the economic region like the EU (Coleman and Perl, 1999). Thus defined, internationalised policy environments may be further distinguished using two criteria. First, some will feature more public sector activism than others. Public sector activism refers to the degree of direct involvement of politicians and senior public officials in coordinating activity. Thus private actors will take the lead in environments where activism is low, while politicians and civil servants will dominate in highly activist ones. The second criterion is the degree of development of distinct international institutions. In some environments, international institutions will possess a mandate defined in supranational law and a capacity to act that gives them an important role in governance. In others, the nation-state will retain control of international interaction and decision-making in the absence of autonomous international institutions. Using these two criteria, Coleman and Perl (1999) distinguish the four ideal-typical internationalised policy environments identified in Table 20.1. For the purposes of this chapter, three of these are more important namely multilevel governance (MLG), intergovernmental negotiations (IGN) and private regimes.

As Table 20.1 suggests, the EU and the international trade regime illustrate the multilevel governance environment. Institutionalisation at the international level is significant, with bodies like the European Commission, the European Court of Justice and the disputes settlement mechanism of the WTO having significant autonomy from nation-states. Moreover, these institutions are dominated by political not private actors. In contrast, the G8 features less institutional development at the international level and works through regular negotiations between members. Some supranational governance arrangements feature high levels of institutionalisation, but are governed through private

Table 20.1   Variations in supranational governance arrangements

Level of institutionalisation of supranational governing arrangements	Level of public sector activism in governing arrangements	

High	High
	Multilevel governance
	Examples: European
	    Union, International
	    Trade
		Low
		Self-regulatory and
		    private regimes
		Examples: global bond
		    markets, Internet

Low	Intergovernmental
	    negotiations
	Examples: G8,
	    Convention
	    on Biodiversity
		Loose couplings

associations or arrangements. Most notable here are global bond markets where the key actor is the International Securities Markets Association and the Internet.

The nature of internationalised policy environments has implications, in turn, for how associations function. These implications become clearer if we look at Table 20.2, which examines different stages of policy development and asks what kind of policy network is involved, depending on the policy environment (Coleman and Perl, 1999). I distinguish first of all between *national* and *transnational* policy networks. Furthermore, when it comes to transnational policy networks, it is useful to separate out *transnational intergovernmental* ones from *transnational expert* ones. In the former networks, governmental actors monopolise the membership, while in the latter, governmental actors are joined by persons and organisations who have some kind of specialised or expert knowledge.

What research has shown, therefore, is that the relative importance of these types of policy networks vary depending on the nature of the policy environment in which the association is working. If we compare the MLG and the IGN policy environments, transnational and national policy networks are involved in setting agenda in MLG, but national policy networks remain the dominant sites for this function in the IGN environment. When it comes to the design and formulation of policies, both types of transnational networks take precedence in the MLG environment, while national networks remain the most important in the IGN environment. Finally, when it comes to the implementation of policy, national policy networks remain prominent, but do share responsibilities more with transnational expert policy networks in the MLG environment.

The future of associational governance: challenges

If this analysis is valid, then we can draw from it several challenges that associations will need to address if they are to function effectively in the current globalising era:

- *What steps must be taken to influence national or EU government bodies operating in a global forum?* The key issue here is gaining access. If one is working in a MLG environment where an organisation like the WTO is involved, how accessible is it? How open are key committees to NGOs like associations? How transparent is the global institution? How does one deal with a lack of openness and transparency? In a way, the problem may be compounded when one is working in an IGN environment. Clearly, it will be crucial here to influence a national or EU governmental body participating in the negotiations. That said, these negotiations often tend to be more inaccessible than those taking place at a formal global institution.
- *How does an association exercise influence at the global level?* The global policy environment tends to be more chaotic, less consistent, and less transparent than policy environments at the national or EU levels. Does an association build up its own capacity for functioning at this level? Does it form a confederation with other national and EU associations seeking influence at this level on behalf of a given sector or profession? Or is it better to avoid this confederation model and to leave it to individual corporations or persons, whose interests are most profoundly affected by global developments, to form a distinct, direct membership organisation.
- *How does an association compile the expertise and technical knowledge necessary for influence at supranational levels?* As this chapter has emphasised, technical knowledge and expertise are important currencies of exchange for influence in internationalised policy environments. How do associations come by the necessary expertise? Do they build it up in-house? Do they develop an organisational strategy for tapping members for expert knowledge when it is needed? Do they contract out to consulting firms or to think tanks for the knowledge?
- *How does an association decide what information is crucial for its own effectiveness and for its members?* This chapter has also stressed that information is a crucial resource both for associations and for their

Table 20.2 International policy environments, policy community types, and the policy process: rank order of importance

Stages of policy Development/type of internationalised policy environment	Definition, discussion and selection of policy options	Formulation of policies	Implementation of policies
Multilevel Governance	TN and National Policy Communities all involved	1. TN-intergovernmental 2. TN-Expert 3. National	1. National and TN-expert equally involved 2. TN-intergovernmental
Intergovernmental negotiations	1. National 2. TN-Expert	1. National 2. TN-Expert	1. National 2. TN Expert
Private regimes	TN	1. TN 2. National	1. TN 2. National
Loose couplings	TN	Temporal participants in a transnational issue network	Loosely linked local issue niches

TN denotes Transnational.

members in the current environment. There is a tremendous amount of information available, only some of it useful for these purposes. How does one construct the filters to get the information one needs? How does one search out the information that is crucial, but perhaps not obviously available?

- *How do associations set up procedures for scanning events and for information at national, regional and global levels?* As we have seen, globalisation is more than an economic process. It involves important changes in how associations and how their members situate themselves. Many corporations and professionals are thinking of themselves as operating in a global space just as much as a traditional national space. As they take on this more global orientation to what they are doing, they will be doing different kinds of things, develop new needs, give less emphasis to traditional needs, and be searching for new kinds of information. Associations will have to adjust their own scanning procedures for meeting the changes in the needs of their members.

- *What are best practices for working collaboratively with other associations?* As noted above, horizontal, collaborative forums where a range of associations and government actors contribute to agenda-setting, policy design and policy implementation are becoming more and more common. Policy advocacy thus will differ from that found in traditional bilateral exchanges with government agencies and other state bodies. These new horizontal forums involve strategic bargaining and working together to solve problems. Operating in these environments requires particular skills and knowledge.

- *What new opportunities exist for governance roles that might not have been available before?* Of particular importance here may be the internationalised policy environments termed 'private regimes'. What distinguishes private regimes from the MLG and IGN policy environments is the relative absence of state institutions. This governance path might be taken by sectors of the economy that have globalised very quickly, sufficiently quickly that nation-states cannot keep up to the process nor exercise significant control over what is happening. The path might also be taken by sectors where state regulation has been rather weak at the nation-state level. We move to private regimes rather than 'loose couplings' when the concentration of economic power in corporate actors appears to be quite high.

There is reason to believe that private regimes may occur more frequently at global levels than they will at the national or EU levels.

There is no world government, there is no equivalent of the European Commission operating at the global level. What do we find is a great variety of institutional arrangements, most of which featuring less involvement by state bodies and less governance authority and power than are found at the national level. This environment therefore can take on a certain anarchic character. Anarchy is healthy sometimes, but economically destructive at others. Usually, some kinds of rules for economic activity are necessary. In the absence of state or governmental bodies, these functions may be filled by associations or alliances of associations that set up codes of conduct or other self-regulatory mechanisms. These opportunities will be available for many associations.

In summary, the future of associational governance in this globalising era may very well lie in how well associations meet these kinds of challenges.

21
Conclusions
Justin Greenwood and Alfons Westgeest

A 'scientific' conference is designed for exploration, debate, and development of the subject matter, with individual participants free to put forward and test their own ideas rather than to conform to a common research design, or a common set of approaches. The papers selected from the conference are presented in this spirit, although each was conceived, selected and grouped so as to address a particular theme. The first set of papers addressed factors in the environment of EU business associations that cause variation in their abilities to unify their members interests and secure compliance with common goals. The second set of papers addressed factors of change, and case studies in managing change. The third group examined the special position of cross sectoral and employers organisations, while the contribution by Bill Coleman joins this chapter as a concluding one. This final chapter, seeking to bring together the main issues raised by the different chapters presented here, is the only one in the collection that was not presented at the conference itself.

The uniqueness of this exercise has been to bring together a group of practitioners with academic analysts to examine EU business associations. This is the first book collection dedicated to the subject, and a rare combination of authors. Inevitably, the different styles evident from the different chapters reflect our different orientations and traditions and backgrounds, yet by and large we have met our original challenge to communicate with each other.

The narrow scope of EU business associations

In his environmental analysis, Bennett counsels us to understand associations through the motivation and dynamics of their membership. Most EU business associations were established by their members (or an entrepreneur) to undertake political representation, and networking, functions and all the activities these entail. Despite developing some-way beyond the *comités de liaison* function that many started life as, most EU business associations still undertake a much narrower range of functions than those undertaken by national associations. Hollings-worth *et al.* reflect that:

> In all modern economies, companies have associated with each other to collect information about production levels and prices, to conduct joint research and development, to promote standardization, to engage in technology transfer and vocational training, to channel communication and influence to state agencies, to formulate codes of conduct, to negotiate with labor, and even to decide on prices, production goals, and investment strategies.
>
> (1994: 7)

While there are exceptions, EU business associations do not have significant resources devoted to functions such as training, export pro-motion, research and development or technology transfer, or to the economic development of their constituencies. They are also limited by EU, national and international competition policy in the tasks they can undertake. Whereas many national associations arose historically in response to the needs of their members to manage competition,[1] such a task is now completely outlawed under modern EU law. That is, there are limitations to the value that EU business associations can add to their members by moderating the forces of competition. Their efforts in addressing competition issues are focused on political decision-making, either in seeking regulation to mitigate the effect it has on member interests, or in opposing it. EU regulation is a product of a wider agenda of 'deregulation', yet deregulation requires a system of rules, or reregula-tion, to govern market exchange and promote competition and the free flow of goods and services in the EU. In this way, 'deregulation' distri-butes costs and benefits, but where these are distributed narrowly then a typical outcome is competitive interest group politics (Wilson, 1995). As remarked in our introductory chapter, this is both a source of, and a curse for, EU business associations.

A further consequence of the narrow remit of EU business asso-ciations is that they do not need to develop a comprehensive range of special incentives in an effort to attract members. While national associations devote a good deal of their energies to recruiting members who may not be particularly interested by their political environment,

EU associations draw from a constituency of members who, by and large, are already politically active. That is, EU business associations were established by members in order to fulfil their needs for political representation and networking at the EU level, and in consequence there has never really been a need to provide these members with a wider range of services. As was argued in Chapter 1, participation in EU business associations is often normal political behaviour, or 'habit', and rarely involves undertaking a 'cost-benefit' calculation. By and large, subscribing members are either associations of national associations, whose *raison d'être* is collective action and who need no special appeal, or large firms who are well able to look after themselves and do not need special membership incentives such as access to discounted business services. This is not to say that 'incentives' are absent, but they are of a different kind, often based around the *costs of non-membership* identified in Chapter 1. That is, for most members a 'choice' doesn't really arise; participating is something that has to be undertaken. As a speaker at the conference, Hanns Glatz from DaimlerChrysler remarked, 'there is hardly any corporation that does not participate in a number of business associations' (Glatz, 2001). This speaker went on to remark that 'business is obliged to develop basic common positions' because of the pressure placed by EU institutions to work through associations (ibid). In the circumstances that participation is more or less obligatory, member pressures to develop their associations are not the top priority.

There are other factors that lead to low membership pressure for associational development. Members have avenues of EU public affairs management other than their associational affiliations. The fragmented power structure of the EU means that each and every one of them has a number of 'channels' to choose from, ranging from those in member-states to those in Brussels. These choices often vary on an issue by issue basis, partly dependent upon the particular EU decision-making instruments in force. Some members have the resources to invest in their own public affairs presence in Brussels, and are large enough to have their own direct routes to the corridors of power. Maria Green Cowles makes the point in her contribution to this volume that under these circumstances, members are bound to 'by-pass' their associations, and the lack of dependence by members upon their associations similarly means that there will be a lack of corresponding pressure for associational development. Bennett's work presented in Chapter 2 suggests that these types of influences are likely to be most prevalent where there are large corporate businesses in small associations.

Chapters by Coleman, Boléat and Timmerman all point to how the process of mergers and acquisitions raise challenges for associations. The first two of these authors also make the point that there may be a wider trend of reduced dependence upon associations, heralded by the IT revolution, where association members are easily able to access information direct that at one time was supplied to them by their association. If associations believe that the need for information is one of the key factors that keeps their organisation together, the conclusion may be that the association needs to concentrate its efforts on the informal information sources that networking brings. The loss of potentially vital information is clearly one of the major factors in the cost of non-membership calculus, and the quality of the network on offer may well be an issue of increasing importance for formal associations. Here, too, there are potential competitors, in the form of the plethora of informal network clubs in Brussels that have grown up around corporate and association public affairs managers. In response, some associations in sectors affected by these have tried to increase the number of social opportunities for their members in the hope that enhanced familiarity and trust between members might help cohesion. While trust can be a key glue of associations, it cannot be artificially produced, or manufactured too quickly, but in trying to do just these things, some associations have fallen foul of Boléat's advice to avoid the trap of being seen as 'tourism organisations'.

This raises the wider question, once more, of what members use their associations for. The external environment factors that cause variation were extensively reviewed in the papers grouped together in the first section of this collection. In some cases, the association is the mainstay of public affairs management for members, or a very significant part of it. A symptom of this level of commitment is the degree of people resources that companies often contribute to the association. At the conference, Jan-Peter Huges, from Akzo Nobel, recounted how at any one time the company for which he works has 70 people involved in meetings inside CEFIC (Huges, 2000). But in other cases, the *cost of non-membership* motivation leads the member to deliberately seek a low profile association, particularly in sectors where it is likely to be routinely difficult for members to find common positions. If the member motivation is thus, there will hardly be a pressure for associational development, and this appears to be at the root of some of the problems in service sectors described by Irina Michalowitz. Bennett suggests that these tendencies are likely to be greatest in small associations organising large firms, and brings to our attention the useful observation from elsewhere in the literature on associations that large firms seek both involvement and control.

Hans-Werner Müller provides some confirmation for this perspective by coming to it from the opposite starting point, in that associations representing smaller firms lacking the means to find alternatives are less challenged by this problem. While 'size matters', as the latter author argues, so to do the factors of variation identified in the first section of this collection, on 'understanding the environment'. For instance, some sectors may contain such a variation by firm size that there are completely different interests at stake, with large firms seeking to use the association to achieve liberalisation, and medium-sized firms most at risk from the competition seeking protectionism. In such circumstances, the best that can be done is for each party to prevent the other from gaining the upper hand. As Irina Michalowitz remarks, associations facing these circumstances can never be 'effective'.

While the EU is a competitive public affairs environment, the competition is mainly between specialist interests, rather than between associations competing for members. The landscape of EU associations is highly fragmented and specialised, and directory readings can yield amusing examples, such as the natural sausage casing manufacturers' association. In some product areas, there are highly specialised associations representing subsectors, such as glass. Here, there are specialised associations representing the interests of firms producing container glass, flat glass, glass fibres, technical glass, cut glass, as well as a standing committee of the glass industries. Apart from smart puns about the glass industry being fragmented, the example, which is not uncommon, yields the serious point that the overall impact of business in EU public affairs can be reduced by its organisation into sometimes competing specialisms in the product chain, or in business areas. While Oliver Blank provides an interesting case study that appears to buck the trend of specialism (Chapter 11), the main factor responsible seems to be more the changing sense of sectoral definition as a result of merging technologies in the IT and telecoms domains, than member demands for greater breadth.

All associational systems are subject to the competing tensions of the logic of membership on the one hand, and the logic of influence on the other (Streeck and Schmitter, 1981). The first of these, *the logic of membership*, encourages members to work in small number associations organised around a very narrow specialism, because these features make it easy for them to reach common positions, while each member gains a relatively higher share of the cake of any 'lobby achievements' (Olson, 1965). The second, *the logic of influence*, encourages broader, more encompassing associations in order to satisfy the requirements of public authorities for policy making, and to avoid competing positions being articulated in public policy. While each of these influences is present in the EU, the logic of membership is stronger in political systems that lack the ability to act as patrons for (i.e. to 'licence') associations, in the manner described in our introductory chapter to this volume. In the case of the EU, its fragmented power structure is once again at the root of this problem, producing a disjointed landscape of (often competing), specialist associations that weaken the overall impact of business in EU public affairs. Added to the 'associational by-pass' created by the same issue of a fragmented power structure and multiple access points, this creates quite a problem. In his chapter, Zygmunt Tyszkiewicz notes how EU institutions can take advantage of this competition through 'divide and rule' tactics, either between competing associations, or between competing interests within associations. He also remarks that 'it is becoming a physical impossibility for the EU institutions to give them all a proper hearing', and plausibly projects an exacerbation of the problem after enlargement.

This specialisation can result in the colonisation of specialist 'issue niches', where an association (as opposed to an informal network) is organised not around a subsector, but a highly specialised issue. This might be a cross-sectoral issue in the product chain (such as AIM, the European Brands Association), or it might be a sectoral specialism (such as ACE, Action on Cartons and the Environment). Beyond this, it might be part of a process of mutual accommodation between associations, whereby associations occupy to avoid competing with one another. Hanns Glatz, speaking from his position as the public affairs manager of a major German-American company, also remarked in his presentation that 'there are hardly any private business associations that compete for customers, as it is usual in the US' (Glatz, 2001). Associations can acquire a reputation for specialising in a particular issue, and associations with otherwise potentially similar interest constituencies can avoid competing for members. This work is most closely associated with the work of Browne, who argues that:

> An organised interest, in effect, gains a recognizable identity by defining highly specific issue niches for itself and fixing its activities within that niche...various organised interests within a policy domain accommodate one another, usually by focusing on their own increasingly narrow demands.
>
> (Browne, 1990: 502)

Similarly, Schmitter argues that:

> associations may appear to have defined their domains in ways that imply competition while in practice coming to less obtrusive arrangements under which they agree not to try to lure away each other's members or to share key resources and even leaders or to engage in a subtle division of labour *vis-à-vis* potential interlocutors.
>
> (Schmitter, 1992: 441).

Is associational autonomy the key?

In consequence of their degrees of specialisation, and their narrow range of functions, EU business associations have a smaller resource base than do national associations. While some of the associations led by authors in this collection have relatively substantial levels of resources (see, particularly, the contributions by Bulteel and Devos), even the most well endowed of these have fewer resources than do their larger members. Beyond these clutch of top associations, resources get thinner still. In his chapter, Zygmunt Tyszkiewicz observes that 'most EU business associations remain chronically under resourced and thus ill equipped to perform the tasks demanded of them.' Data collected by Greenwood in the mid-1990s, drawn from a postal questionnaire among 224 associations indicated a median secretariat size of 3–3.5 full time equivalent staff. Seven per cent (15) of this sample had no staff at all, while 20 per cent (30) had a turnover of less than €20 000 (Greenwood, 1997). In these latter organisations, there is no prospect whatsoever that an association can develop a monopoly of expertise upon which its members can be dependent, or internal specialisation by function which is a starting point for the development of such expertise.

Wyn Grant performs an invaluable role in this collection in making available a common heritage of research on associations in national contexts undertaken in an earlier era. One of the key points he summarises is that associations charged with narrow functions (such as EU associations) also have income streams that are over dependent upon member subscriptions, and lack the independent streams they need to develop their own expertise. 'In summary', he concludes, 'a less developed association is likely to be reactive; a more organisationally developed association is likely to be pro-active.'

There are of course innovative models in which associations without any staff or premises can work very well, and one example is provided in the chapter by Christophe Lecureuil and Simon Ward, which generated a lot of interest at the conference. Zygmunt Tyszkiewicz opens his chapter with the observation that 'with minimal resources (EU business associations), consistently perform miracles on behalf of their members.' But there is a danger that a low level of resourcing creates both instability, a point Franz Traxler makes in his chapter, and an over dependency by associations upon their members for resources. As a consequence of this latter problem, many EU business associations lack the key quality of autonomy that predicts associational strength. Philippe Schmitter sums up the point nicely:

> Effective associations need to be resourceful and autonomous to define and sustain a course of action over the long run that is neither linked exclusively to the immediate preferences of their members nor dependent on the policies or partners and agencies external to their domain.
>
> (Schmitter, 1992: 438–9)

In his chapter, Rudolf Beger, who has himself bravely walked this tightrope, notes a general unwillingness for members to assign the necessary autonomy that EU associations need, and sees this as the principal cause of the 'lowest common denominator' problem. A senior Commission official in DG Enterprise recounted at the conference how one EU business association manager came to a meeting and said he could not talk with them as he had been mandated not to cooperate (White, 2000). Beger's remedy for this problem, borne of his own experiences, is unequivocal:

> A modern association management must lead its members rather than do what it perceives as what the member companies 'really want' or what they have been told by their members. They must feel responsible for bringing their members' commercial goals into line with their own strategic political vision and with societal expectations. To be able to do this, a business association management must have the independence, the courage and the intellectual political abilities to do this difficult job. This requires strong personality and strength, credibility internally and externally, with the communication target groups and political vision.

Bill Coleman's description of a 'policy capable association' in the preceding chapter shows just how far the association in David White's example is from this ideal. In one of his earlier contributions to the subject, he reflected that:

> as a participant in policy-making, it (the policy capable association) is more that the sum of the interests of one or the other. It takes on a life of its own and is able to rise above the short-term, particularistic interests of its members. It not only can see beyond, to the medium and longer term, it can define for its members what their interests are within this broader perspective.
>
> (Coleman, 1988: 51)

To be able to undertake this delicate task, an EU association needs to avoid capture by any one specialised interest, to exceed its members appreciation of EU public affairs, to have an independent supply of resources of funding and expertise, a decision-making structure which provides insulation from control by any one member, and highly skilled leadership. This is a rare combination indeed, but those who have these qualities, in conjunction with the environmental factors that favour collective action identified in our introductory chapter, appear to have the winning formula.

Developing autonomy by design

Factors such as the growing interdependence of policy fields, specialisation of firms, intensified market competition, and expanding inter- and intra-sector trade, lead Traxler to detect a clear trend towards associational governance becoming ever more complex. Yet there are a number of features that can be addressed by associational design in an attempt to manage this complexity and to maximise cohesion. Traxler draws our attention to the different procedures that some national associations have developed to process different interests, and in particular those between employer, and product market interests. Here, the lesson seems to be the capacity of the association for differentiation of its functions, and specialisation. At a practical level, this is once again about resources. Over time, a number of associations have sought to address their lack of resources by admitting large firm members directly. This can help in spreading influence where such firms exist alongside national association members, but where the association becomes a representative only of company members, so it is possible that a small number of large members will come to dominate.

To avoid this problem, associations need to insulate themselves by design, such as spreading affiliation fees, and voting influence between members. This is a very delicate balance to achieve, although the tripartite structure described by Devos appears to meet the criteria, including the use of a constitutional spread in the weighting of votes. Although very few associations vote much, the presence of qualified majority voting rules concentrates the minds of members, and governs their tactics, in coming to collective decision making. However, if the votes are spread too thinly, the large firm members, who expect to have more influence over the work of the association than their smaller brethren, may pose a threat of exit. In order to avoid this, there is either a constitutional link between firm size, affiliation fees, and votes carried, or an informal trade off between large firm, and small firm, members whereby the former agree to bankroll the association in return for more influence. The challenge is to provide this weighting of influence towards those who provide the lion's share of resources, without making the association too dependent upon any one category of member. The chapter by Alfons Westgeest and Bruno Alves provides a lead here, with its emphasis upon the neutrality of moderators to mediate conflicts, whether these arise between members, or between members and the management. These sources of neutrality also offer the prospect for associations to insulate themselves from short-term member demands, so as to enable the association to take risks in favour of the long-term perspectives of member interests described by Coleman. Here the governing body, and particularly the President, have a key role to play. While member participation is important, there is a balance to be struck in that micro management and over monitoring will reduce the autonomy of the association and its management, and hence its ability to add value to its members.

Another constitutional possibility geared at diluting the possibility of over dependence, this time upon members taken a whole, is to ensure that seats on the key decision making structures are elected by the membership as a whole, rather than acting as delegates from individual members. Another is to ensure that decisions do not require the approval of all affiliates (Schmitter and Streeck, 1981). As confirmation of this, Bob Bennett (Chapter 2) finds a relationship between an executive driven structure (rather than a member or council driven structure) and high membership densities.

The end is nigh

There is no sector in which relationships between the EU and business are conducted wholly through an associational intermediary. Very few

EU associations undertake the highly developed roles of economic governance that require them to have the capacity to bind their members to the agreements struck with governments. These functions are common in 'corporatist' systems of interest intermediation, where associations take on functions of public governance, but rare in fragmented systems of competitive, 'pluralist' interest representation. Pestoff describes a scheme of 'direct debit fines' administered by Swedish associations, in which members are required on joining to provide their full banking details together with authority for the association to levy fines direct from their account without further recourse to the member (Pestoff, 2000). These fines, sometimes at a substantial level, are levied automatically for transgressions, so as to maintain discipline for the wider good of the members, and to keep the integrity of agreements negotiated on their behalf with governments.

The inability of any one European institution to monopolise governance powers and enter into exclusive agreements with associations means that EU business associations could not be expected to have developed such capacities. In consequence, EU business associations must not be measured on the scale of 'cohesiveness' by the yardsticks by which some of their national associations can be. Put simply, they are different animals, and require different treatment by both analysts, members, and users. In their own terms, they can bring value to each of these purposes. While they have limitations, these limitations are not an inflexible given. Pressed to identify one factor that yields most promise to raise their horizons, we place our bets on the capacity of autonomy. While some of the ideas to realise this are contained in this volume, we expect our next volume, following from our 2002 conference addressed to this topic, to yield the most productive stimuli for analysts and practitioners alike.

Note

1 For instance, in 1938 nearly 50 per cent of Germany's industrial output was subject to price and production controls which were devised and managed by trade associations acting through the devolved authority of government (Schneiberg and Hollingsworth, 1991).

Bibliography

Bachrach, P. and Baratz, M. S. (1970) *Power and Poverty. Theory and Practice* (New York/London).

Baran, P. and Sweezy, P. (1968) *Monopoly Capital* (Harmondsworth: Penguin).

Bennett, R. J. (1993) *Britain's Chambers of Commerce: A national network development study* (Association of British Chamber of Commerce, London).

Bennett, R. J. (1999a) 'The impact of European economic integration on business associations: the UK case', *West European Politics*, **47**(2), 240–57.

Bennett, R. J. (1999b) 'Business associations: their potential contribution to government policy and the growth of small and medium-sized enterprises', *Environment and Planning C: Government and Policy*, **17**, 593–608.

Bennett, R. J. (1999c) 'Explaining the membership of sectoral business associations', *Environment and Planning A*, **31**, 877–98.

Bennett, R. J. (1999d) 'Business routes of influence in Brussels: explaining the choice of direct representation', *Political Studies*, **XLVIII**, 240–57.

Bennett, R. J. (ed.) (1997) *Trade associations in Britain and Germany: responding to internationalization and the EU*, Anglo-German Foundation (London and Bonn).

Bennett, R. J. and Robson, P. J. A. (2002) 'Exploring the market potential and bundling of business association services', *Journal of Services Marketing* (forthcoming).

Bennett, R. J., Bratton, W. A. and Robson, P. J. A. (2000) 'Business advice: the influence of distance', *Regional Studies*, **34**, 813–28.

Bennett, R. J., Robson, P. J. A. and Bratton, W. A. (2001) 'The influence of location on the use by SMEs of external advice and collaboration', *Urban Studies* (forthcoming) extended version in WP190 (University of Cambridge, ESRC Centre for Business Research).

Bernstein, M. (1955) *Regulating Business by Independent Commission* (Westport, Conn: Greenwood).

Betts, P. and Groom, B. (2001) 'Industrialists urge faster EU reform: group says heads of state have failed to deliver on after Lisbon summit', *Financial Times*, 20 March, p. 1.

Boléat, M. (1996) *Trade association strategy and management* (Association of British Insurers, London).

Bolger, A. (2001) 'Financiers move to support single market', *Financial Times*, 2 March.

Bratton, W. J., Bennett, R. J. and Robson, P. J. A. (2002) 'Critical mass and economies of scale in the supply of services by business support organizations' (forthcoming).

Browne, W. (1990) 'Organized interests and their issue niches: a search for pluralism in a policy domain', *Journal of Politics*, **52**(2), 477–509.

Buchanan, J. M., Robert, D. T. and Gordon, T. (eds) (1980) *Towards a Theory of the Rent-Seeking Society* (Texas).

Bundesverband der Deutschen Industrie (BDI) (2001), www.bdi-online.de.

Bundesverband der Deutschen Tourismuswirtschaft (1999) Jahrbuch (Bonn).

Butt-Philip, A. and Gray, O. (1996) *Directory of Pressure Groups in the EU* (Cartermill: Harlaw).

Calmfors, L. and John, Driffill (1988) 'Bargaining structure, corporatism and macroeconomic performance', *Economic Policy*, 6, 14–61.

Castells, M. (1996) *The Rise of the Network Society* (Oxford: Basil Blackwell).

Chandler, A. D. (1990) *Scale and scope: the dynamics of industrial capitalism* (Cambridge, MA: Belknapp Press).

Chubb, J. (1983) *Interest Groups and the Bureaucracy: The Politics of Energy* (Stanford).

Coe, N. M. and Townsend, A. R. (1998) 'Debunking the myth of localized agglomerations: the development of a regionalized service economy in southeast England', *Transactions, Institute of British Geographers NS*, 23, 385–404.

Coen, D. (1997) 'The evolution of the large firm as a political actor in the European Union', *Journal of European Public Policy*, 4(1), 91–108.

Coleman, W. D. and Grant, W. (1984) 'Business associations and public policy: a comparison of organisational development in Britain and Canada', *Journal of Public Policy*, 4, 209–35.

Coleman, W. D. (1997) 'Weathering the storm: associational governance in a globalizing era', in Hollingsworth, J. R. and Boyer, R. (eds) *Contemporary Capitalism: The Embeddedness of Institutions* (New York: Cambridge University Press).

Coleman, W. D. and Perl, A. (1999) 'International policy environment and policy network analysis', in *Political Studies*, XLVII(4), 691–709.

Coleman, W. D. and Porter, T. (2000) 'International institutions, globalization and democracy: assessing the challenges', *Global Society*, 14(3), 377–98.

Coleman, W. D. (1988) *Business and Politics. A Study of Collective Action* (Kingston).

Cosh, A. D. and Hughes, A. (eds) (1998) *Enterprise Britain; Growth, innovation and public policy in the small and medium sized enterprise sector 1994–97* (ESRC University of Cambridge, Centre for Business Research).

Cowles, M. G. (1994) *The Politics of Big Business in the European Community: Setting the Agenda for a New Europe*, unpublished Ph.D thesis (The American University).

Cowles, M. G. (1995a) 'Setting the agenda for a new Europe: the ERT and EC 1992', *Journal of Common Market Studies*, 33(4), 501–26.

Cowles, M. G. (1995b) *German Big Business and Brussels: Learning to Play the European Game*, AICGS Seminar Paper No. 15 (American Institute for Contemporary German Studies, The John Hopkins University, Washington, November).

Cowles, M. G. (1996) 'The EU Committee of AmCham: the powerful voice of American firms in Brussels', *Journal of European Public Policy*, 3(3) 339–58.

Cowles, M. G. (2000) 'The transatlantic business dialogue: transforming the new transatlantic dialogue', in Pollack, M. and Schaffer, G. (eds) *The New Transatlantic Dialogue* (Boulder, CO: Rowman and Littlefield).

Cutler, A. C., Haufler, V. and Porter, T. (1999) *Private Authority and International Affairs* (Albany: State University of New York Press).

Domhoff, G. W. (1967) *Who rules America* (Englewood Cliffs).

Domhoff, G. W. (1970) *The Higher Circles. The Governing Class in America* (New York).

Drahos, M. (2001) *Convergence of Competition Laws and Policies in the European Community* (Deventer: Kluwer).

Drahos, M. and van Waarden, F. (2001) *Regulatory Convergence through Markets, States or Courts? A Case Study of National Competition Policies*, paper presented at the ECPR Joint Sessions, Grenoble, April.

Edwards, M. (2000) *NGO Rights and Responsibilities* (The Foreign Policy Centre, London).

ESF (2001) 'GATS 2000 European services network memorandum of understanding', 21 October 1998, and agreement on European services network, 26 January 1999, www.esf.be/f-e-abou.htm.

ETOA, ETC/CET, ETAG, WTTC (2000) *Europe's Tourism. How important is it?* Joint Brochure, (Great Britain: Hensal Press).

Euro Banking Association (2000) www.abe.org/.

Euroconfidentiel (1999) *World Directory of 9300 Trade and Professional Associations in the EU* (Genval, Euroconfidentiel).

Europe 2000 (1990) 'Industrialists drive for a stronger Europe. Interview with Prof. Dr Wisse Dekker', 2(2), 17–9.

European Banking Federation (2001) www.fbe.be/f_e_abou.htm#top.

European Commission (1999) *Directory of Interest Groups in the European Union*, *http://europa.eu.int/*comm/sgc/lobbies/index_en.htm.

Fielder, N. (2000) 'The origins of the single market', in Bornschier, V. (ed.), *State-Building in Europe* (Cambridge: Cambridge University Press).

Financial Times (1997) 'Observer: rounding off', 8 April.

Financial Times (2000) 6 December.

Frank, S., Kowalski, M. and Zuber, S. (2001) 'Schon gebucht? Focus', no. 9, 204–14

Gardner, J. N. (1991) *Effective Lobbying in the European Community* (Deventer: Kluwer).

Garner, R. (1993) 'Animals', *Politics and Morality* (Manchester: Manchester University Press).

Glatz, H. (2001) *Why Large Firms Join and Stay in Associations*, paper presented to the conference on 'The Effectiveness of EU Business Associations', Brussels, 18–22 September 2000, http://www.ey.be/EYBE/Site.nsf/Pages/EnconfFrame.

Grant, W. (1993) *Business and Politics in Britain*, 2nd edn (London: Macmillan).

Grant, W. (2000) *Pressure Groups and British Politics* (London: Macmillan).

Grant, W. (ed.) (1987) *Business Interests, Organizational Development and Private Interest Government: An international comparative study of the food processing industry* (Berlin: de Gruyter).

Grant, W. (1993) *Business and Politics in Britain* (London: Macmillan).

Greenwood, J. (1997) *Representing Interests in the European Union* (London: Macmillan).

Greenwood, J. (2000) *The Impact of Europeanization and Globalization on National Patterns of Interest Intermediation*, paper presented at the Conference at the European University Institute, Florence, 1–3 June.

Greenwood, J. and Ronit, K. (1992) 'Established and emergent sectors: organized interests at the European level in the pharmaceutical industry and the new biotechnologies'.

Harrison, B. (1997) *Lean and Mean: the changing landscape of corporate power in the age of flexibility* (New York: Guildford Press).

Haverland, M. (1998) *National Autonomy, European Integration and the Politics of Packaging Waste* (Amsterdam: Thelathesis).

Held, D., McGrew, A. Goldblatt, D. and Perraton, J. (1999) *Global Transformations: Politics, Economics and Culture* (Stanford, CA: Stanford University Press).

Hirschman, A. O. (1970) *Exit, voice and loyalty* (Cambridge, MA: Harvard University Press).

Hirschman, A. O. (1982) *Shifting involvements: private interest and public action* (Oxford: Basil Blackwell).

Hollingsworth, J. R., Schmitter, P. C. and Streeck, W. (eds) (1994a) 'Capitalism, sectors, institutions and performance', *Governing Capitalist Economies: Performance and Control of Sectors* (New York: Oxford University Press).

Hollingsworth, J. R., Schmitter, P. C. and Streeck, W. (1994b) *Governing Capitalist Economies: Performance and Control of Economic Sectors* (Oxford: Oxford University Press).

Huges, J.-P. (2000) *What Members Use Associations For*, paper presented to the conference on 'The Effectiveness of EU Business Associations', Brussels, September 18–22, http://www.ey.be/EYBE/Site.nsf/Pages/EnconfFrame.

Illeris, S. (1994) 'Proximity between service producers and service users', *Tijdschrift voor Economische en Sociale Geografie*, 85, 294–302.

Illeris, S. and Rasmussen, J. (1992) *Regionalising af technologisk service: En evaluering af Industriministeriets initiativ 1998–1992* (Institut for geografi, Samfundsanalyse og Datogi, Report 84, Roskilde).

Jacobi, O., Keller, B. and Müller-Jentsch, W. (1998) 'Germany: facing new challenges', in Ferner, A. and Hyman, R. (eds) *Changing Industrial Relations in Europe* (Oxford: Blackwell), pp. 190–238.

Jordan, A. G. (1997) 'What drives associability at the European level? The limits of the utilitarian explanation', in Greenwood, J. and Aspinwall, M. (eds) *Collective Action in the European Union: Interests and the New Politics of Associability* (London: Routledge), pp. 31–62.

Jordan, G. and Davidson, S. (2000) 'Science and scepticism: expertise and political decisions', *Public Policy and Administration*, 15, 58–76.

Jordan, G. and Maloney, W. (1977) *The Protest Business?* (Manchester: Manchester University Press).

Keller, B. and Sörries, B. (1999) 'Sectoral social dialogues: new opportunities or more impasses?', *Industrial Relations Journal*, 30, 330–44.

Kotler, P. and Bloom, P. N. (1984) *Marketing professional services* (Englewood Cliffs, NJ: Prentice-Hall).

Landmarks Publications (1999) *European Public Affairs Directory 1999* (Brussels: Landmarks Publications).

Majone, G. (1994) 'The rise of the regulatory state in Europe', *West European Politics*, 17(3), 77–101.

Marks, G., Hooghe, L. and Blank, K. (1996) 'European Integration from the 1980s: State-Centric v. Multi-level Governance', *Journal of Common Market Studies*, 34, 343–78.

Mazey, S. and Richardson, J. (1993) *Lobbying in the European Community* (London: Sage).

Mclaughlin, A. M., Jordan, G. and Maloney, W. A. (1993) 'Corporate lobbying in the European community', *Journal of Common Market Studies*, 31(2), 191–212.

Mills, P. K. and Margulies, N. (1980) 'Towards a pure typology of service organizations', *Academy of Management Review*, 5(2) 255–65.

Millward, N., Stevens, M., Smart, D. and Hawes, W. R. (1992) *Workplace Industrial Relations in Transition* (Aldershot: Dartmouth).

Mitnick, B. M. (1980) *The Political Economy of Regulation* (New York).

Müller-Jentsch, W. (1998) 'Der wandel der unternehmens- und arbeitsorganisation und seine auswirkungen auf die interessenbeziehungen zwischen arbeitgebern und arbeitnehmern', *Mitteilungen aus der Arbeitsmarkt- und Berufsforschung*, **31**, 575–84.

O'Farrell, P. N., Hitchens, D. M. W. N. and Moffatt, L. A. R. (1992) 'The competitiveness of business service firms in Scotland and south-east England: a matched pairs analysis', *Regional Studies*, **26**, 519–33.

O'Farrell, P. N., Moffat, L. A. R. and Hitchens, D. M. W. M. (1993) 'Manufacturing demand for business services in a core and peripheral region: does flexible production imply vertical disintegration of business services?', *Regional Studies*, **27**, 385–400.

Olson, M. (1965) *The Logic of Collective Action: Public Goods and the Theory of Groups* (Cambridge, MA: Harvard University Press).

Olson, M. (1971) *The Logic of Collective Action: Public Goods and the Theory of Groups*, 2nd edn (Cambridge, MA: Harvard University Press).

Olson, M. (1982) *The Rise and Decline of Nations. Economic Growth, Stagflation and Social Rigidities* (New Haven: Yale University Press).

Olson, M. (1983) 'The political economy of comparative growth rates', in Mueller, D. C. (ed.) *The Political Economy of Growth* (New Haven: Yale University Press).

Paun, D. (1993) 'When to bundle or unbundle products', *Industrial Marketing Management*, **22**, 29–34.

Pedler, R. H. and van Schendelen, M. P. C. M. (eds) (1994) *Lobbying in the European Union Companies, Trade Associations and Issue Groups* (Aldershot: Dartmouth).

Perry, M. (1992) 'Flexible production, externalisation and the interpretation of business service growth', *Service Industries Journal*, **12**, 1–16.

Pestoff, V. (2000) *Europeanisation and Globalisation of Business Interest Associations – exit provides two or more voices, but implies no loyalty*, paper delivered at a workshop on 'Europeanisation and its Impact on National Forms of Business Associability', Florence, 1–3 June.

Phillips, D., MacPherson, A. D. and Lentnek, B. (1998) 'The optimum size of a producer service firm facing uncertain demand', *Environment and Planning A*, **30**, 129–42.

Pizzorno, A. (1978) 'Political exchange and collective identity in industrial conflict', in Crouch, C. and Pizzorno, A. (eds) *The Resurgence of Class Conflict in Western Europe since 1968*, vol. II (London: Macmillan).

Porter, M. E. (1998) *On competition* (Cambridge, MA: Harvard Business Review Press).

Posner, R. A. (1974) 'Theory of economic regulation', *Bell Journal of Economics and Management*, **5**(2), 335–58.

Pred, A. (1977) *City systems in advanced economies* (Chichester: John Wiley).

Preussag (2001) Group at a Glance, www.preussag.de/en/konzern/group_at_a_glance/index.html.

Reinicke, W. (1998) *Global Public Policy* (Washington, DC: Brookings).

Rosamond, B. (2000) *Theories of European Integration* (London: Macmillan).

Schattschneider, E. E. (1962) *The Semisovereign People: A Realist View of Democracy in America* (Hinsdale).

Schmitter, P. C. (1992) 'The consolidation of democracy and representation of social groups', *American Behavioural Scientist*, **35**, (4–5) March/June, 422–449.

Schmitter, P. C. and Streeck, W. (1981) *The Organization of Business Interests: Studying the Associative Action of Business in Advanced Industrial Societies*, Max Planck Institute for the Study of Societies, discussion paper 99/1.

Schneiberg, M. and Hollingsworth, J. R. (1991) 'Can transaction cost economics explain trade associations?', in Czada R. M. and Windhoff-Heritier, A. (eds) *Political Choice: Institutions, Rules and the Limits of Rationality* (Campus: Frankfurt), pp. 199–231.

Scholte, J. A. (2000) *Globalization: An Introduction* (Basingstoke: Palgrave).

Shell (2000) *Listening and Responding: the Dialogue Continues* (Shell International Petroleum Co. Ltd., London).

Shonfield, A. (1982) *The Use of Public Power* (Oxford: Oxford University Press).

Stigler, G. J. (1971) 'The theory of economic regulation', *Bell Journal of Economics and Management*, **2**, 3–21.

Stopford, J. and Strange, S. (1991) *Rival states, rival firms: Competition for world market share* (Cambridge: Cambridge University Press).

Streeck, W. and Schmitter, P. C. (1981) '*The organization of Business Interests: a Research Design to Study the Associative Action of Business in the Advanced Industrial Societies of Western Europe*', Labour Market Policy discussion papers, International Institute of Management, Berlin.

Streeck, W. (1989) 'The territorial organization of interests and the logic of associative action: the case of the *handwerk* organization in West Germany', in Coleman, W. D. and Jacek, H. J. (eds) *Regionalism, Business Interests and Public Policy* (London: Sage).

Streeck, W. and Schmitter, P. C. (eds) (1985a) *Private Interest Government: Beyond Market and State* (London: Sage).

Streeck, W. and Schmitter, P. C. (eds) (1985b) 'Community, market, state and associations? the prospective contribution of interest governance to social order', *Private Interest Government: Beyond Market and State* (London: Sage), pp. 1–29.

Tate, C. N. and Vallinder, T. (eds) (1997) *The Global Expansion of Judicial Power* (New York: New York University Press).

Teulings, C. and Hartog, J. (1998) *Corporatism or competition. An international comparison of labour market structures and their impact on wage formation* (Cambridge: Cambridge University Press).

Tordoir, P. P. (1994) 'Transactions of professional business services and spatial systems', *Tijdschift voor Economische en Sociale Geografie*, **85**, 322–32.

Traxler, F. (1991) 'The logic of employers' collective action', in Sadowski, D. and Jacobi, O. (eds) *Employers' Associations in Europe: Policy and Organisation* (Baden-Baden: Nomos), pp. 28–50.

Traxler, F. (1993) 'Business associations and labour unions in comparison: theoretical perspectives and empirical findings on social class, collective action and associational organizability'. *British Journal of Sociology*, **44**, 673–91.

Traxler, F. (1995) 'Farewell to labour market associations? organized versus disorganized decentralization as a map for industrial relations' in Crouch, C. and Traxler, F. (eds) *Organized Industrial Relations in Europe: What Future?* (Aldershot: Avebury), pp. 3–19.

Traxler, F. (1998) 'Employer and employer organisations', in Towers, B. and Terry, M. (eds) *Industrial Relations Journal. European Annual Review 1997*, 99–111.

Traxler, F. (2000) 'Employers and employer organizations in europe: membership strengh, density and representativeness', *Industrial Relations Journal*, **31**, 309–17.

Traxler, F. and Schmitter, P. C. (1995) 'The emerging euro-polity and organized interests', *European Journal of International Relations*, **1**, 191–218.

Traxler, F., Blaschke, S. and Kittel, B. (2001) *National Labour Relations in Internationalized Markets. A Comparative Study of Institutions, Change and Performance* (Oxford: Oxford University Press).

Unger, B. and van Waarden, F. (1999) 'Interest associations and economic growth', *Review of International Political Economy*, **6**(4), 425–67.

Union of International Associations (UIA) (1999) *Yearbook of International Organizations* (Frankfurt: Bowker-Saur).

United Nations (1997) *World Investment Report 1997: Transnational Corporations, Market Structure and Competition Policy* (Geneva: United Nations).

Useem, M. (1984) *The inner circle: Large corporations and the rise of business political activity in the US and UK* (Oxford: Oxford University Press).

van Apeldoorn, B. (2000) 'Transnational class agency and European governance: the case of the European round table of industrialists', *New Political Economy*, **5**(2), 157–81.

van Apeldoorn, B. (forthcoming) *Transnational Capitalism and the Struggle over European Integration* (London: Routledge).

Van der Pijl, K. (1998) *Transnational Classes and International Relation* (London: Routledge).

van Dinteren, J. H. J. (1987) 'The role of business-service offices in the economy of medium-sized cities', *Environment and Planning A*, **19**, 669–86.

van Waarden, F. (1989) *Organisatiemacht van belangenverenigingen. De ondernemersorganisaties in de bouwnijverheid als voorbeeld* (Amersfoort and Leuven: Acco).

van Waarden, F. (1992) 'Emergence and development of business interest associations, an example from The Netherlands', *Organization Studies*, **13**(4), 521–61.

van Waarden, F. (1995) 'Employers and employers' associations', in van Hoof, J., Huiskamp, R. and van Ruysseveldt, J. (eds) *Comparative Industrial and Employment Relations* (London, Thousand Oaks, New Delhi: Sage), pp. 68–108.

van Waarden, F. (1995) 'The organizational power of employers' associations compared. cohesion, comprehensivenesss and organizational development', in Crouch, C. and Traxler, F. (eds) *Organized Industrial Relations in Europe: What Future?* (Aldershot: Avebury), pp. 45–97.

Versluis, E. (2000) *Comparison of the Conditions for Effective Compliance of the Seveso II Directive in Spain and the Netherlands*, paper presented at a workshop on regulatory enforcement in Southern Europe, European University Institute, Florence.

Vogel, S. (1996) *Freer Markets, More Rules. Regulatory Reform in Advanced Industrial Countries* (Ithaca: Cornell University Press).

Weiss, L. (1998) *The Myth of the Powerless State*, (London: Polity Press).

Weitbrecht, H.-J. (1969) *Effektivität und Legitimität der Tarifautonomie* (Berlin: Duncker und Humblot).

White, D. (2000) 'What the institutions need from collective business: a view from the commission', paper presented to the conference on 'The Effectiveness of EU Business Associations', Brussels, 18–22 September, http://www.ey.be/EYBE/Site.nsf/Pages/EnconfFrame.

Wilson, J. Q. (1995) *Political Organizations* (Princeton: Princeton University Press).

Wilson, T. L. and Smith, F. E. (1996) 'Business services 1982–1992: growth, industry characteristics, financial performance', *Industrial Marketing Management*, 25 163–71.

Wright M. C. (1956) *The Power Elite* (London/Oxford/New York).

WTO (1997) 'Economic effects of services liberalization', Background Note by the Secretariat, Council for Trade in Services, p. 2, S/C/W/26, 97–4342.

Index

Author's articles appear where page numbers are **bold**.

Abbey Life, 88
Academie Avignon, 192
accountants, 20, 39
ACE, *see* Action on Cartons and the Environment (ACE)
ACEA (Association des Constructeurs Européens d' Automobiles), 202
ACOM, *see* Consultative Assembly of Member Companies (ACOM)
Action on Cartons and the Environment (ACE), 228
Adamson-BSMG Worldwide, 2
Advisory Committee on Public Procurement, 188
AEGON, 203
aeronautics, 47
AFEG, *see* Consultative Assembly of Affiliated Groups (AFEG)
AFEM, *see* Consultative Assembly of Member Federations
affiliations, associational, 9, 225
AGF, 88
Agilent, 116
Agnelli, Giovanni, 66, 203
AGORIA, 116
agricultural sector, 49
  GDP, 133
  variation, 57
AIM, 6, 228
air carriers, 134
air transport, 40
airlines, 86–7
Airtouch, 87
Akzo Nobel, 71, 226
Alcatel, 116
Alliance for Cartons and the Environment, 5–6
Allianz, 88, 203
Alves, Bruno, **143**, 232

AmCham EU, *see* EU Committee of the American Chamber of Commerce
AMCs, *see* Association Management Companies (AMCs)
American firms, 10, 66–8, 74
American Society of Association Executives (ASAE), 148
Amsterdam, 43, 177
  Treaty of, 49
AMUE, *see* Association for Monetary Union in Europe (AMUE)
anarchy, 222
ANIE, 116
ANIEL, 116
animal protection movement, 61
anti-dumping, 57
anti-trust penalties, 5
Apple, 116
architects
  regulation, 48
  service sector, 138
ASAE (American Society of Association Executives), 148
ASSINFORM, 116
Association des Constructeurs Européens d'Automobiles, *see* ACEA
Association for the Monetary Union of Europe (AMUE), 202
Association Management Companies (AMCs), 143
  change agents, 143–53
  development, 145
  structure, 145, 146
Association of Hotels, Restaurants and Cafés in Europe (HOTREC), 134
associations, *see* business associations
Austria, 4, 116
  OBI project, 53
Autogrill, 126

Auto-Oil, 123
Axa, 88, 203

Bad Honnef, 172
Bangemann, Martin, 74
banks and banking, 20, 40, 49,
    87–9
  associations, 233
  central, 216
  financial services, 139
  lobbying, 139
  mergers, 87, 93
  regulation, 90
  regulators, 89
  service sectors, 132, 138
BASF, 71
Basle Committee on Banking
    Supervision, 90
Bass, 87, 126
Bayer, 199
BCC, *see* British Chambers of
    Commerce (BCC)
BDA, *see* Bundesvereinigung der
    Deutschen Arbeitgeberverbände
    (BDA)
BDI, *see* Bundesverband des Deutschen
    Industrie (BDI)
Belgium, 96, 116
  collective agreements, 170
Bennett, Robert J., **15**, 223, 225, 232
Beger, Rudolf, **79**, 230
Berlin, 73
Bertelsmann, 71, 74
best practice
  trade associations, 90
Betamax, 6
BEUC, 76
BIAs, *see* business interest associations
    (BIAs)
biotechnology, 211
Bitcom, 136
BITKOM, 116
Blank, Oliver, **115**, 227
BNP, 87
Boléat, Mark, **85**, 226
book publishing, 40
brand development
  business associations, 19
Bratton, William, 29

Britain (United Kingdom), 16–17,
    24–5, 55–6, 68, 85, 92,
    94–5, 116
  ad hoc groups, 70
  animal protection movement, 61
  bank mergers, 87
  business associations, 18
  devolution, 90
  employer associations, 166
  financial services, 89
  insurance companies, 88
  Labour Party, 61
  MORI survey, 62
  OBI project, 53
  petrol protests, 62
  political parties, 61
  surveys, 21
  trade associations, governance, 97
British Chambers of Commerce (BCC),
    16, 29
Brittan, Sir Leon, 137
broadcasting
  competition policy, 6
Brown, Ron, 72
BSE, 60
BTW, 136
  service sectors, 140
  structure, 134
building societies, 88–9
  deregulation, 89
  regulators, 89
  UK, 85
Bulgaria, 102
Bull, 116
Bulteel, Paul, **109**, 229
Bundesverband des Deutschen
    Industrie (BDI), 68, 135,
    137–8
  ESF, 138
  service sectors, 136–7
Bundesvereinigung der Deutschen
    Arbeitgeberverbände (BDA),
    166
bundling, 15
  business associations, 17, 22–3, 28
  services, 18
  surveys, 21
bureaucracies, 81–2
  alliances, 83

BurgerKing Europe, 126
bus operators, 134

business associations
  ad hoc, 70
  administration, 96
  advisors, 19
  affiliations, 9
  alliances, 83
  amalgamations, 167
  AMCs, 145
  anti-trust penalties, 5
  associations of, 64
  autonomy, 54, 230
  banking, 233
  Britain, 18, 94
  bureaucracies, 82
  case studies, 31
  centralisation, 40, 43–5
  CEO-based, 70
  change agents, 148
  changes in policy-making, 216
  collective agreements, 166
  collective contracts, 210
  Commission input, 4
  common advocacy, 101
  companies, 10, 50–1
  competition, 101, 229
  competition law, 42
  competition policy, 6
  competitiveness, 8
  comprehensive, 33
  conflicts, 227
  construction, 42
  consultants, 19, 95
  consumers, 228
  Convergence of IT,
    Telecommunications and the
      Media, 120
  corporatism, 79
  costs, 17, 19
  courts, 35
  critical mass, 17–20
  decision-making, 50, 80, 93, 102,
      129
    compromises, 81
  deregulation, 109–14
  development, 71
  dialogue, 60

differential interests, 157
director, 16
distribution, 164
diversity, 16
economies, 15, 20
effectiveness, 15–29, 64, 122–3,
    157, 159
employer, 157, 160–70
employers associations, 34, 53,
    160–1, 164, 167
  amalgamations, 167
environment, 2, 25, 57
ERT, 194
EuroCommerce, 6
evolution, 49, 52, 64, 101
examination, 223
expectations, 84, 101–2
expertise, 41
external economies, 24–5
financial services, 139–40
funding, 180
German, 41
Germany
  BDI, 136
globalisation, 87–8, 110, 209–222
governance, 96–8, 144, 148,
    157–170, 209–10, 212
ICT, 119
information, 90, 91
input, 5
international, 107, 123
Internet, 90–2, 94–5, 98, 144
IT, 119
key economic management criteria,
    28
labour market interests, 162
law firms, 41
leadership, 47
legal framework, 48
legal system changes, 40
lobbying, 27–8, 49, 51, 93, 141
local chamber, 19
management, 80, 84, 95–6, 230
management companies, 143–53
market, 3, 92
market penetration, 24
members
  competition, 96
  mergers, 86–8

business associations (*Continued*)
  membership, 8–10, 17–18, 27, 88,
      93, 101, 166
    trust, 8
  mergers, 43–4, 87, 93, 167, 226
  mixed, 168
  national, 9, 44, 72, 73, 124,
      171–81, *see also* national
      associations
  NGOs, 21, 62
  OBI project, 53
  operating environment, 86
  opportunities, 86
  organisational development, 53–4,
      210
  outsourcing technology, 95
  peak, 167, 168, *see also* peak
      associations
  perceptions, 172
  policy networks, 217
  politics of production, 59
  privatisation, 89
  product market, 157, 160–70
  product market interests, 160
  professional, 16, 46
  rationalisation, 92, 180
  regional, 45
  regulations, 36, 40
  representativeness, 178
  representativity, 169
  reputations, 176
  research, 179, 214
  resources, 175, 224, 230–1
  restructuring, 92, 93, 98, 178
  role, 15–16, 21, 56, 60, 63, 66, 76,
      83–5, 98, 102, 114, 115, 125,
      141, 143, 152, 158, 173
  role of state, 34–5, 42
  sector and sectoral, *see* sector and
      sectoral associations
  sector change, 122–5
  sector-specific, 165
  self-discipline, 33
  self-regulation, 37, 42, 222
  service sectors, 131–42
  services, 90, 91
  SMEs, 189
  specialisation, 227–8, 231
  specialist, 89

  specialization, 164, 167
  staff, 96
  status, 48
  structures, 97, 115, 146–7,
      174, 232
  sub-national, 90
  sub-national legislatures, 55
  subscription income, 86–7
  subscriptions, 86, 229
  subsidies, 41
  surveys, 15, 21
  systems, 30–2
  TABD, 73
  technology, 90
  TECs, 23
  The Netherlands, 44
  threats, 86
  TNCs, 204
  tourism, 133–5
  traditional, 75–6
  UEAPME, 189
  UNICE, 64–5, 67, 165, 171
  unions, 159, 165
  utilities, 89
  vertical portals, 92
  websites, 91, 94–5
  yardsticks, 233
business interest associations (BIAs),
    see business associations
California, 55
  air pollution regulations, 82
Canada
  OBI project, 53
car manufacturing, 86
  trade associations, 93
Carbon and Steel, 183
CBI, *see* Confederation of British
    Industry (CBI)
CEEP, 173
CEFIC, 2, 46, 64, 69, 76, 102–3, 106,
    202, 226
  communications, 105–6
  competitiveness, 104–5
  decision-making, 103
  ERT, 104
  incorporation, 102
  information source, 103
  reforms, 101–8
  role, 102–4

sector associations, 102
structure, 107
UNICE, 104
cement
associational effectiveness, 7
competition policy, 6
centralisation, 34, 40, 43
associations, 44
BIAs, 43, 45
decision-making, 33
employers, 44
globalisation, 212
hindrances, 44
unions, 44
CET, 133
chambers of commerce, 18, 21
business associations, 28
critical mass, 22
economies of scale, 22
EU Structural Funds, 24
local, 20
market penetration, 23
SMEs, 24
TECs, 24
Charlotte, 73
Cheltenham and Gloucester building
society, 88
chemical industries, 40, 57, 106
associational effectiveness, 7
centralisation, 45
CEFIC, 102–5
ICCA, 108
mergers, 45
transportation, 103
chemical weapons, 108
Chicago, 73
chocolate industry, 161
CIAA, 46
Cincinnati, 73
Cisco, 116
codes of practices, 162
pharmaceutical industry, 163
Coleman, William D., **209**, 223, 226,
230, 232
collective action, 6, 43–4, 204, 231
AMCs, 159
trade associations, 126
collective agreements, 162, 166, 168,
170

collective bargaining, 53, 161–3
employer associations, 166
collective contracts
associations, 210
College of Commissioners, 176
Comité des Organisations
Professionelles Agricoles (COPA),
46
comitology, 35, 36
EU Committee of AmCham, 2, 64, 68
development, 69
global trade, 72
Committee of Permanent
Representatives, 56, 177
business associations, 177
EU associations, 177
Committee of the Regions, 48–9,
177
common advocacy, 101
Common Agricultural Policy, 47,
84
communications, 17, 19, 62, 71, 74,
84, 98, 102, 105, 118, 124
broadband, 144
business associations, 123
CEFIC, 105–7
GBDe, 74
globalisation, 211
IT, 119
regulators, 117
SMEs, 187
technologies, 120
companies, 195, 203
business associations, 4, 10, 25, 28,
50–1, 91, 226
chemical, 102
diversity, 80
energy, 71
ERT, 197
global, 215
Internet, 92
lobbying, 25, 27
research, 224
service, 138
size, 72
surveys, 62
tourism, 133
US, 67, 68
Compaq, 116

competition, 32, 44, 212, 227
  associations, 228–9
  CEFIC, 105
  electricity, 109
  financial services, 139–40
  global, 195
  globalisation, 80, 213–14
  internal, 96
  laws, 34, 36–8, 41
    BIAs, 42
  lobbying, 20
  market, 231
  policy, 5, 224
    decision-making, 6
    European Court of Justice, 67
  TNCs, 201
competitiveness, 55
  bureaucrats, 175
  CEFIC, 104, 107
  ERT, 198
  ICT, 117
  Lisbon package, 70
  regulations, 82
  SMEs, 186
  TABD, 204
  trade associations, 8
  UNICE, 171
Competitiveness Advisory
    Group, 204
computers, 83, 86
  trade associations, 93
concentration, 19, 25, 28, 43,
    86–8
  globalisation, 212
  sector changes, 122
  sectoral, 7
Condor, 133
Confederacao da Indústria
    Portuguesa, 167
Confédération des Industries
    Agro-alimentaires, 46
Confédération Européenne des
    Fédérations de l'Industrie
    Chimique, 46
Confederation of British Industry
    (CBI), 68
Confederazione Autonoma Sindicati
    Artigiani, 164
Confindustria, 164

construction industries
  associational effectiveness, 7
  Dutch, 42–3
  EU law, 40
  GDP, 132
  unions, 44
consultants, 39
  associations, 19
  influence, 52
  numbers, 47
  trade associations, 95
Consultative Assembly of Affiliated
    Groups (AFEG), 107
Consultative Assembly of Member
    Companies (ACOM), 107
Consultative Assembly of Member
    Federations (AFEM), 107
Consultative Committee
  food, 129
consumers, 22, 31, 47, 55, 63, 76
  business associations, 228
  consultative organisation, 49
  Convergence of IT,
    Telecommunications and the
    Media, 120
  convergence of technologies, 118
  e-commerce, 75
  EICTA, 116
  electricity, 110
  EMRA, 126
  energy, 71
  ESC, 48
  EURELECTRIC, 113
  industrial, 71
  international trade
    politics, 144
  Internet, 94
  lobbyists, 52
  organisations, 183
  sector changes, 122
  SMEs, 184
  umbrella groups, 76
Consumers International, 76
contracts, 28, 39
Convergence of IT,
    Telecommunications and the
    Media, 120
COPA, 46, 57
COPA-COGECA, 46

copyright
Directive, 144
co-regulation, 5
e-commerce, 74
COREPER, 177, *see also* Committee of
Permanent Representatives
corporatism, 79, 83
cotton, 45
The Netherlands, 43
Council of Ministers, 56–7, 176–8
Court of Justice, 56
courts, 35, 42
layers, 39
political, 38
Cowles, Maria Green, **64**, 225
critical mass, 15, 20
business associations, 17–19, 24, 28
chambers of commerce, 22
sector associations, 21, 22
surveys, 21
TECs, 22
Cromme, Gerhard, 196
customers, *see* consumers
cyber security, 75
Czech Republic, 102, 116
Czechoslovakia, 90

DaimlerChrysler, 71, 72, 87, 225
dangerous chemical substances Seveso
II directive, 36
Dansk Arbeijdsgiverforenining, 167
Dansk Industri, 167
Davignon, Etienne, 69, 195, 203
decision-making
AMCs, 148, 151–2, 159
associations, 102, 146, 158, 163, 175,
217, 231–2
employer, 162–3
national, 175
trade, 50, 93, 126, 169
business associations, 80, 168
CEFIC, 103
centralisation, 33–4
competition policy, 6
EMEA, 36
EMRA, 128
EU, 57, 175, 179
processes, 180–1
European Parliament, 177

ICT, 119
influencing, 21, 57, 81, 183, 224–5
multilevel governance, 56
regulation, 90
SMEs, 188
structures, 151
UEAPME, 191
DEHOGA, 134
Dekker, Wisse, 69, 195, 199
Delors, Jacques, 47, 172, 174, 197
Denmark, 116
employer associations, 164
OBI project, 53
DER, 133
deregulation, 5, 39, 109
BIAs, 42
European integration, 37
financial services, 89
influencing, 224
Internet, 120
markets, 88
trade associations, 86
utilities, 89
deterritorialisation, 210
Deutsche Bank, 203
devolution, 90
Devos, Jean-Marie, **101**, 229
differential interests
associations, 157
digital divide, 75
directives, EU, 36–8, 42, 48, 59–60,
110, *see also* regulations
Copyright in the Information
Society, 144
Electronic Commerce, 144
ERT, 195
general, 70
Internal Electricity Market, 109–10
packaging waste disposal, 37
process, 175
single market, 179
Work Councils, 68
director associations, 16
disengagement, 151
distribution, 44, 59, 103, 144
service sectors, 132
dockyards
The Netherlands, 43
unions, 44

Dow Europe, 71
drink industry
consultative organisation, 49
drugs, 108
Dun & Bradstreet, 71

EACEM, *see* European Consumer
Electronics Association (EACEM)
EBA, *see* European Banking Association
(EBA)
ECJ, *see* European Court of Justice
ecologists, 47
consultative organisation, 49
lobbyists, 52
e-commerce, 64, 71, 74–5
directives, 144
financial services, 139
Economic and Social Committee
(ESC), 48, 177
role, 49
economies of scale, 15, 18–20, 24
BIAs, 44
business associations, 28
chambers of commerce, 22
sector associations, 22
surveys, 21
economies of scope, 15, 19–20, 24
ECTEL, 116, 120
Edelman Public Relations, 62
EEG, *see* European Enterprise Group
(EEG)
EFPIA, *see* European Federation of
Pharmaceutical Industry
Association (EFPIA)
EICTA, *see* European Information and
Communications Technology
Industry Association (EICTA)
EITO, *see* European Information
Technology Observatory (EITO)
electricity, 5, 89, 109–10
customers, 110
deregulation, 113
liberalisation, 110
mergers, 88, 109
privatisation, 109
service sectors, 140
electricity industry
competition, 109
integration, 113

electronic commerce, 71, 74
convergence of technologies, 118
EICTA, 116
SMEs, 184, 187
taxation, 117
tourism, 134
trade, 144
electronics industries, 119
EMEA, 38, 40
decision-making, 36
employers, 2, 34, 166, 167
centralisation, 44
ESC, 48
labour market, 161
organisations, 53
regulation, 163
employers' associations,
161, 165, *see also* business
associations
decision-making, 162–3
labour market interests, 164
logic of membership, 166
Nordic, 166
number, 167
trade associations, 34, 160–1, 164
amalgamations, 167
trade unions, 175
UNICE, 196
employment, 40
energy industry, 122
food industry, 127, 128
SMEs, 184, 186
terms, 161
TNCs, 201
tourism, 132, 136
EMRA, *see* European Modern
Restaurants Association, The
(EMRA)
encryption, 71
ENERG-8, 64, 70–1
energy, 39
CEFIC, 105, 107
companies, 70
consumption, 103
GDP, 132
market, 71
sector changes, 122
entrepreneurship
SMEs, 187

Environment, the
    CEFIC, 103
    chemical industry, 106, 108
environmental action groups
    international trade politics, 144
environmental law, 40
environmental protection, 4
environmentalists, 60
Ericsson, 72, 116
Ernst & Young, 1
ERT, *see* European Round Table of
    Industrialists (ERT)
ESC, *see* Economic and Social
    Committee (ESC)
ESF, *see* European Services Forum
    (ESF)
ESN, *see* European Services Network
    (ESN)
ESPRIT, *see* European Strategic
    Programme in Information
    Technology (ESPRIT)
ESRC Cambridge University,
    Centre for Business Research
    Survey, 21, 29
Esso, 69
Estonia, 102
ETAG, 133
ETNO, 136
ETOA, *see* European Tour Operators'
    Association (ETOA)
ETUC, 172, 196
ETUI, 176
EU law, 36, 38, 40, 42, 224
EU regulation, 5
EU Structural Funds, 24
Euratom, 66
EURELECTRIC, 5, 109–12
    customers, 113
    role, 112–13
Euro, 128, 139, 211
    SMEs, 184
European Banking Association (EBA),
    139, *see also* Fédération Banquaire
    Européen (FBE)
EUROBIT, 120
    industry associations, 116
EuroCommerce, 6
European Association of
    Beetgrowers, 46

European Banking Federation, *see*
    Fédération Banquaire Européen
    (FBE)
European Brands Association, *see* AIM
European Chemical Industry Council,
    see CEFIC
European Committee of Sugar
    Manufacturers, 46–7
European Consumer Electronics
    Association (EACEM), 121
European Court of Justice, 35, 38, 217
    competition policy cases, 67
European Enterprise Group (EEG),
    68–70, 202
    UNICE, 69
European Federation of Pharmaceutical
    Industry Associations (EFPIA), 162
European Forum, 173
European Information and
    Communications Technology
    Industry Association (EICTA), 2,
    115–17, 120–1
    Convergence of IT,
        Telecommunications and the
        Media, 120
    globalisation, 117
    industry associations, 117–19
    membership, 116
    merger, 116
    mobile communications, 117
    objectives, 120
    role, 117–18
    structure, 116–19
    websites, 117
European Information Service, 2
European Information Technology
    Observatory (EITO), 118
European integration, 3, 35, 38, 42,
    162, 195
    markets, 37
    privatisation, 39
European Modern Restaurants
    Association, The (EMRA), 61, 126–30
    Consultative Committee, 129
    food safety, 130
    governance, 127
    industry associations, 128
    role, 127, 129–30
    structure, 126

European Organisation for craft
    and SMEs, 182, *see also*
    UEAPME
European Parliament, 42, 51, 56, 59,
    129, 177, 182
    decision-making, 177
European Public Affairs Directory, 46
European Round Table of Industrialists
    (ERT), 64, 66, 69–70, 194–205
    access, 197–8, 201
    Association International avec un
        But Philantropique, Scientifique,
        et Pédagogique, 199
    associations, 202
    CEFIC, 104
    Competitiveness Advisory Group, 204
    development, 69
    EEG, 69
    effectiveness, 194, 198, 204
    evolution, 198–9, 202
    governance, 196
    Groupe des Présidents, 200
    influence, 194
    internal market, 198
    lobbying, 195–6
    membership, 199
    merger with GdP, 199
    power, 197
    role, 194, 196–8, 200, 202
    Single Market program, 67
    strategy, 198
    structures, 194–6, 198
    TABD, 203
    TNCs, 194, 197, 199, 204
    UNICE, 196–7, 199, 202, 204
    uniqueness, 195
European Services Forum
    (ESF), 137–8
    GATS, 137, 142
    lobbying, 138, 141
    service sectors, 138
    structure, 138
    UNICE, 138
European Services Network
    (ESN), 137
European Social Model, 185
European Strategic Programme in
    Information Technology
    (ESPRIT), 69

European Tour Operators' Association
    (ETOA), 133–4
EUROPIA, 124
extreme right wing parties, 31

farmers, 46, 83, 123
    consultative organisation, 49
FBE, *see* Fédération Banquaire
    Européen (FBE)
FDI, *see* foreign direct investment (FDI)
Federal Economic Chamber, 4
Fédération Banquaire Européen (FBE),
    139, *see also* European Banking
    Federation
    e-commerce, 139
    financial services, 139
    internal competition, 139
    structure, 139
federations, 177, 202
    AMCs, 145
    business associations, 20, 25
    EU associations, 9
    Internet, 144
    sectoral, 173
FEEI, 116
FEI, 116
FEII, 116
FIAT, 66, 195, 203
financial services, 88, 139
    associations, 141
    deregulation, 89
    economies of scale, 89
    mergers, 93
    service sectors, 131–2, 138
Financial Services Authority, 89
Finland, 116, 191
First, 133
food industries
    consultative organisation, 49
    fast, 61
    new age politics, 60
    quality, 127
    regulation, 90
    safety, 47, 128–30
    The Netherlands, 43
foreign direct investment (FDI), 67
    EU, 72
    US, 72
Företagen, 116

France, 47, 53, 116
  bank mergers, 87
  financial services, 139
  SMEs, 191
franchising, 127, 129
  EMRA, 126
  regulation, 129
fund managers
  opinion-forming, 62

G7, 216
G8, 71, 216–17
gas, 89
  liberalisation, 110
  mergers, 88
  sector changes, 122
GATS, *see* General Agreement on Trade
    in Services (GATS)
GBDe, *see* Global Business Dialogue on
    e-commerce (GBDe)
GDP, *see* Groupe des Présidents
General Agreement on Trade in
    Services (GATS), 114, 137, 141
  ESF, 137, 142
  service sector, 138
genetically modified seeds, 60
Germany, 56, 116
  bank mergers, 87
  employer associations, 164, 166
  financial services, 139
  OBI project, 53
  peak associations, 53
  service sectors, 131, 132, 136
  telecommunications, 135
  tourism, 133
Glatz, Hanns, 225, 228
Global Business Dialogue on
    e-commerce (GBDe), 64, 71, 74–6
  development, 73, 74
globalisation
  airlines, 87
  associational governance, 209–22
  communication, 211
  competition, 80
  concentration, 212
  deterritorialisation, 210
  EICTA, 117
  issues, 123
  legal services, 39

logic of influence, 213
logic of membership, 212–13
market concentration, 89
markets, 88, 90
mergers, 87
public policy making, 216
rationalisation, 87, 212
sector changes, 122
service sectors, 132, 136
technologies, 211
TNCs, 201, 204
trade associations, 86, 88, 93, 96, 110
WTO, 76
Goodys, 126
governance, 58, 214
  AMCs, 143, 151, 152
  associational, 32, 34, 85, 153, 162–5,
      168–9, 210, 212, 231
  globalisation, 209–222
  role, 215
  TNCs, 204
  associations, 8, 30, 96–7, 157–60
  EU, 233
  bureaucrats, 98
  employer associations, 161
  EMRA, 127
  ERT, 196
  EU, 3, 172, 203
  mechanisms
    markets, 214
  multi-level, *see* multilevel
      governance (MLG)
  role, 217, 221–22
governance mechanisms, 209
Grant, Wyn, **53**, 229
GRE, 88
green parties, 31
Greenpeace, 62
Greens Group, 51
Greenwood, Justin, **1**, **223**, 229
Groupe des Présidents (des Grandes
    Entreprises Européennes), 40, 66,
    70, 199
  ERT, 200
  merger with ERT, 199
  role, 200
  service sectors, 132
  skills shortages, 118
  tourism, 132

Guéguen, Daniel, **46**
Gyllenhammar, Pehr, 69, 195, 203

Hapag-Lloyd, 133
HDI project, 32, 43
health, 60, 103, 105
   chemical industry, 106, 108
   chemicals, 106
   safety, generic, 32
hospitality industry, 87, 93
hotels
   service sectors, 133
   trade associations, 93
HOTREC, *see* Association of Hotels,
   Restaurants and Cafés in Europe
   (HOTREC)
HP, 116
Huges, Jan-Peter, 226
Hungary, 102, 116
Hyder group, 89

IACA, *see* International Air Carriers
   Association (IACA)
IBM, 67, 71, 116
ICCA, *see* International Council of
   Chemical Associations (ICCA)
Iceland, 191
ICI, 66, 69, 71
ICL, 71, 116
ICRT, *see* International
   Communications Round Table
   (ICRT)
ICT, *see* Information and
   Communications Technology (ICT)
   national associations, 120
IGN, *see* intergovernmental
   negotiations (IGN)
IKT Norge, 116
IMO
   ICCA, 108
Indra, 116
industrial relations, 53
   associations, 169
   SMEs, 186
industry associations, *see also*
   business associations
Industry/Government ad hoc
   Council, 67
Infineon, 116

Information and Communications
   Technology (ICT), 115–16, 119–20
   competitiveness, 117
   convergence of interests, 119
   Convergence of IT,
      Telecommunications and the
      Media, 120
   EICTA, 121
   experts, 118
   globalisation, 118
   industry associations, 116, 119–20
   products, 118
   skills shortage, 117–19
information generation, 4
information technology
   convergence, 118
   EUROBIT, 116
   trade associations, 86, 213
Information Technology Agreement, 73
Information Technology Roundtable, 69
insurance, 40, 49, 88
   mergers, 93
   regulation, 90
   regulators, 89
   service sector, 138
   trade associations, 93
Intel, 116
intellectual property, 71, 75, 103
   chemical industry, 108
   law
      CEFIC, 103
      protection, 71
      rights, 75
Intercontinental, 87
interest associations, *see* business
   associations
intergovernmental negotiations
   (IGN), 217–19, 221
Internal Market, 187
   ERT, 195
Internal Public Affairs Forum, 67
International Air Carriers Association
   (IACA), 134
International Chamber of Commerce,
   137
International Communications
   Round Table (ICRT), 71
International Council of Chemical
   Associations (ICCA), 107–8

International Organisation for
  Standardisation (ISO), 108
International Securities Markets
  Association, 218
international trade law, 101
Internet, 62, 72, 91, 94–5
  convergence of technologies, 118
  International Securities Markets
    Association, 218
  pace of change, 115
  regulation, 120
  regulations, 144
  service sectors, 136
  trade associations, 90–2, 94, 98
introduction services, 131
Ireland, 116, 167
ISO, *see* International Organisation for
  Standardisation (ISO)
IT, 6, 116
  costs, 17
  regulations, 118
Italtel, 116
Italy, 116
  employer associations, 164
  OBI project, 53
ITB, 116
ITEK, 116
IVSZ, 116

Japan, 56, 199
Japanese firms, 74
journalists
  numbers, 48
  opinion-forming, 62
judicial review, 35, 38
juridification, 38
  BIAs, 41–2
  privatisation, 39

knowledge spillovers, 20
KNP BT, 71

labour market interests, 161, 163–5,
    167–8
  employer associations, 160
  lobbying, 162
Labour Party
  Britain, 61
Lafarge, 195

Lannoye, Paul, 51
law firms, 39
  lobbyists, 41
  numbers, 47
lawyers, 20, 39, 68
  BIAs, 44
  political entrepreneurs', 41
  regulation, 48
Lecureuil, Christophe, **126**, 230
legal system, 35, 38
  BIAs, 40
  fragmentation, 39
Leverhulme Trust, 29
Leysen, André, 197, 203
liberalisation, 39, 72, 89, 110, 114
  AMCs, 145
  globalisation, 213
  sector changes, 122
  service sector, 138
  service sectors, 132, 137, 140
  TABD, 204
  trade, 203
libraries, 17
lifestyle politics, 63
Liikanen, Erkii, 187
Lisbon package, 70
Lithuania, 102
Lloyds TSB, 88
lobbying and lobbyists, 15, 28, 47–8,
    64, 69, 166, 196
  banking, 139
  corporate, 51
  development, 66, 67
  dual strategy, 51
  effectiveness, 50
  EICTA, 117
  ERT, 196, 198–9
  ESF, 138
  farming, 51
  influence, 51
  IT, 119
  labour market interests, 162
  landscape, 47
  law firms, 41
  perceptions, 182
  professionalisation, 66
  regulation, 48
  role, 84, 183
  rules, 48

lobbying and lobbyists (*Continued*)
  SMEs, 28, 188, 190
  strategies, 51
  TNCs, 201
  tourism, 134
  UEAPME, 192
  US, 68
local chamber associations, 19
local chambers, *see* chambers of
    commerce
logic of excludable collective
    services, 18
logic of individual services, 18
logic of influence
  AMCs, 159
  business associations, 57, 61, 63,
      169, 212, 227
  employer associations, 160, 166, 168
  globalisation, 213
  OBI project, 33–4, 54–5
  resources, 59
  service provision, 18
logic of membership, 212
  AMCs, 159
  business associations, 58, 63, 162,
      227
  employer associations, 160, 166, 168
  EU, 228
  food processing, 60
  globalisation, 213
  OBI project, 33–4, 54–5
logic of organisation
  associations, 212
logic of protest, 61, 63
Longin Group, 67
LTU, 133
Lucent, 116
Luxembourg Compromise, 66

Madrid US–EU, 72
management economics, 16, 17
Mannesmann, 87, 135, 137
manufacturing, 173
  ENERG-8, 70
  ICT, 120
  national associations, 74
Marconi, 116
market access
  CEFIC, 105

market penetration, 15, 17–21
  business associations, 19, 23–5, 28
  external economies, 24
marketing, 19
  business associations, 19
  costs, 20
  tourism, 134
markets, 3, 5–6
  bond, 218
  concentration, 89
  currency, 210–11
  deregulation, 88
  electricity, 109
  financial services, 89
  global, 212
  globalisation, 88, 90
    EICTA, 117
  governance mechanisms, 214
  liberalisation, 72, 213
  mergers, 93
  regulation, 32
  role of state, 34–5, 37
  self-regulation, 34
  trade associations, 86
Matsushita, 116
McDonald's, 93
McDonald's Europe, 126
media, 2, 47, 60–1, 70–1, 75, 172
  skills, 60
membership associations, 202
Mercedes-Benz, 71
Merck Sharp & Dohme, 67
merger and acquisition activity, 7
mergers, 7, 87–8
  associations, 167, 213–14, 226
  banking, 87
  BIAs, 44
  building societies, 86
  chemical industry, 45
  EICTA, 116
  electricity, 109
  ERT and GdP, 199
  financial services, 89
  globalisation, 87
  industries, 93
  insurance, 88
  sector changes, 122
  tourism, 133
  trade associations, 87, 92, 96

metalworking
The Netherlands, 43
Miami, 74
Michalowitz, Irina, **131**, 226, 227
micro businesses
lobbying, 28
micro-enterprises, 184
micromanagement, 149, 151
Microsoft, 116
Europe, 71
milk, 49
powdered, 161
MLG, *see* multilevel governance
mobile phones, 62
service sectors, 136
monetary policy, 216
market forces, 89
Monnet, Jean, 65
monopolies
public, 39
representational, 41
MORI survey, 62
Motorola, 116
Müller, Hans-Werner, **182**, 227
multilevel governance (MLG), 4,
56–7, 217–19, 221
multi-sectoral associations, 173, 181
restructuring, 179
Mutual Recognition Agreements, 73

NAM, *see* National Association of
Manufacturers (NAM)
National Association of Manufacturers
(NAM)
UNICE, 73
national associations, 202, 224, *see also*
business associations
AMCs, 145
collective action, 225
decision-making, 175
development, 44
EU, 4, 40, 49, 180
associations, 9
processes, 181
financial services, 139–40
ICT, 116, 119–20
international associations, 123
manufacturing, 74
mergers, 93

multi-sectoral associations, 181
procedures, 231
research, 176, 179, 229
resources, 229
service sectors, 136, 141
size, 44
structures, 174
tourism, 135
UNICE, 68, 69
yardsticks, 233
NatWest, 87
NCR, 116
NEC, 116
Neckermann, 133
Netherlands, The, 31, 36–7, 116
association management, 96
BIAs, 43
collective agreements, 170
law firms, 41
non-litigious culture, 35
OBI project, 53
new age
direct action, 63
politics, 60, 61
new economy, 72, 76
trade associations, 15
New Transatlantic Agenda
(NTA), 72–3
New York, 74
NGOs, 62
access, 219
business associations, 21, 62
lobbying, 51
numbers, 47, 49
role, 63
sector changes, 122
status, 48
trust, 62
WTO, 144
Nice Summit, 49
Nokia, 72, 116
Nordsee, 126
NORMAPME, 192
Nortel, 116
Northern Ireland, 90
Norway, 116, 167
Nouvelles Frontières, 133
NTA, *see* New Transatlantic Agenda
(NTA)

OBI project, 34, 43
OECD
    CEFIC, 105
    ICCA, 108
Oil, sector changes, 122
Olivetti, 195
Olivettilexikon, 116
Olson, Mancur, 43
Organisation of Business Interests
    project, 31–3, 53, 54, 55
outside input, 3–4
outsourcing, 120
    trade associations, 95
ownership, 7, 87, 124
    concentration, 212

packaging waste disposal
    directive, 37
Paribas, 87
Paris, 74, 137, 199
peak associations, *see* business
        associations
    employer, 167
    Germany, 53
petrol protests, 62
PHARE Business Support Programme,
    121
pharmaceutical industries, 36, 40,
    162
    associational effectiveness, 7
    centralisation, 45
    codes of practices, 163
    EMEA, 40
    regulation, 162
    self-regulation, 162
Philips, 66, 69, 116, 195, 199, 203
Pilkington, 71
pluralism, 30
Poland, 102
policy networks, 199, 217–19
political representation, 8, 224, 225
politics of bargaining, 59
politics of collective consumption,
    59, 61
politics of production, 59–61
pollution, 59, 80
    MORI survey, 62
    negotiations, 81, 82
    regulations, 82, 90

Portugal, 191
pressure groups, 61, 62
Preussag, 133, 137
privatisation, 39
    BIAs, 42
    electricity, 109
    sector changes, 122
    trade associations, 86, 89
Prodi, Romano, 172–3
product market interests, 157, 161–3,
    165, 167–9, 231
    trade associations, 160
professional associations, 16
    Britain, 18, 21
public health, 47
public interest groups, 6
public sector activism, 217
public transport, 39
publishing, 71
    vertical portals, 92
pulp, 6

R&D
    EICTA, 117
    generic, 32
    ICT, 120
Rank-Xerox, 67
rationalisation
    associations, 180
    globalisation, 87, 212
    insurance companies, 88
    sector changes, 122
Ravenstein Group, 67, 70
regulation and regulations, 4–5,
    30, 34, 36–7, 48, 118, 174,
    see also directives
    banking, 90
    BIAs, 36, 42
    California, 55
    CEFIC, 105
    centralisation, 44, 45
    competitiveness, 82
    e-commerce, 74
    franchising, 129
    global, 89
    globalisation, 214, 221
    ICT, 119
    influencing, 224
    insurance, 90

Internet, 120, 144
market failures, 32
pharmaceutical industry, 162
product market, 164
role of state, 40
securities industries, 90
The Netherlands, 44
regulators
specialist, 89
regulatory agencies, 36, 38, 40
BIAs, 42
public monopolies, 39
regulatory authorities
centralisation, 45
Reinicke, Wolfgang, 215–16
reinsurance, 88
representativity, 124, 159, 169
research, 9, 21, 29, 31, 61–2, 128, 176
Acadamié Avignon, 192
associations, 176
companies, 224
EU associations, 179
policy networks, 218
SMEs, 187, 191
resources
BIAs, 41
Responsible Care, 104
CEFIC, 106
chemical industry, 105
ICCA, 108
restaurants, 126
service sectors, 134
restructuring, 41, 92
associations, 180
business associations, 178
financial services, 140
multi-sectoral associations, 179
tourism, 133
UNICE, 171
retail and retailing
associational effectiveness, 7
EU law, 40
service sectors, 132
Reuters, 71
Rewe, 133
Richardson, Keith, 199
risk management
chemicals, 106
river transport, 42

road transport, 42
Robson, Paul, 29
Rome, 73
Treaty of, 48, 186
'Rond Point Schumann' man, 60
Round Table, *see* European Round
Table of Industrialists (ERT)
Royal Bank of Scotland, 87

SAF, 166
safety, 36, 47, 90
chemical industry, 108
food, 127, 128, 129, 130
Schmitter, Philippe, 31, 33, 55
OBI project, 53
Scotland, 90
Scottish Parliament, 55
Scottish Power, 89
Scottish Widows, 88
Seattle, 76, 144
Secretary Generals, 8
sector and sectoral associations, 137,
165, 171, 173, *see also* business
associations
CEFIC, 102
critical mass, 21, 22
economies, 20
economies of scale, 22
environment, 25
external economies, 24
German, 68
lobbying, 15
market penetration, 23
product market interests, 165
role, 21, 171
staff, 23
sector change
business associations, 122–5
securities industries
regulation, 90
SEDISI, 116
self-regulation, 4–5, 32, 37
BIAs, 42
e-commerce, 74
employer interests, 163
markets
role of state, 34
pharmaceutical industry, 162
The Netherlands, 44

service industries
  national associations, 74
service sectors, 131–42, 226
  financial services, 138, 139
  resources, 141
  tourism, 136
SET, 116
Seveso II directive, 36
Seville, 72, 73
SFIB, 116
Shell, 62, 66, 199
shipyards, 45
Siemens, 116, 203
Simon, David, 198
Single European Market, 69
single issue parties, 31
Single Market program, 67, 70
skills shortages, 118
Slovakia, 102
Slovenia, 102
small and medium-sized enterprises
    (SMEs), 16, 21, 41, 173–4, 183,
    185–8, 192
  Academie Avignon, 192
  chambers of commerce, 24
  definition, 188
  development, 186
  electronic commerce, 184
  employment, 184
  equality of opportunity, 186
  EU, 183–6
  Euro, 184
  European Social Model, 185
  exports, 184
  Germany
    tourism, 133
  finance, 187
  franchising, 127
  growth, 184
  influence, 182
  Internal Market, 187
  lobbying, 28, 188, 190,
    192
  multi-sectoral associations,
    179
  NORMAPME, 192
  numbers, 184, 189
  policy, 187
  research, 191, 192

resources, 175
  role, 183–5, 191
  Single Market, 186
  size, 189
  social partner, 193
  specifics, 16
  standardisation, 191–2
  structure, 183
  surveys, 15
  UEAPME, 186–7, 189,
    192
  UNICE, 205
Social Dialogue, 127
Social Partners, 127, 193
social security, 41, 42
social services, 40
Sony, 71, 116
Southern Water, 88
Spain, 36, 72, 116
  employer associations, 164
  financial services, 139
  OBI project, 53
specialism of interest, 10
Specialist Working Groups
  CEFIC, 105
SPIS, 116
steel
  associational effectiveness, 7
  competition policy, 6
Stockholm, 203
Streeck, Wolfgang, 31, 33, 54,
    55
  OBI project, 53
street action, 123
strikes
  employers, 34
  local, 43
subsidiarity, 48, 168
  horizontal, 216
subsidies, 33, 48
  BIAs, 41
  The Netherlands, 44
sugar, 46, 49
  beet, 61
  farmers, 61
  industrial users, 61
  lobbying, 51
Sun, 116
Sutherland, Peter, 197

Sweden, 116, 166
associations
amalgamations, 167
employer associations, 164
OBI project, 53
SWICO, 116
Swiss car party, 31
SWISSMEM, 116
Switzerland, 116
employer associations, 164
OBI project, 53

TABD, *see* Transatlantic Business
Dialogue (TABD)
taboo catalogues, 166
taxis, 123
TBL-ITF, 116
technology and technologies, 113,
117
communications, 120, 144
convergence, 118
e-trade, 144
globalisation, 211
ICT, 116
pace of change, 115
regulation, 119
SMEs, 187
specialisms, 227
TECs, *see* Training and Enterprise
Councils (TECs)
chambers of commerce, 24
telecom services, 39
telecommunications, 87, 211
convergence, 118
industry associations, 116, 135
mergers, 87
service sectors, 132, 136–7, 140
utilities, 89
Thales, 116
Third Generation Wireless standards,
73
Thomson Multimedia, 116
Thomson Travel, 133
Thyssen, 71
Timmerman, Jan J. F., **122**, 226
TNCs, 199
associational governance, 204
dominance, 201
employment, 201

ERT, 194–5, 197, 204
European Enterprise Group, 202
European Round Table of
Industrialists (ERT), 199
globalisation, 201
lobbying, 196, 201
TABD, 203
UNICE, 202
Tokyo, 74
Total, 203
tourism, 135, 139, 140
associational effectiveness, 7
associations, 134, 138, 141, 226
employment, 132, 136
markets, 133
national associations, 134
restructuring, 140
service sectors, 131, 132, 137
Trade Association Forum, 94
trade associations, *see* business
associations
trade disputes
EICTA, 117
trade journals, 92
Trade Policy Society, 76
Training and Enterprise Councils
(TECs), 21, 23–4
business associations, 21–3, 28
critical mass, 22
EU Structural Funds, 24
Transatlantic Business Dialogue
(TABD), 64, 71–6, 143
development, 72
e-commerce, 74–5
ERT, 203, 204
TNCs, 203
Transatlantic Consumers
Dialogue, 76
Transatlantic Environmental
Dialogue, 76
transnational corporations,
see TNCs
transport, 17, 37, 40, 47
chemical industry, 108
service sectors, 132, 134
transport law, 40
transport sector, 40
Traxler, Franz, **157**, 196, 230–1
Treaty of Amsterdam, 49

Tricon Restaurants International, 126
truck drivers, 123
TUI, 133, 134
Turkey, 102
Tyszkiewicz, Zygmunt, **171**, 199,
    228–30

UAP, 88
UEAPME, 2, 173, 182, 186
    EU, 191
    lobbying, 192
    objectives, 189
    SMEs, 187–90, 192
    social partner, 193
    structure, 183
    trade, 189
UNEP
    ICCA, 108
UNICE, 2, 46, 64, 65, 67–9, 73–4,
    76, 137–8, 141, 172–4,
    178–9, 181
    Advisory and Support Group, 69
    benchmarking studies, 171
    CBI, 68
    CEFIC, 104
    ERT, 196–7, 199–200
    ESF, 138
    European Enterprise Group, 68–9
    European Round Table of
        Industrialists (ERT), 204
    European Services Forum (ESF),
        138
    restructuring, 202
    service sectors, 137
    SMEs, 205
    staff, 171
    TFCs, 204
    TNCs, 202
    trade associations, 165
    WTO, 137
    WTO Services Working Group, 138
Unilever, 66, 199
Union Européenne de l'artisanat et des
    petites et moyennes entreprises,
    see UEAPME
unions, 33, 55, 172, 176
    associations, 44
    business associations, 34, 159, 164
    centralisation, 44

comprehensive, 33
    employer associations, 175
    globalisation, 214
    international trade politics, 144
    labour market, 161
    local/regional level, 43
    representations, 183
    role, 184
    TNCs, 201
    trade associations, 165
unique selling point (USP), 19
United Kingdom, *see* Britain
    ad hoc groups, 70
    bank mergers, 87
    devolution, 90
    employer associations, 166
    OBI project, 53
    trade associations
        governance, 97
United States, 53, 55–6, 138
    animal protection movement, 61
    EU, 72
USP, *see* unique selling point
    (USP)
USSR, 90
utilities, 37, 88
    telecommunications, 89

van Apeldoorn, Bastiaan, 70, **194**
van Waarden, Frans, **30**
VDMA, 135
vertical portals, 92
VHS, 6
Viag, 135
V-ICT, 116
vocational training, 32, 191, 224
    SMEs, 185, 188
Vodaphone, 87
voluntary associations, 163
volunteers, 19, 153
Volvo, 69, 195, 199
Von Geldern, M., 66
Vredeling proposal, 67, 68, 69

Wales, 89, 90
war industry, 183
Ward, Simon, **126**, 230
water utilities, 88, 89
Weber, Max, 83

websites, 94
  EICTA, 117
  outsourcing, 95
  subscriptions, 91
  trade associations, 91, 94, 95
WEGO, 92
Welsh Assembly, 55
Westgeest, Alfons, **1**, **143**,
    223, 232
Whitbread, 126
White Papers
  Governance, 3, 5
  Strategy for a future chemicals
    policy', 106
White, David, 230
Wirtschaftskammer Österreich
    (WKÖ), 168
Works Councils
  directive, 68
workers' syndicates, 48
  consultative organisation, 49
World Tourism Organisation, 134
  structure, 135
World Trade Organisation, *see* WTO
World Travel and Tourism Council
    (WTTC), 132–4

WTO, 47, 57, 132, 216
  disputes settlement mechanism,
    211, 217
  GATS, 137
  ICCA, 108
  international trade politics,
    144
  MLG, 219
  Seattle, 76
  service sectors, 141
  services, 137
  Services Working Group, 138
  Third World, 144
  Trade Policy Review
    1997, 132
WTTC, *see* World Travel and Tourism
    Council (WTTC)

Xerox, 116

Yugoslavia, 90

Zentralverband des deutschen
    Handwerks, 41